𝔈locutionary

The principles of Elocution, with exercises and notations

Alexander Melville Bell

Alpha Editions

This edition published in 2019

ISBN : 9789353955397

Design and Setting By
Alpha Editions
email - alphaedis@gmail.com

"ELOCUTIONARY MANUAL."

THE

PRINCIPLES

OF

ELOCUTION,

WITH

EXERCISES AND NOTATIONS.

BY

ALEXANDER MELVILLE BELL,

Author of " VISIBLE SPEECH," " PRINCIPLES OF SPEECH AND DICTIONARY OF
SOUNDS," " EMPHASIZED LITURGY," " STANDARD ELOCUTIONIST,"
" ESSAYS AND POSTSCRIPTS ON ELOCUTION," " SOUNDS AND
THEIR RELATIONS," " LECTURES ON PHONETICS,"
" ENGLISH LINE-WRITING," " WORLD
ENGLISH," &c., &c., &c.

SIXTH EDITION.
REVISED AND ENLARGED.

New York:
N. D. C. HODGES,
874 Broadway.

New York:
EDGAR S. WERNER,
108 East 16th St.

London:
PAUL, TRENCH, TRÜBNER & CO.

PREFACE.

An outline of the Principles detailed in this volume constitutes the first Section of the " STANDARD ELOCU-TIONIST"—a book of which upwards of one hundred and fifty thousand copies have been sold. The present is the SIXTH EDITION of the parent Work. This will be found improved in quality of paper, &c. ; and a portrait of the Author has been added.

WASHINGTON, D. C.,
May, 1893.

EXTRACTS FROM FORMER PREFACES.

FIRST EDITION.

In the preparation of this Work the Author has endeavoured to write not merely for the use of pupils, to whom a defective description in the book may be orally supplemented in the class-room, but for those to whom such additional instruction is not and cannot be available. How far he has succeeded in this remains to be proved. He has studied to preserve the utmost simplicity of arrangement, and to avoid overloading principles by unnecessary rules. He has not followed in the steps of any preceding writer, either as to his Theory or his plan of developing it; but he has observed Nature for himself, and recorded his observations after his own fashion. The Science of Elocution seemed to him to want an A B C, and he has endeavoured to supply the deficiency.

EDINBURGH, *November*, 1849.

SECOND EDITION.

Two years ago the Author published his "New Elucidation of the Principles of Speech and Elocution,"—a work which has been so favourably received among Critics, and so rapidly disposed of, that he has been induced to prepare an ELOCUTIONARY MANUAL adapted for use in classes, as well as for private students.

This Volume may be considered as a Second Edition (but entirely re-written) of the Elocutionary Sections of the larger work. The Fundamental Theories, and the Details of Articulation and Defective Speech are condensed; the Principles of Orthoepy, Vocalization, and the Art of Reading, more copiously illustrated; and a full Practical Treatment of the subject of GESTURE has been added; besides an extensive Collection of Poetical and Dramatic Quotations marked for Exercise in Expressive Reading.

All the Extracts are alphabetically collected in one general Index in the Table of Contents, so as to form a DICTIONARY OF EMOTIVE QUOTATIONS : and the Table of Contents, generally, is arranged as a minute Reference-Index to the subjects treated of in the Volume.

The Author has to acknowledge his obligations to his father, Alex. Bell, Esq., Professor of Elocution, London; and to his brother, D. C. Bell, Esq., Professor of Elocution, Dublin, for their critical perusal of this Work in its progress through the Press.

EDINBURGH, 1852.

iv

THIRD EDITION.

In the present Edition the whole of the Notations have been revised, and many new paragraphs have been added in each Division of the Work. The Introductory Essay and the Section on EMPHASIS are entirely new, and a large number of additional Exercises and Illustrations have been given under the various Heads of Inflexion, Expressive Exercises, Gesture. The Work will now, it is hoped, be found still more worthy of the flattering encomiums it has received from the Press and the Professional Public.

EDINBURGH, 1859.

FOURTH EDITION.

The Third Edition of the " ELOCUTIONARY MANUAL" having been for some time out of print, and the work being still in steady demand, the Author has been induced to prepare a New Edition, with the improvements suggested by his long experience. Such a duty he cannot hope to be again called on to undertake; and, as his " PRINCIPLES OF ELOCUTION"—first published in 1849— have had a manifest influence on subsequent elocutionary literature, he desires to extend and perpetuate that influence by a final revision of the Theories and Exercises, which were the fruit of original study and observation thirty years ago.

TUTELO HEIGHTS, BRANTFORD,
ONTARIO, CANADA, *July*, 1878.

FIFTH EDITION.

In this fifth edition of the " PRINCIPLES OF ELOCUTION " all the directions and exercises have been again revised, and to a great extent re-written. Much new matter has also been added, including the entire series of " READING EXERCISES MARKED FOR EMPHASIS, CLAUSE, AND PITCH" (pp. 145 to 156). The work is now as perfect as the Author's best efforts can make it. In this form, therefore, it has been for the first time electrotyped in preparation for continued and extended use.

1525 THIRTY-FIFTH STREET,
WASHINGTON, D. C.,
September, 1887.

CONTENTS.

PART THIRD.—MODULATION AND EXPRESSIVE DELIVERY.

GENERAL INDEX OF EXTRACTS.

Prose passages are distinguished by an asterisk (*).

XIV CONTENTS.

XVI   CONTENTS.

PRINCIPLES OF ELOCUTION.

INTRODUCTORY ESSAY.

Elocution does not occupy the place it reasonably ought to fill in the curriculum of education. The causes of this neglect will be found to consist mainly of these two : the subject is undervalued, because it is misunderstood ; and it is misunderstood because it is unworthily represented in the great majority of books, which take its name on their title page ; and, also by the practice of too many of its teachers, who make an idle display in Recitation the chief, if not the only, end of their instruction.

When we point to the fact, that public speaking is a part of the professional duty of every Clergyman and Advocate, and no unusual part of the social duty of a private citizen ; and that Public Speaking involves two distinct requirements,—a knowledge of what to say, and how to say it ; and when we farther advert to the fact, that in the whole course of school and college education, either for private citizens or public speakers, only one of these requirements is systematically provided for, the inadequacy of the provision to the requirements cannot but be manifest. We naturally ask, "why is this?" The reason, perhaps, may simply be, that *so it is!* We are all slaves of custom, and cannot, without much difficulty, be brought to alter existing arrangements, however unreasonable. We are too apt to lazily acquiesce in things as they are, however wrong, and passively accept the doctrine that "whatever is, is right."

1

But, besides this natural conservatism, this unreason, which is the principal cause of the maintenance of all error, there is another cause which is indeed a reason for the anomaly referred to, although the reason itself will be admitted to be unreasonable: a prejudice exists against the cultivation of *manner* in Delivery. Prejudice,—that Reason's very opposite,—denounces manner as if it was a thing of no *matter*. "Manner" and "Matter" are spoken of as antagonists in Oratory. But what is matter without manner? Matter is the native unquarried rock; Manner is the chiseled statue, or the sculptured palace. Matter is the chaos "without form and void" when "darkness brooded over the face of the earth;" Manner is the rolling globe launched in the flood of light, and beautified with hill and dale, ocean and streamlet, herb, and tree, and flower. Manner is the manifestation of all matter; and no matter can be known but by the manner of its presentment.

This is equally true of intellectual as of physical material. The matter of the finest oratory may lie hidden within the brain, worthless and unappreciated; as the marble of that sweetest creation of the sculptor—the "Greek Slave"—lay buried in its native hill, till Powers arose that could unveil its symmetry and grace. And it depends entirely on the speaker's skill,—his power over manner—whether he fashion his matter into a paving stone or a Medicean Venus.

But this prejudice has a moral root from which it derives all its vitality:—"The eloquence that fascinates may be employed to dazzle and seduce. It may be used to make the worse appear the better reason." True, but the greater the attractiveness of Eloquence for purposes of mere amusement, or for more unholy ends, the stronger is the reason and the more imperative the duty to master its refinements, and utilize its influence in all good and sacred causes.

The adage cannot be too often repeated that whatever is worth doing at all, is worth doing well; and we may add, the worthier any object of effort, the higher should be the standard of efficient execution. Slovenliness is intolerable in the meanest business. How much more so in the highest, and especially in that which has an aim beyond all earthly objects!

But by whom is this prejudice entertained? Who are they that shake the head at oratorical refinement in the pulpit, and denounce preparatory study of " manner " as " theatrical?" Are they the eloquent of the Church, the ornaments of their profession, speakers refined by culture, or endowed with natural powers of eloquence? No! They are those only who are themselves destitute of any pretensions to effectiveness. No man who is conscious of the ability to speak effectively can undervalue the power, and none who is not competent in this respect, can judge of its value or pronounce it worthless.

The study of Oratory is, however, hindered by another prejudice, founded—too justly—on the ordinary methods and results of elocutionary teaching ; the methods being unphilosophical and trivial, and their result not an improved manner, but an induced mannerism. The principle of instruction to which Elocution owes its meanness of reputation may be expressed in one word,— Imitation. The teacher presents his pupils with a model or specimen of reading or declamation, and calls on them to stand forth and do likewise. The model may be good, bad, or indifferent ; it is, at all events, tinged with the teacher's own peculiarities, and the pupils, in their imitative essays, can hardly be expected to distinguish between these accidents of style and the essentials of good delivery which may be embodied in the model. Thus, becoming accustomed to imitate the former, they naturally confound them with the latter. Each pupil, too, has his own peculiarities, already more or less developed—arising from structural differences in the organs of speech, from temperament, or from habit,—the result of previous training or of previous neglect. These fixed idiosyncrasies and tendencies, mingled with the imitated peculiarities, form a compound style, which, whatever its qualities, can hardly fail to be unnatural. Besides, as imitation is in a great degree an unconscious act, habits are thus formed of the existence of which the subject of them is entirely ignorant. In no other way can we account for those monstrous perversions of style which are so common, and so patent to all but, apparently, the speakers themselves. The very purpose of a philosophical system of instruction should be—to give us a standard by which to measure our own shortcomings and, primarily, by which we can discover them.

But it may be urged by adherents of the imitative methods of instruction, that they do not teach by imitation alone ; that they teach by Rule, and merely illustrate rules by their model readings, in imitating which the pupils consciously apply the rules. There has been far too much of this teaching by "Rules" in all departments of education. The rules of nature are few and simple, at the same time extensive and obvious in their application. These are PRINCIPLES rather than rules, and it is the highest business of philosophy to find out such. Principles alone are worthy of the student's care. These he cannot too perfectly "learn and con by rote." But the rules of elocutionary books are not of this kind. The latter are cumbersome in number, limited in application to certain forms of grammatical construction, and very far from obvious in their use. Some principle must be involved in every rule. Rules are but logical deductions from understood principles ; and, often, a single principle will be found to underlie a whole category of rules. If Principles are understood, the mind will deduce rules for itself, but the knowledge of the most elaborate code of rules may be possessed without acquaintance with a single principle. Besides, in actual practice, rules cannot be applied. They keep the mind in leading-strings which prevent self-effort, and destroy natural freedom, being rather fetters than assistances to one who has learned to walk alone. For instance, a certain movement of voice implies incompleteness of statement, and its mechanical opposite implies completeness. A knowledge of this simple Principle involves at once a knowledge of more than half the rules for Inflexion with which Elocutionists have bewildered their students. The mind can grasp this principle and carry it along without effort through all the complexities and involutions of composition ; but if, instead of this, the student is made to learn all the possible arrangements of words in sentences, and to apply a separate "Rule" for each new form, he can never bring his rules into spontaneous application. He may apply them, or fancy that he applies them, in the reading of selected sentences, but beyond this he cannot carry them a step without feeling them an incumbrance and a hindrance to mental action. Constant thinking of inflection proves fatal to *reflection*. What a student chiefly requires to know, is *how* to vary his voice ; if his own judgement and appreciation of the sense, in connection with defined principles, do not inform him *when* to do so, the most minute direction by Rules will be of little service. The *mechanics* of expression are what he must master, if he would use and manifest his mind in reading ; but he must be unfettered in their application, in order that he may develop and improve his manner without acquiring the formality of mannerism.

Elocutionary Exercise is popularly supposed to consist merely of Recitation, and the fallacy is kept up both in schools and colleges, where Elocution is said not to be wholly neglected, because an hour is occasionally set apart for a competitive display of the declamatory powers of the pupils or students. This is a miserable trifling with an art of such importance,—an art that embraces the whole Science of Speech, as well as sentimental expression. With as much justice might it be said that music was attended to, if a class were called on once or twice a week, or half a dozen times a session, to whistle a popular air in competition for a prize. Music is both a Science and an Art. So is Elocution ; and such an amount of attention as is limited to the occasional " spouting " of passages learned anywhere or anyhow, is to Elocution merely what whistling is to music. The cultivated orators of old esteemed Delivery the chief of all the arts of Oratory, and they " being dead yet speak to us : " and they should do so with authority, for the letter of their eloquence is still the model in our colleges. We admire the orations of Demosthenes : so did contemporary judges ; but they tell us that truly to appreciate these compositions we must have *heard* them ! How would the Grecian " Thunderer" esteem our modern wisdom, in practically reversing, as we do, the relative importance of writing and of speaking well ! Oratory, doubtless, is not now an art of such high consequence as it was before the invention of the printing press, and the general diffusion of knowledge through its blessed agency; but the sphere of oratorical influence, though narrowed, is yet large, and within that sphere the value of an effective Delivery is as preponderating as it ever was.

Oratory was of old a very comprehensive subject, and its study was the labour of a life. It included almost every department of general knowledge, and mental and moral discipline, as well as Pronunciation, or what we now call Elocution or Delivery. The latter department was the one most sedulously cultivated, as being that on which all the rest depended for successful exhibition. Hoary hairs were considered indispensable to the consummate orator, that his manner might be duly refined with that art which hides itself; and also because his laborious preparations were supposed to require the length and vigour of the youth and prime of life. Consistently with this, Oratory was emblematized under the figure of an Old Man, threads of amber issuing from his lips, and winding into the ears of deferential auditors. Our modern orators expect to jump into the rostrum and oratorical ability at once, and without preparation even for the primary requisite of public speaking—distinct Pronunciation. They expect to find the amber in their mouths, born with them ;—like Dogberry, who thought that "to write and read comes by nature." They expect to drop the native substance from their lips—as the princess in the fairy tale did pearls—at every opening. But men are not orators by birth, and the amber of eloquence is seldom found save as the rich deposit of assuetude and science.

Elocution may be defined as the EFFECTIVE EXPRESSION OF THOUGHT AND SENTIMENT, by Speech, Intonation, and Gesture. Speech is wholly conventional in its expressiveness, and mechanical in its processes. Intonation and gesture constitute a Natural Language, which may be used either independently of, or as assistant to, speech. Speech, in all the diversities of tongues and dialects, consists of but a small number of articulated elementary sounds. These are produced by the agency of the lungs, the larynx, and the mouth. The lungs supply air to the larynx, which modifies the stream into whisper or voice ;

and this air is then moulded by the plastic oral organs into syllables, which, singly or in accentual combinations, constitute words. These words are arbitrarily appropriated to the expression of ideas, and thus we have Language,— variously intelligible in every community, but the same in its elements, throughout the world.

Elocution, as it involves the exercise of language, must embrace the Physiology of Speech—the mechanics of vocalization and articulation. A knowledge of the conventional meanings of words is of course also implied, but this may be obtained independently of Elocution, in the modern sense of the term. The student of Elocution, then, should be made acquainted with the instrument of speech, *as an instrument*, that all its parts may be under his control, as the stops, the keys, the pedals, and the bellows, are subject to the organist. These principles of Instrumentation are equally applicable to all languages, and the student who has mastered them, in connection with his vernacular tongue, will apply them to the pronunciation of any foreign language with which he may become acquainted.

Elocution has also a special application to the language or dialect employed, that the elements and vocables of each may be pronounced according to its own standard of correctness ;—that being correct in one which is incorrect in another. Thus, in the elocution of the northern British, the Irish, the New England and other American dialects of our tongue—for all dialects may have their elocution, or effective utterance—the vowels a and o, and the letter r, have different pronunciations from those which obtain in the southern dialects of England. The student of elocution should be capable of discriminating these and all similar differences. He should not be enslaved to the peculiarities of any dialect; he may, when occasion requires, speak English like an Englishman, Scotch like a Scotchman, and Irish like an Irishman ; but his reading should not be imbued with the characteristics of Irish, of Scotch, or of any local pronunciation, when he delivers the language of Shakespeare, of Milton, or of Addison.

The differences that distinguish dialects are quite susceptible of assimilation to any standard. Just as a piece

of music can, by a skilful player, be transposed in execution to a different key from that in which it is written, so
language can, by one skilled in the characteristics of dialects, be transposed in pronunciation from one dialect
into another.

But local peculiarities manifest themselves in varieties
of *intonation* as well as of syllabic pronunciation. As
the tones of speech have all a natural expressiveness,
there is rarely any difficulty in acquiring command over
them. The "science of sweet sounds" can only be
effectively studied by those who have "an ear" for
music, but the expressive tones of speech can be distinguished and efficiently executed, even by those who are
destitute of the musical faculty. This department of elocutionary discipline is of high importance, as it involves
the exercise of much judgement in discriminating the
analogies of sound to sense.

The peculiarities of tone, which characterize dialects,
consist, for the most part, of repetitions of the same
species of inflexion, clause following clause in a sort of
tune, which prevails merely by the force of habit. The
voice of every individual is apt to partake too much of a
uniformity of melody; but we have no difficulty in understanding the intention of the speaker, notwithstanding
the sameness or the habitual fluctuations of his tones.
This proves the folly of attempting, by any set of Rules,
to impose a system of intonation as a standard for all
voices. There is scarcely a sentence which will not
admit of just expression by half a dozen, or ten times as
many, modes of vocal inflexion. What is wanted is not a
Rule for this or that species of sentence, but a power
over the voice generally, to redeem it from monotony; a
knowledge of the various modes of conveying sense; and
an appreciation of the special sense to be conveyed. To
aim at anything more than this would be to destroy the
speaker's individuality, and to substitute formality and
mannerism for versatility of natural manner. In reference to inflexion, elocutionary training has for its object
mechanical facility, and definiteness of execution, rather
than uniformity of application. It is the mistake of Mr.
Walker's, and all similar Rules, that they tend to produce

the latter result only ; one which is neither desirable nor strictly possible,—which is, in fact, unnatural.

Inflexion is associated with accent, or emphatic stress, and this is regulated by the sense to be conveyed. The laws of emphasis form a study of the highest intellectual value, which has been too little investigated and systematized. No department of Elocution can compare with this in importance ; yet not only has it been superseded in books, by unnecessary Rules for Inflexion, and in schools by thoughtless imitation, but these rules, and all exercise founded on them, constantly violate the laws of accent. Here is one point in which almost absolute uniformity must prevail among all good readers. Set practice right in respect to emphasis, and inflexion cannot go far wrong.

Every sentence or clause is susceptible of various meanings, according as its different words are rendered prominent by emphasis. " There will always be some word or words more necessary to be understood than others. Those things which have been previously stated, or which are necessarily implied, or with which we presume our hearers to have been preacquainted, we pronounce with such a subordination of stress as is suitable to the small importance of things already understood ; while those of which our hearers have not been before informed, or which they might possibly misconceive, are enforced with such an increase of stress, as makes it impossible for the hearers to overlook or mistake them. Thus, as it were in a picture, the more essential parts of a sentence are raised from the level of speaking, and the less necessary are, at the same time, sunk into a comparative obscurity ! " *

How awkwardly ambiguous is the reading of those who have no principle to guide them in the selection of emphasis,—the distribution of the light and shade of speech ! One verse of Scripture—a peculiarly difficult one to hap-hazard readers—is rarely delivered correctly. This is the 25th verse of the 24th chapter of the Gospel by Luke :—"O fools, and *slow* of heart to believe all

* " Practical Elocutionist." London, 1842.

that the *prophets* have spoken !" The reproof conveyed
here is that the disciples addressed were "slow to believe;" but, by a faulty clausing of the sentence, separating these allied words, and a misplaced emphasis,
precisely the opposite censure seems to be intended : " O
fools, and slow of heart, to *believe* all that the prophets
have spoken."

It is the business of Elocution to teach the student three
things important to be known : 1st, How to discover all
the meanings that any passage may embody ; 2nd, How
to express the several meanings, supposing each of them
to be just ; and, 3rd, How to ascertain the true interpre-
tation, or the sense intended by the author. In all these
processes, and especially in the last, much judgement will
manifestly be required. Indeed, it may be questioned
whether *any* study is more directly calculated to exercise
the mind in all its faculties than the investigation of the
precise meaning of a standard author. It is true that the
critical acumen to appreciate the sense may be possessed
without the ability to express it ; and herein is manifest
the necessity of vocal training, to give the judicious inter-
preter a command over the mechanics of expression, that
he may "make the sound an echo to the sense."

The succession of the accents in sentences constitutes
what is called Rhythm. This succession is regular in
metrical composition, and irregular in prose. The regu-
larity of rhythmus in poetry, while it favours a musical
delivery, is very apt to lead the voice into a tuneful movement, where music is not intended ; and the result is that
nauseating intermixture of the tones of speaking and of
singing which is denoted canting or sing-song. There can
be no doubt that the school methods of *scanning*, and of
reading poetry by the line, are directly productive of this
worst and most prevailing oratorical taint. It is but rarely
that a reader can be found whose voice is entirely free
from this blemish ; and the habit is speedily extended from
poetry to prose, so that the expressive irregularity of pro-
saic rhythm is entirely lost in the uniformity of time to
which the reader's voice is set. Pinned, as it were, on
the barrel of an organ, his accents come precisely in the
same place at every sentential revolution, striking their

emphasis, at one turn, upon a pronoun or a conjunction, and, at another, impinging sonorously on an article or an expletive.

> " 'Tis education forms the infant mind ;
> Just as the twig is bent, the tree 's inclined."

The little green twigs in the Grammar School are sedulously bent into the barrel-organ shape, and pegged to play their destined tune by systematic teaching ; and when the tiny twig-barrel has swelled into a full-grown cylinder, and rolls forth its cadences in far-sounding pitch, the old pegs are still there, striking the old chords in the old way.

What have children, or men either, to do, in reading, with trochees, iambi, dáctyls, amphibrachs, or anapæsts? They are all pests together. Scanning, or the art of dividing verse into the " feet " of which it is composed, is a practice that should not be left " a foot to stand upon." It confounds every element of natural pronunciation, calling long " short," and short " long ;" separating the syllables of the same word, and uniting the syllables of different words, in a way that would be almost too monstrous for belief, were we not so habituated to the " scanning " art from our earliest " twig "-hood, that we have great difficulty in scanning its full stupidity. While this wretched pedantry is taught in our schools, so long must our pulpits bring forth the normal increase of such seed, in singsong, drawling, and unnaturalness.

The subject of Rhythmus has been involved in much obscurity by the way in which writers have treated of it ; and even Elocutionists have been so far misled under the influence of early education, as to adapt their reading exercises to the accustomed measures, and divide their sentences into bars of equal time. It is difficult to characterize the folly of such divisions as the following, quoted from a well-known work :—

> " While the | stormy | tempest | blows
> While the | battle | rages | long and | loud."

> " Where is my | cabin door | fast by the | wild wood?
> Sisters and | sire | *did you | mourn for its | fall?"

These bars are terrible bars to progress in the art of reading—barriers of nonsense in the way of sense !

The marks of punctuation are taught in schools as measures of the pauses in reading. Children are told to stop at all the " stops," and only at the stops, and to proportion their stopping to the supposed time-value of the stops. But the marks of punctuation have no relation to time; nor are they at all intended to regulate the pauses of a reader. They have a purpose, but it is not this. They do, in the majority of cases, occur where pauses should be made, but they do not supply nearly the number of pauses that good reading requires. They simply mark the grammatical construction of a sentence. While word follows word in strict grammatical relation, no comma is inserted, though many pauses may be indispensable ; and wherever any break occurs in the grammatical relation of proximate words, there a comma is written, though, often, a pause would spoil the sense. Commas are placed before and after all interpolations that separate related words—adjective and noun, adverb and adjective, pronoun and verb, verb and object, &c. ;—but they are not written while words follow each other *in direct and mutual relation*. Punctuation has thus no reference to delivery ; it has no claim to regulate reading; and nothing but ignorance of a better guide could have led to the adoption of the grammatical points to direct the voice in pausing.

Some writer has happily expressed the principle of pausing in a metrical form, which is worth committing to memory, although the reader will find something more definite in the section on "Verbal Grouping : "

> " In pausing, ever let this rule take place,
> Never to separate words, in any case,
> That are less separable than those you join ;
> And, which imports the same, not to combine
> Such words together as do not relate
> So closely as the words you separate."

The subject of Antithesis and the relation of antithesis to emphasis, is one in which the Rules of Elocutionists are not only superseded by a fundamental law, but in which the rules are often at variance with the natural Principle. There is a grand distinction in the expressiveness of the tones of speech, which has been insufficiently attended to. The vocal inflexions are primarily two,—

an upward and a downward movement. These express the sentiments of appeal to the hearer, in the rising movement, and of assertion from the speaker, in the falling turn. The union of these simple movements with one accent, or impulse of stress, produces two compound tones, which express the same sentiments with a suggestive reference to the *antithesis* of the utterance. No great observation was necessary to discover that all emphasis implies antithesis ; but Elocutionists have jumped to the conclusion that the converse of this principle must needs be likewise true, and that all antithesis implies emphasis. As if, because every potato is undoubtedly a vegetable, every vegetable must of course be a potato ! Upon this false assumption, rules for the inflexion of antithetic sentences have been founded, which led to a constant up and down alternation of the voice on opposed words, than which nothing can be more at variance with the natural law of emphasis, or with its invariable manifestation in the spontaneous utterance of conversation. It is only when verbal opposition is *inferred* and not fully expressed, that we have a genuine instance of the figure of Antithesis, and nature has provided us with a distinctive intonation by which the antithetic idea may be unmistakeably suggested. When the opposition is complete in terms, the tones of antithesis are not required, and the emphasis follows the general law, by which the idea new to the context, or uppermost in the speaker's mind, is rendered prominent by mere accentual stress, and with simple tones. It is no less true in Elocution than in physics, that the brightest light casts the deepest shadow. The light of emphasis on any word throws a shade of subordination on all allied words, the darker and more concealing in proportion to the lustre of the emphasis. Among speakers whose tones are adjusted by artificial rules, we look in vain for this " night side of nature," this shadow of the illuminated thought. Each word of every contrasted pair of words is thrown mechanically into equal prominence, with the effect expressed by Pope in his " Essay on criticism : "

> " False eloquence, like the prismatic glass,
> Its gaudy colours spreads on *every* place."

We may follow out the Poet's idea, and add a converse couplet :—

> True eloquence the lens's part must play,
> And blend the colours in one *focal* ray.

With many speakers who aim at being emphatic without knowing how to be so, every leading *grammatical* word—noun and verb,—or every *qualifying* word—adjective and adverb—is delivered with an intensity of stress which defeats its own object, and is as destitute of intelligent effect as that tame and drawling monotony in which others indulge, where nothing rises above the level of constant dulness. Words are emphatic or otherwise, not in virtue of their inherent grammatical rank, but of the relation they bear to each other *in the context*. The discriminating principle which marks this relation is called *accent* in reference to combinations of syllables, *emphasis* in reference to groups of words, and *modulation* in reference to successions of sentences. But it is the same art in all its applications, governed by the same intellectual perception of relative proportion and comparative importance.

The student is now referred to the body of the Work for a full development of Principles. Enough has been said here to prove that Elocutionary Art is something more than merely imitative ; that it has more intellectual exercises than the sentimental declamations usually associated with the name ; and that, if it has been encumbered with useless Rules, it is not destitute of guiding Principles.

DIRECTIONS FOR USING THIS WORK.

To the Private Student.

When you consult a Teacher for instruction in Elocu-tion, your attention is, for the time, limited to special points—those in which your delivery requires correction, or those to which the Teacher gives precedence. The duly-qualified instructor is, of course, competent to direct his pupils in ANY of the departments of his art; but he does not, in every case, allow his lessons to range over ALL departments.

In this Book you have a teacher — prepared to give instruction in Theory, or direction in Exercise, in any department of the Art of Delivery : but you must, in order to self-improvement, do for yourself what you cannot avoid under the living teacher—namely, confine your attention, at first, to those points in which you specially need help, and overlook all else till they are mastered.

There is a great art in learning even from the best of teachers. Some pupils will draw out precisely what they require, and profit rapidly ; others—"receptive" only,— will, from a longer period of instruction, derive much less advantage. The art of learning from a BOOK is of course still more dependent on the student himself. The secret of success is undoubtedly the same in both cases : ATTEND EXCLUSIVELY TO ONE POINT AT A TIME.

A cursory examination of the whole ground of study is sometimes advantageous as a preliminary,—especially when it is undertaken merely to assist in the selection of a Department for exercise ;—but a desultory perusal of a practical work—on such a practical subject as elocution— can lead to no satisfactory result. Therefore :—Treat this Book as a *viva voce* Teacher : Give heed exclusively to the section before you : Practise the exercises prescribed, and look neither backward nor forward until you have mastered the Lesson in hand.

Do you belong to either of the following classes of speakers?

I. Your voice is feeble—it is smothered—it is strained —you are soon fatigued by vocal effort—you become hoarse—breathless—giddy—the muscles of your throat, chest, abdomen, are rendered sore by public speaking.—

15

For you, until you have changed these characteristics, this Book has only ONE LESSON—the management of RESPIRATION.

II. Your pronunciation is faulty—it is indistinct—it slurs syllables—it is peculiar in some element—it is provincial—it is foreign—it is guttural—it is nasal.—Study first the details of VOWELS, ARTICULATION, and ACCENTUATION.

III. Your tones are unvaried—they are limited to a narrow range—they are tunefully recurrent—they are vaguely meandering—they are screechy—they are croaky —they are drawling.—Begin with the mastery of INFLEXION.

IV. Your reading is governed by sentences—by breath-limits—in poetry by lines—your pauses by the marks of punctuation — your primary and secondary clauses are undiscriminated.—Study SENTENTIAL ANALYSIS and the principles of CLAUSING and PAUSING.

V. Your delivery is ponderous— it is flippant—it is rhythmical—it is uniform—it is pointless.—Commence with the principles of EMPHASIS.

VI. Your general style is dull—it fails to arrest attention— it is harsh—it is unsympathetic.— Begin with MODULATION and EMOTIVE EXPRESSION.

VII. Your action is awkward—it is angular—it is stiff —it is jerking—it is repetitive—it is indefinite. Study first the section on GESTURE.

VIII. You feel yourself to be ineffective, but are not conscious of the particulars in which you fail.—Learn the NOTATIONS of Inflexion and Expression, and READ the notated and emphasized passages, until you acquire a definite knowledge of the source of your ineffectiveness ; for consciousness of a fault is the necessary preliminary to its correction.

IX. You simply desire to understand the subject as a matter of interest; or you wish to master it for the purpose of teaching.—Begin at the beginning and go through THE WHOLE WORK.

The previous editions of this "Manual" have met with many appreciative and successful disciples. This finally revised edition should prove even more widely useful to new generations of Elocutionary students.

PRINCIPLES OF ELOCUTION.

PART FIRST.

PRONUNCIATION.

I. GENERAL PRINCIPLES.

1. SPEECH is the audible result of a combination of *mechanical* processes, separately under the government of volition, and conventionally expressive of ideas.

2. As, in learning to play upon an instrument of music, it is indispensable to be practically acquainted with its mechanical principles, so, in studying the Art of Speech, it is of consequence that the learner be familiar with the structure and working of the instrument of Speech.

3. But this important fundamental knowledge is not anatomical in its nature. The pianist does not require to understand the arrangement of the interior of his instrument,—its pegs and wires, and hammers and dampers —but to be familiar with its keys, and with the principles of digital transition, so that he may gallop over its gamuts without stop or stumble. The violinist does not need to know the details of shape and fastening of the parts of the fiddle-frame, but he must have perfect acquaintance with the working of the pegs, the stopping of the strings, and the drawing of the bow. The flutist does not require any knowledge of the arts of turning and boring the block from which his instrument is formed, or of the mathematical calculations and nice relative measurements which regulate the holing; but he must thoroughly understand how to blow, to tongue, and to "govern the ventages," so as to make it "discourse its eloquent music." And so, the SPEAKER does not require to learn of how many, and of what muscles and cartilages the larynx is

3

formed, and by what sets of "motors" and "antagonists" the various organs of speech are influenced : such knowledge may be a welcome addition to his stock of information, but he cannot bring it into any practical use in speaking. He should, however, comprehend clearly the dynamic principles of the vocal instrument, and the mechanical means by which the various sounds and articulations of speech are produced and modified.

4. The instrument of speech combines the qualities of a wind and of a stringed instrument : voice being produced by means of a current of air impelled from a sort of bellows—the lungs—and modified by contraction or expansion of the voice-channels, and by tension or relaxation of the vibrating membranes.

5. The speaking machine, while thus resembling in certain points the organ and the violin, is characteristically distinct from all instruments of music in its unique apparatus of *Articulation;* which embraces the *pharynx;* the *nares* or nostrils ; the *palates*, soft and hard ; the *tongue;* the *teeth;* and the *lips.*

6. In the management of the Breath, and of the Organs of Articulation, lie the mechanical principles with which the speaker should be practically familiar, in order to enable him to use his oratorical powers healthfully, in energetic and protracted efforts, and with ease, grace, and precision at all times.

7. ELOCUTION, or Delivery, comprehends, besides the principles of salutary respiration, distinct articulation, and correct pronunciation, those of mental and emotional Expressiveness, by tones, gestures, &c.

8. Regulating the Expressive, as well as the Articulative departments of Elocution, are various mechanical principles with which the student should be experimentally familiar, that he may be gracefully effective in every effort ; in nothing giving offence to the eye or ear of taste, or " o'erstepping the modesty of nature."

II. PRINCIPLES OF RESPIRATION.

9. Speech consists of variously modified *emissions* of breath. Breath is thus the material of Speech. The

lungs must, therefore, be well supplied with air before speech is commenced, and they must be kept so supplied during the whole progress of speech. The very common fault of dropping the voice feebly at the end of a sentence, arises in great measure from a faulty habit of respiration : and many personal inconveniences, sometimes painful and serious, accrue to the speaker, from insufficient, too infrequent, or ill-managed respiration.

10. The amount of air ordinarily inspired for vital wants is quite insufficient for vocal purposes. Speech must be preceded by a deeper than common inspiration, and sustained by replenishments of more than common frequency.

11. The lungs are supplied with air by the expansion of the cavity of the chest; and they are made to yield the air they contain by its contraction from the pressure of its walls and base.

12. The cavity of the chest is conical in form, tapering from its muscular base,—the diaphragm,—by the ribs and clavicle to the windpipe.

13. The chest is expanded by the bulging of the ribs, the raising of the clavicle (or breast-bone), and the descent or flattening of the diaphragm. Expiration may be produced either by means of the bony frame-work, or of the muscular base of the chest. The latter is the correct mode of vocal expiration; the former is exhausting, and often injurious in its consequences.

14. Too much importance cannot be attached to the formation of a habit of easy respiration. The walls of the chest should not be allowed to fall in speaking, but the whole force of expiration should be confined to the diaphragm. Clavicular respiration is the prevailing error of those who find speaking or reading laborious. When the respiration is properly conducted, vocal exercise should be unfatiguing even though long continued ; and the longer it is practised the more should it be conducive to health.

15. The inspirations in speaking must be noiseless. Audible *suction* of air is as unnecessary as it is ungraceful. To avoid this fault, let the passage to the lungs be but open, and *expand the chest;* the pressure of the

atmosphere will then inflate the lungs to the full extent of the cavity created within the thorax.

16. The common Scotch bagpipe gives an excellent illustration of the comparative efficacy of a partial, and of a complete inflation of the lungs. See the piper, when the bag is only half filled, tuning the long drones :—how his arm jerks on the wind-bag !—And hear the harsh and uneven notes that come jolting out from the pressure ! Then see him, when the sheep-skin is firmly swelled beneath his arm :—how gently his elbow works upon it ! while the clear notes ring out with ear-splitting emphasis. Let the public speaker learn hence an important lesson. He but plays upon an instrument. Let him learn to use it rationally—in consciousness, at least, of the mechanical principles of the apparatus. For, as the instrument of speech is more perfect than anything the hand of man has fashioned, it surely must, when properly handled, be " easier to be played on than a pipe !"

17. There is an important point of difference, however, between the human speaking machine and artificial wind instruments like the bagpipe or organ. These latter have separate passages for the entrance and exit of the air, while the instrument of speech has but one channel by which the air is received and delivered. Through the aperture of the glottis,* all the breath must pass both in inhalation and exhalation. These acts must therefore be alternate, and cannot possibly take place at the same time ; while, in playing on artificial instruments, the air is both drawn in and expelled simultaneously by separate apertures.

18. Speaking being an expenditure of breath, pausing must be regularly alternate with utterance, to supply the waste of breath. The speaker must not exhaust his stock before he takes a further supply, but he must aim

---

* The GLOTTIS is the narrow aperture of the trachea or wind-pipe, situated behind the root of the tongue. Its action in closing or opening the passage to the lungs may be felt in *coughing*. The effort that precedes the cough shuts the glottis, by contact of its edges ; and the explosive ejection of breath in the cough arises from the sudden opening of the glottis by the separation of its edges.

at keeping up a constant sufficiency, by repeated inhalations. This is the *principle* which the bagpipe teaches. The most momentary pause will be found long enough to give opportunity for adding to the contents of the chest easily and imperceptibly.

19. A clear sonorous voice uses comparatively little breath : consequently the purer the voice the easier the utterance. The chest would be uncomfortably distended if the unexpended breath were held in at pauses. Pauses should therefore be synonymous with *change* of breath.

20. In addition to the power and ease that are gained by a proper management of the respiration, the speaker derives the further advantage of a good carriage of the bust. This contributes in no slight degree to give the young orator a feeling of *confidence* in addressing an audience. Fear naturally collapses, and courage expands the chest ; and the cultivation of the habit of keeping the chest expanded in speech imparts courage, and prevents that perturbation of the breathing which bashfulness and diffidence occasion to the unpractised speaker.

Respiratory Exercises.

21. To gain the power of fully and quickly inflating the lungs the following exercise will be useful. Prolong the simple vowel sounds musically to the full extent of expiratory power : silently replenishing the lungs and recommencing the sound as expeditiously as possible. The voice should begin softly, swell out vigorously, and then " knit sound to silence," by the most gentle termination. Thus :

< >	< >	< >	< >
e	ah	aw	oo, &c.

After a little practice the sound should be continued clearly for the space of from 25 to upwards of 30 seconds. This exercise is equally advantageous to the singer as to the speaker.

22. The same principle of exercise in connection with articulation may be obtained in *counting*. Pronounce the numbers from one to a hundred, deliberately and distinctly, with as few breathings as possible. *Note* the

numbers after which the breath is inspired, and compare
the results of the exercise at different times.

23. To gain the power of *keeping* the chest expanded
and the lungs well filled, by frequent and imperceptible
inspirations, the following exercise will be of service :—
After due preparatory elevation of the chest, pronounce
a long series of numbers with a gentle and instantaneous
expansion of the chest *before each number;* and continue the exercise for some minutes at a time, without a
single pause for breathing. This may be found difficult
and laborious at first, but practice will speedily impart
facility.

24. These respiratory exercises will be found of the
highest utility in cases of CONTRACTED CHEST or WEAK
LUNGS. Persons engaged in sedentary occupations, the
dyspeptic, and the convalescent, would find in them gym-
nastics of the most salutary nature, without leaving the
office or the chamber.

25. To strengthen weak respiration the practice of energetic reading in a strong loud whisper, or "gruff"
voice, will prove beneficial. Above all, exercise in the
open air will be found of advantage. The ancient rhet-
oricians practised declamation while walking or running
up a hillside before breakfast, or standing by the sea-shore,
face to the wind, and endeavoring to out-bellow the
tempest.

26. Respiratory exercises should not be practised immediately after a full meal. The distension of the stomach
prevents the free play of the diaphragm. The public
speaker should therefore be sparing before any important
oratorical effort, and defer making up the deficiency until
he has made his bow to the audience.

III. PRINCIPLES OF VOCALIZATION.

27. VOICE is the name given to that sound which is
formed in the Larynx,* by the passage of the compressed

------

* The LARNYX is that cartilaginous box-like structure which
surmounts the trachea, causing the protuberance in front of the
neck, known as "Adam's apple." Its aperture is a lengthened
slit, the upper extremity of which is called the *superior glottis*,
and the lower the *inferior glottis.*

air from the lungs, through the contiguous edges of the glottis. It being important that the student should clearly understand the mechanical formation of voice, we offer the following simple and homely illustrations.

28. The principle on which vocal sound is formed is the same as that by which a blade of grass or a slip of ribbon is made to produce a sound by being placed between the lips while the breath is strongly impinged against them. But the most perfect imitation of voice, as well as the most exact imitation of the laryngeal aperture—the glottis—is obtained by the approximation of two fingers, say the fore and middle fingers of the left hand, holding them nearly to the middle joints in the right hand, and forcing the breath between their moistened edges. The aperture thus obtained between the fingers, from the knuckles to the next joints, is of about the same size as that of the glottis; and the sound produced by the vibration of its edges, remarkably resembles glottal voice, and exemplifies many of the vocal principles. Comparative openness of the aperture produces grave sounds, and contraction, acute sounds: slackness of its edges causes huskiness or whisper, and tension gives clearness and purity of tone. A knowledge of these principles should assist the speaker in correcting habits of defective or impure sonorousness of voice.

29. Variations of Pitch in the voice are thus produced by variations in the condition and dimensions of the glottis. Something, too, depends on the elevation or depression of the whole larynx; as we see coarsely exemplified by untrained singers, who toss the head upwards, or burrow the chin in the chest, as they squeak or croak at the extremities of the voice. In running over the vocal compass, the larynx may be felt descending with the gravity of the tones, and ascending with their acuteness. The head, of course, should be quiescent. A sympathetic motion of the head or eye-brows is a common but offensive accompaniment to the movements of the voice among untutored speakers.

[Exercises on the vocal movements—speaking tones—will be found under the head of Inflexion.]

30. The voice may be formed by a soft and gradual

vibration, or by an abrupt and instantaneous explosiveness
of sound. The latter mechanism of voice is often employed in energetic, emphatic speech; and the orator
should be able, at will, to adopt it with any degree of
, force from *piano* to *forte*. The pronunciation of the
vowel sounds with something of the effort of a cough,*
but without its breathiness, will develop the power of
producing this intensive vocal effect. Thus:—inhale a
full breath, and eject the vowel sounds directly from the
throat; avoiding, in the most forcible effort, any bending
or other action of the head or body.

31. Huskiness of voice may be the result of diffidence,
of disease, or of over-exertion. With the first and last
of these we have to do. The mechanical cause is a relaxation of the vocal ligaments. Rest will generally
restore the voice when over-exertion is the cause of its
depravity; and the "coup de la glotte" will purify it,
and contribute to give confidence when the first is the
modifying circumstance. In temporary affections of the
voice, warm mucilaginous drinks, and many confectionery
preparations will be of service. Dryness of the mouth
will be relieved by a small particle of powdered nitre
placed upon the tongue. Habits of temperance are the
best preservative of the voice.

32. The voice is variously modified in quality by the
relative arrangement of the organs of the mouth,—the soft
palate, the tongue, the teeth, and the lips. The various
configurations of the vocal channel, and of the oral aperture, by the plastic soft organs, the tongue and lips, give
rise to *vowel* diversity. The contraction of the arch of
the fauces, by enlargement of the tonsils, or by too close
approximation of the root of the tongue to the soft palate,
produces a *guttural* depravity of tone: laxity of the soft
palate, causing it to hang from, and uncover, or only partially close, the nares (the pharyngeal openings of the
nostrils) produces a *nasal* modification: too close approximation of the jaws, especially the falling back of
the lower teeth behind the upper, gives rise to a *dental*

---

* This exercise ("coup de la glotte") is recommended to singers
in the excellent and philosophical Treatise on the Art of Singing,
by M. Garcia, of Paris.

impurity ; and contraction or inequality of the labial aperture—by elevation of the lower lip above the edges of the lower teeth, by depression of the upper lip below the edges of the upper teeth, by contact of the corners of the lips, by pouting, or by opening the mouth unequally to one side—produces a *labial* modification. These labial habits affect not only the quality of the voice, but also many of the vowel and articulate formations.

33. The quality of the voice is said to be gutturally, dentally, or labially depraved, when the approximation of the organs is so close as to produce a degree of guttural, dental, or labial *vibration*, in addition to the true sonorous vibration of the glottis.

IV.—PRINCIPLES OF VOWEL FORMATION.

34. The voice, as formed in the glottis, may be said to be destitute of vowel quality. It is *moulded* into vowel shapes as it flows out of the mouth. The following simple experiment will give a clear idea of the nature of vowel formation.

35. Open the mouth to the greatest possible extent—with the lips naturally drawn back, so that the edges of the teeth are visible—and emit an utterance of voice : it will sound *ah!* Continue sounding this vowel while you gradually cover the mouth firmly with the hand, laying the fingers of the left hand on the right cheek, and slowly bringing the whole hand across the mouth : the vowel quality of the sound will be changed with every diminution of the oral aperture, progressively becoming *aw, oh, oo,* as the palm gradually covers the mouth.

36. The apparatus of the mouth is wonderfully calculated to effect the most minute and delicate changes with definiteness and precision. The *tongue* and the *lips* are the chief agents of vowel modification. When the tongue is evenly depressed, and the lips are fully spread, the voice has the vowel sound *ah;* when the tongue contracts the oral channel—by rising convexly within the arch of the palate, leaving only a small central passage for the voice—the vowel quality is *ee;* and when the labial aperture is contracted to a small central opening—the vowel

quality is *oo*. These vowels then, *ee*, *ah*, and *oo*, are the extremes of the natural vowel scale : the closest *lingual* vowel is *ee;* the closest *labial*, *oo;* and the most *open* sound, *ah*.

37. From the mutual independence of the vowel modifiers—the lips and the tongue,—it will be obvious that their various positions may be assumed either separately or simultaneously. Thus we may put the tongue into the position *ee*, and the lips into the position *oo* at the same instant ; and we shall produce a vowel, which combines the qualities of *ee* and *oo*, and is different from both ; just as two colours intermixed, such as blue and yellow, produce a third,—green,—which combines their effects, and differs from either element of the compound. The close labio-lingual vowel, resulting from the simultaneous formation of *ee* and *oo*, is the German ü—a sound often heard in some of the Irish and American dialects, instead of *oo*, or *u*.

38. Two other vowels of the Labio-lingual class are such very common European sounds, that an additional illustration, with reference to them, may not be superfluous. The lips in the position ō, and the tongue in the position ā, produce the broad variety of French û—the same as the Scotch vowel in *fruit*, *shoe*, &c. ; and the lips in the position aw, with the tongue in the position ĕ (ell), produce the French eu or the German ö. If, therefore, the vowel oo be sounded, or the vowel ō, or the vowel aw, the mere advance of the tongue will produce the corresponding Labio-lingual vowels without any change in the position of the lips. Thus, retract and advance the tongue while the lips retain the positions oo, ō, aw, and the sounds will be alternately :

oo ü,	oo ü,	oo ü
ō û,	ō û,	ō û
aw eu,	aw eu,	aw eu

39. In the system of " Visible Speech " three classes of purely *lingual* vowels are recognized, as modified by the " Back," the " Front," or the (" Mixed ") Back and Front, of the tongue. At each of these three parts of the tongue three distinct vowels are formed by the " High," " Mid," or " Low " position of the tongue in reference to

the palate ; and of each of the nine vowels so produced
there is a " Wide " variety, caused by expansion of the
faucal cavity behind the tongue. There are thus eighteen
vowels of the lingual class provided with separate symbols.
Each of these eighteen vowels yields a " Round " or la-
bialized variety ; so that the Alphabet of Visible Speech
contains 36 simple vowels. The number is extended by
diacritic signs to no fewer than 180 possible shades of
vowel quality, for which a distinctive notation is given.
It is impossible by means of ordinary letters to tabulate
the Universal Alphabet with intelligibility ; although
these vowels are all written by only six primary symbols
in " Visible Speech."

40. The following Table contains a classification of
English Vowel sounds in the order of their formation,
commencing with that which has the most contracted
lingual aperture.

41. *English Vowel Scheme, and Numerical Notation.*

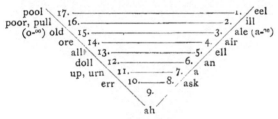

Combinations.

8–2 isle ; 8–16 owl ; 12–2 oil ; y–16 cure ; y–17 cue.

42. In order to bring this scheme into practical application, the student must discard *letters* as names of the
sounds, and adopt instead a *numerical* nomenclature, in
accordance with the arrangement in the Table. Thus,
he must associate the sound *ee* with Number 1, and speak
of the vowel in the words b*e*, f*ee*, t*ea*, k*ey*, ce*i*l, f*ie*ld,
pe*o*ple, p*i*que, &c., as uniformly No. 1., independently
of the diverse vowel letters which represent the sound.
And so with all the other vowels. He has to deal with
sounds, not letters.

43. The key words in the Table contain the vowel sounds to which the numbers refer. The student should make himself expert at vocal analysis, so as to be able to pronounce the vowels *alone* with the exact sound which they receive in the words. He will probably experience some difficulty at first in isolating the " short" sounds correctly,—especially the 2d and 6th vowels,—without the customary assistance of an articulation to " stop" them. But as there is no particular quantity or duration *essential* to any vowel, he should make himself able to pronounce all the sounds independently, with both long and short degrees of quantity.

44. The terms *long* and *short* are here used with reference only to sounds which are identical in quality or formation. Vowels are commonly spoken of as relatively long and short, when they are utterly unlike in every characteristic of sound. Thus *i* in *ill* is called the *short* sound of " I," the *long* sound of which is heard in *isle;* and *u* in *us*, the *short* sound of " U," the long sound being heard in *use*. In the more definite nomenclature by *numbers*, these " short " sounds are respectively the 2nd and 11th vowels.

45. The" long" or name-sounds of the alphabetic vowels are : A = 3, E = 1, I = 8-2, O = 15, U = y-17 ; and their "short" sounds are : A= 6, E = 5, I= 2, O = 12, U =11.

Vowel Exercises.

46. The following words exemplify each of the English vowels in their various modes of orthography.

47. FIRST VOWEL, *represented by* e, i, æ, ae, ay, ee, e'e, ea, ei, eo, ey, eye, ie, œ, uoi ; *as in* eve, fatigue, minutiæ, aerie, quay, bee, e'en, eat, conceive, people, key, keyed, field, antœci, turquoise ; religion, sedate, prefer, vehement, peculiar, enough, decide, between, œtites, assuetude, idea, aureola, sphere, shire, bier, belief, unique, priest, police, treaty, seizure, ægis, amphisbœna, œdema, peevish, meagre, league, siege, scream, fiend, wean, ease, breeze, frieze, achieve, trustee, ennui, ye, thee.

48. SECOND VOWEL, *represented by* a, e, i, o, u, y, ai, ay, ea, ee, ei, ey, ia, ie, ui, uy; *as in* cabbage, pretty, ill, women, busy, hymn, mountain, Monday, guineas,

breeches, forfeit, monkey, parliament, sieve, build, plaguy;
orange, England, alkali, ashy, fancies, oxygen, servile,
cottage, marriage, miniature, business, vineyard, cygnet,
abyss, hyssop, citron, chintz, vivify, dizziness, invisible,
miracle, spirit, livelong, vigil, give, film, bilge, finger,
singer, precipice, premises, vestige, virility, valleys.

49. THIRD VOWEL, *represented by* a, ai, ao, au, ay,
aye, ea, ei, ey, eye, oi ; *as in* age, aim, gaol, gauge, pay,
aye, steak, vein, obey, preyed, connoisseur ; aerial, archai-
ology, ukase, emigrate, portrait, clayey, vacate, weigher,
half-penny, phasis, plaice, complacent, obeisance, bait,
great, straight, ache, quaint, able, layer, azure, hey-day,
maiden, zany, gala, jailor, sago, scabrous, shame, they've,
lathe, baize, chaise, rein-deer, vain, veil, bewail, vagrant,
neigh, dismay, inveigh, allay, grey, gay, yea.

50. FOURTH VOWEL, *represented by* a, e, aa, ae, ai,
ay, ea, e'e, ei, ey ; *as in* fare, ere, Aaron, aer, air, prayer,
wear, ne'er, heir, eyre ; daring, fairy, heiress, Mary,
chary, scare-crow, lair, therein, where'er.

51. FIFTH VOWEL, *represented by* a, e, u, ae, ai, ay,
ea, ei, eo, ie, ue ; *as in* many, ever, bury, Michaelmas,
said, says, health, heifer, leopard, friend, guess ; erratic,
erroneous, effect, effeminate, embezzle, eccentric, except,
executor, extend, dreaded, essence, headless, segment,
freshness, emptiness, jeopardy, feoff, death, etiquette,
wealth, elsewhere, burial, beryl, ferret, pellet, rennet,
jealous, zenith, pleasure, regiment, legend, emblem,
brethren, helmet, velvet.

52. SIXTH VOWEL, *represented by* a, aa, ai ; *as in*
amber, Canaan, raillery ; atlantean, vagrant, translate,
woodland, annual, atlas, capital, passion, patent, relapse,
statue, tapestry, waft, wax, altitude, balcony, amaranth,
arid, ballad, cavalry, galaxy, gaseous, harass, paragraph,
album, band, flag, plaid, glad, pageant, scandal, value,
harangue.

53. SEVENTH VOWEL, *represented by* a ; *as in* abode,
adapt, again, alone, arouse, charade, dragoon, fanatic,
oasis, pagoda, idea, paralysis, saliva, saloon, syllable,
sofa, drama.

54. EIGHTH VOWEL, *represented by* a ; *as in* bath,
cast, castle, brass, fasten, master, pass, past, repast, sam-
ple, staff, task, vast.

55. NINTH VOWEL, *represented by* a, e, au, ea, ua ; *as in* ardour, clerk, haunt, hearty, guardian ; artificer, barbaric, harpoon, narcotic, parhelion, sarcastic, lunar, dotard, arch, artifice, carpet, hearth, hearken, startle, tartar, aunt, can't, draught, laugh, arm, are, barge, farm, sergeant, guardian, alms, balm, calves, malmsey, papa, qualm, salve, father.

56. TENTH VOWEL, *represented by* r, re, er, ir, yr, ear, uer, wer ; *as in* par, here, her, firmness, hyrst, earnest, guerdon, answer ; pier, near, hare, star, war, ore, sure, fire, beaver, fibre, acre, cider, ephir, zephyr, martyr, satire, chirp, earth, bird, fertile, merchant, thirty, vertex, virtue, myrtle, gherkin, irksome, kerchief, verb, firm, sirs, hers, bird, herd, verge, dirge, earn, yearn, early, pearl, sirloin, sterling, whirlwind, err, stir, myrrh, prefer.

57. ELEVENTH VOWEL, *represented by* o, u, eo, io, oa, oi, oo, ou, ow, wo, eou, iou, olo ; *as in* world, done, furnace, ugly, dungeon, motion, cupboard, avoirdupois, blood, journey, young, bellows, twopence, gorgeous, cautious, colonel ; bombast, buffoon, doubloon, sublime, umbrella, unkind, upon, seldom, bankrupt, medium, dubious, jealous, genus, courageous, collection, dudgeon, question, bluff, chough, tough, couple, nuptial, doth, husk, joust, thus, subtle, luscious, luxury, pulp, bulk, gulf, mulct, monk, uncle, borough, brother, colour, cover, cunning, curricle, honey, money, mother, shovel, smuggle, study, thorough, tunnel, worry, colander, dull, dumb, none, buzz, love, tub, hung ; burr, fur, spur, cur, surfeit, worse, work, worm, curly, worldly, urn, absurd, curdle, urge.

58. TWELFTH VOWEL, *represented by* a, o, au, oa, ou, ow ; *as in* want, often, laudanum, groat, hough, knowledge ; observe, occasion, oppose, quadroon, volcano, blossom, coffee, cloth, fossil, doctor, prologue, quantity, quash, squat, topic, twattle, vocative, wash, wasp, watch, conch, frontier, monster, prompt, wampum, cauliflower, chronicle, foreign, grovel, honest, laurel, monad, nomad, olive, provost, qualify, quarrel, sovereign, squalid, volant, warrant, zoology, bond, prong, quadrant, solve, squander, swan, was, wan.

59. THIRTEENTH VOWEL, *represented by* a, au, aw, oa, ou ; *as in* all, taught, law, broad, thought; war, swarthy, warm, auction, awful, balk, bought, caution, falcon, vaunt, halt, plaudit, lawyer, bald, broad, shawl, tall, yawn, faugh, pacha, spa, saw.

60. FOURTEENTH VOWEL, (only before R), *represented by* o, ew, oa, oo, ou, wo, owa ; *as in* ore, sewer, oar, door, four, sword, towards ; original, oriental, forebode, glory, sonorous, coarse, court, courtier, forth, hoarse, porch, source, portly, porte, borne, bourn, forge, gourd, mourn, torn, tournament, untoward, horde, corps, floor, o'er, restore, decorum, horal, pylorus, deportment, victorious, proportion.

61. FIFTEENTH VOWEL, *represented by* o, ao, au, ew, cau, ewe, oa, oe, oo, ou, ow, owe ; *as in* old, Pharaoh, hauteur, shew, beau, sewed, oak, foe, brooch, soul, crow, crowed ; analogy, antelope, apotheosis, arrow, borrow, broccoli, cameo, coeval, colony, colossus, furlough, elocution, nosology, obedient, philosopher, potato, rondeau, zoology, oasis, orthoepy, blowpipe, broach, cocoa, engross, host, jocose, locomotive, narcosis, oak, oat, oath, bolster, poultry, won't, curioso, hautboy, olio, onyx, trover, zodiac, blown, boll, brogue, comb, droll, foal, knoll, mould, nones, parasol, shrove, though, bureau, dough, hoe, holloa, know, lo, owe, throe, sloe, trow, mower, woe.

62. SIXTEENTH VOWEL, *represented by* o, u, oo, ou ; *as in* wolf, pull, look, poor, would ; ambush, bivouac, ferula, fulfil, hurrah, to, into, issue, treasure, book, butcher, cuckoo, cushion, push, puss, put, pulpit, bosom, bully, sugar, woman, woollen, bull, should, stood.

63. SEVENTEENTH VOWEL, *represented by* o, u, ew, oe, oo, ou, ui ; *as in* do, rude, brew, shoe, woo, you, cruise ; roué, truism, bouquet, brutal, flute, fruitage, goose, croup, recruit, ruler, whoop, youthful, remove, rhubarb, ruby, ruthless, bloom, bouse, bruise, lose, peruse, shrewd, accrue, ado, brew, halloo, ormolu, ragout, who, too.

64. DIPHTHONG 8-2, *represented by* i, y, ai, ay, ei, ey, eye, ie, oi, ui, uy, ye, ; *as in* isle, by, naiveté, ay, height, eying, eye, lie, choir, guide, buy, dye ; diameter, iden-

tify, iota, psychology, zodiacal, viaduct, society, hierarch,
bias, lyre, science, cycle, nightly, viscount, vital, icicle,
island, ivy, finite, piebald, sliver, twilight, I'll, I'm, I'd,
blithe, gyve, rhyme, lithesome, bye, fy, awry, thigh, rye,
vie, why.

65. Diphthong 8–16, *represented by* o, ou, ow ; *as in*
accomptant, thou, cow ; vouchsafe, foundation, bower,
coward, vowel, our, couch, cowslip, doughty, bounteous,
countenance, fountain, cloudy, owlet, thousand, browse,
lounge, avow, bough, plough, endow.

66. Diphthong 12–2, *represented by* oe, oi, oy, eoi ;
as in oboe, coin, boy, burgeois ; envoy, rhomboid, boy-
ish, loyalty, moiety, cloister, doit, hoist, oyster, anoint,
jointure, embroider, foible, toilsome, avoid, noiseless,
alloy, joy, destroy.

67. Combination y–16, *represented by* u, as in cure,
durable, nature, obtuse, use (n.), abuse (n.), refuse (n.)

68. Combination y–17, *represented by* u, ue, ui, eu,
ew, eau, iew, yew, you ; *as in* duty, imbue, suit, neuter,
few, beauty, view, yew, you ; superior, utensil, virtue,
interview, tutor, Tuesday, dupe, tune, gewgaw, music,
news, fugue, pursuit, mutual, suture, use (v.), alluvial,
illusive, pollute, involution, abuse (v.), refuse (v.)

V. ANGLICISMS OF VOWEL SOUND.*

69. It will be observed that the *a* and *o* which represent
the 3rd and 15th vowels in the English scheme (par. 41),
have a small *ee* and *oo* printed after these radical letters.
This indicates a peculiar Anglicism ; in which, and some
associated principles, lies the leading difference between
the vernacular dialects north and south of the Tweed.
In Scotland these vowels are *monophthongs*—that is,
their sound is the same from beginning to end, thus a‾‾a
and o‾‾o ; while in England these vowels are *diphthongs*, being tapered from the radical point towards the
closest formation of their respective classes, lingual or

---

* For a minute description of each of the English vowels, the
defects to which they are liable, and the means of correction,—
with copious Exercises,—see " Principles of Speech and Dictionary of Sounds."

labial. *A* tapers towards *e* by the progressive ascent of
the tongue, and *o* tapers towards *oo* by the gradual approximation of the lips. Thus—

obey>ᵉᵉ,	go>ᵒᵒ,
ai>ᵉᵉd,	o>ᵒᵒld.
pla>ᵉᵉgue,	ho>ᵒᵒme,
la>ᵉᵉke,	ho>ᵒᵒpe, &c.

70. In the lists of the 3d and 15th vowels, there is no
word containing the letter R after the vowel. This omission is not accidental. It brings us to another Principle.

71. R in English is articulated but faintly, or not at
all, in the two following positions; 1st, *before any articulation*—or consonant;—2d, at the *end of any word*.
In these situations, R has always a *vowel* sound—that of
er or *ir* in the words *her* and *sir*—the 10th vowel. R
has this vowel effect also when between two vowels, the
first being long, as in weary, fiery, glory, fury. In words
of this class, the R has both its vowel and its consonant
sound. Thus, glory is not glō-ry, but glo(re)-ry. The
vowel-quality of the R is most manifest after the closest
radical vowels. The pronunciation *pee-rage, poo-rest,*
&c., is characteristically Scotch. Such words, to be
Anglicised, must be pronounced *pe-er-age, poo-er-est,*
&c.

72. *Exercise on the Double Sound of R:*—Eyry,
ear-ache, leering, nearer, peeress, merest, airy, unwary,
fairy, Mary, heiress, garish, soaring, gory, boreas, jury,
alluring, Moorish, fiery, wiry, showery, towering.

73. The 3rd and 15th vowels are, as shown above,
closing diphthongs—that is, the vowel aperture is smaller
at the end than at the beginning of the sound. A *syllable*
may consist of either an opening or a closing combination
of vowels, but it cannot combine with these any sound
that reverses the progression. The vowel sound of R,
(No. 10) is a very open sound, and could not, therefore, be pronounced after the closing diphthongs *A⌣e* or
O⌣oo in one syllable. Either the diphthongal A and O
must be contracted into *monophthongs*, or the R must be
articulated. The latter expedient would be *un*-English:
the former is adopted. The closing diphthongal termination of the A and O is dropped, and the radical vowel

3

sound is slightly *opened* for easier combination with the very open element 10. Thus, instead of No. 3, we pronounce No. 4, and instead of 15, we pronounce 14, before R in the same syllable.

74. In this way a distinctiveness is maintained in the pronunciation of such words as *lair* and *layer*, *lore* and *lower*, &c. The firsts of these pairs of words are monosyllables (4‿10 and 14‿10), and the seconds are dissyllables (3-2-10 and 15-16-10).

75. The 14th vowel is intermediate in formation to *oh* and *aw*. The rapid alternation of these sounds will blend them into No. 14; or the effort to pronounce an *O without using the lips* will probably at once give the exact effect.

76. The difference between English and Scotch pronunciation in such words as *air* and *ore* is very marked: the *R* being strongly *articulated* in Scotland, and the *A* and *O* having the same sound before R as before other articulations.

VI. SCOTTICISMS OF VOWEL SOUND.

77. VOWEL 1, too short; as in *feet, people, mean, steel*, &c.—Vowel 1, as No. 3, short; as in *deal, meal, seat, conceit*, &c., pronounced dăle, măle, &c.

78. Vowel 2, too open; as in *fill, crib, dig, him*, &c., pronounced nearly as fĕll, crĕb, dĕg, hĕm,* &c.—Vowel 2, as No. 1, short, as in *religion, individual, vicious,* &c., pronounced rĕleegion, ĕndĕveedual, veecious, &c.—Vowel 2, nearly as No. 11; as in *will, wind, wish*, &c., pronounced wŭll, wŭnd, wŭsh, &c.

79. Vowel 3, a monophthong. Vowel 3, a diphthong compounded of Nos. 4 and 1, as in *aye, pay, jail, tailor,* &c., pronounced nearly as ĕh-ee, pĕh-ee, jĕh-eel, &c.—Vowel 2, as No. 5 (long); as in *nation, education, gracious*, &c., pronounced nehtion, grehcious,† &c.;—Vowel

---

* The vowel in these cases is an abrupt utterance of the sound of No. 4 (English Vowel Scheme, par. 41).

† This is less a colloquial than an oratorical and especially a Pulpit Scotticism.

3, as No. 5 (short) ; as in *paint*, *lady*, *trade*, &c., pronounced pĕnt, lĕddy, trĕd, &c.

80. Vowel 4, as No. 3 (monophthong) ; as in *Mary*, *heiress*, &c., pronounced Mā-ry, ai-ress, &c.

81. Vowel 5, as No. 1 ; as in *deaf*, *breast*, *seven*, &c., pronounced dĕĕf, brĕĕst, &c.—Vowel 5, as No. 2 ; as in *twenty*, *ever*, *never*, *ef-*, *em-*, *en-*, *ex-*, &ç., pronounced twinty, iver, niver, if-, im-, in-, &c.—Vowel 5, long instead of short; as in *guess*, *smell*, &c.—Vowel 5, as No. 3 (monophthong) ; as in *death*, *edify*, &c., pronounced daith, &c.—Vowel 5, too open ; as in *very*, *perish*, &c., pronounced varry, parish, &c.—Vowel 5, pronounced with an abrupt sound of No. 4 ; as in *merry*, *cherry*, &c.

82. Vowel 6, as No. 3 ; as in *apple*, *axe*, *pacify*, &c., pronounced aiple, aiks, &c.—Vowel 6, as No. 5 ; as in *cap*, *Saturday*, *salary*, &c., pronounced kep, sĕturday, &c.—Vowel 6, as No. 9 (short) ; as in *man*, *gas*, *am*, *cat*, &c., pronounced măhn, găhs, &c.—Vowel 6, as No. 13 ; as in *wax*, *salmon*, &c., pronounced wawx, sawmon, &c.

83. Vowel 7, as No. 2 ; as in *sofa*, *idea*, &c., pronounced sofy, &c.

84. Vowel 8, as No. 9 (short) ; as in *ask*, *bath*, &c., pronounced ăhsk, &c.—Vowel 8, as No. 5 ; as in *brass*, *grass*, *nasty*, &c., pronounced bress, gress, &c.

85. Vowel 9, too short; as in *parcel*, *carpet*, *half*, &c.—Vowel 9, as No. 13 ; as in *palm*, *papa*, *far*, *star*, &c. ; pronounced pawm, papaw, faur, stawr, &c.- Vowel 9, as No. 5 ; as in *farm*, *heart*, *hearth*, &c. ; pronounced fĕhRm, hĕhrt, hĕhrth, &c.—Vowel 9, as No. 3 ; as in *arm*, *guard*, *sergeant*, &c. ; pronounced aiRm, gaiRd, saiRgeant, &c.

86. Vowel 10, as No. 5 ; as in *err*, *serve*, *person*, *term*, &c. ; prounounced ĕhRR, sĕhRve, pĕhRson, tĕhRm, &c.—Vowel 10, as in *firm*, *circle*, *stir*, *virgin*, *acre*, *paper*, &c. ; pronounced with the abrupt sound of No. 4, referred to in par. 78.

87. Vowel 11, too deep or guttural ; as in *tub*, *cuff*, *cull*, &c.—Vowel 11 (in unaccented termination), as in attent*ion*, geni*us*, atroc*ious*, pronounced with the abrupt sound of No. 4, referred to in the preceding paragraph.

—Vowel 11, (before R,) too short, and the R strongly
articulated—as in *fur, turn, worm,* &c. ; pronounced
fŭʀ, tŭʀn, wŭʀm, &c.

88. Vowel 12, as No. 15 ; as in *cost, morn, fond, copy,
clock,* &c. ; pronounced coast, mourn, &c. Vowel 12 as
No. 11 ; as in *body, nobody,* &c. ; pronounced buddy,
nobuddy, &c.

89. Vowel 13 as No. 9 ; as in *war, saw, call, walk,
warp, quality,* &c. ; pronounced wahr, sah, quahlity, &c.
Vowel 13 as No. 15 ; as in *bought, broad,* &c. ; pronounced, boat, &c.

90. Vowel 14 as No. 15 ; as in *four, sore, door, glory,
story,* &c. ; pronounced fohʀ, glohry, &c. Vowel 14 as
No. 12 ; as in *force, sport, fourth,* &c. ; pronounced
fŏrs, fŏrth, &c. Vowel 14 as No. 17 ; as in *coarse, court,
pour,* &c. ; pronounced cooʀs, pooʀ, &c.

91. Vowel 15 a monophthong. Vowel 15 as No. 2,
in unaccented syllables ; as in *fellow, elocution, analogy,*
&c. ; pronounced felly, analygy, &c. Vowel 15 as No.
3 ; as in *own, alone, toe,* &c. ; pronounced ain, alain, tae,
&c. Vowel 15 as No. 12 ; as in *broken, loaf, coals,* &c. ;
pronounced brocken, lof, colz, &c. Vowel 15 as No. 13 ;
as in *old, cold, fold,* &c. ; pronounced auld, cauld, &c.
Vowel 15 as a diphthong, compounded of Nos. 11 and 17 ;
as in *bowl, soul, mould,* &c. The same vowel is heard,
but the *l* is not sounded, in *boll, poll* (the head), *knoll,
roll,* &c. ; pronounced bow, pow, &c.

92. Vowel 16 as No. 11 ; as in *woman, full, bull,
bush,* &c. ; pronounced wumman, &c. Vowel 16 as
No. 4 (short) ; as in *foot, put;* pronounced nearly fet,
pet.

93. Vowel 17 too short ; as in *pool, fool,* &c. Vowel
17 as the labio-lingual of No. 3 (û French) ; as in *soon,
fruit, goose, shoe,* &c. ; pronounced sûne, frûte, gûse,
shû, &c.—Vowel 17, final, sometimes has the simple
lingual formation correspondent to the above labio-lingual
vowel ; as in *tae* and *dae,* for *too* and *do,* &c. In some
districts closer lingual vowels are used ; as *skill* or *skele*
for *school, fill* for *fool, seen* for *soon, dee* for *do,* &c.

94. Diphthong 8-2, as No. 1, in verbs ending in y ; as
in *gratify, stupify, edify,* &c. ; pronounced grätifee,

stûpifee, äidifee, &c.—Diphthong 8-2, with the Scotch
Vowel referred to in par. 78; as in *find*, *blind*, *sight*,
&c.; pronounced nearly fĕnd, blĕnd, sĕcнt, &c.—Diphthong 8-2 as 9-2—the radical sound very long; as in *fly*,
sky, &c.; pronounced flāh-*y*, skāh-*y*, &c.—Diphthong
8-2, with 5 (long), instead of 8, followed by a very slight
closing effect; as in *I*, *high*, *prize*, &c.; pronounced
nearly as eh-y, heh-y, preh-iz, &c.—Diphthong 8-2,—as
a compound of the Scotch vowel before referred to, and
No. 1; as in *ice*, *fine*, *smile*, &c.; pronounced nearly as
ĕh-ees, fĕh-een, smĕh-eel, &c.
  95. Diphthong 8-16, as 11–17; as in *cloud*, *howl*, *vow*,
thou, &c.—Diphthong 8-16 as No. 17; as in *house*, *proud*,
cow, &c.; pronounced hŏŏs, prŏŏd, cōō, &c.—Diphthong
8-16, as No. 11; as in *pound*, *ground*, &c.; pronounced
pŭnd, grŭnd, &c.
  96. Diphthong 12-2, as 15-2; as in *boy*, *noise*, &c.;
pronounced bō-y, nō-iz, &c.—Diphthong 12-2, pronounced with a compound of the Scotch variety of No. 4
and No. 1; as in *oil*, *oyster*, *joint*, &c.; pronounced
nearly ĕh-eel, ĕh-eester, jĕh-eent, &c.
  97. In the foregoing list of Vowel Scotticisms, no notice
is taken of dialectic changes of *words*, but only of vernacular pronunciations of words used and spelt as in
English.

VII. HIBERNICISMS OF VOWEL SOUND.

  98. VOWEL 1, in some words, pronounced 3 (long,
monophthong); as in *seat*, *meat*, *easy*, &c.; pronounced
sate, aisy, &c.
  99. Vowel 2, (in *y* final) as 1; as in *happy*, *pretty*,
my (unaccented), &c., pronounced happee, mee, &c.
  100. Vowel 3, as a monophthong (long).
  101. Vowel 5, as French "e mute" (the "Mid Mixed"
vowel of Visible Speech); as in *health*, *pleasure*, *friend*,
&c.
  102. Vowels 8 and 9 as 6 (long); as in *bath*, *pass*,
castle, *calf*, *ah*, *papa*, &c.
  103. Vowels 10 and 11, nearly as 12; as in *her*, *sir*,
up, *dull*, *blood*, *worm*, *Dublin*, &c. The true sound

cannot be indicated by Roman letters ; it is the " Low
Mixed Round " vowel of Visible Speech.

104. Vowel 13 nearly as 8 ; as in *all, want, thought,
honest, law,* &c.   The sound is the " Low Mixed Wide
Round " vowel of Visible Speech.

105. Vowel 15, as a monophthong.

106. Vowel 16, in some words, nearly as 11 ; as in
foot, look, stood, put, cushion, &c.

107. Diphthong 8–2 nearly as 13–1 ; as in *why, I,
time,* and all words containing ī.   The true Irish sound
is the same as in par. 103.

108. Diphthong 12–2 nearly as 8–1.   The initial sound
is the same as in par. 104.

109. UNACCENTED VOWELS of all classes, as French
" e mute " (the " Mid Mixed " sound of Visible Speech) ;
as in re*l*igion, d*e*stroy, cabb*a*ge, surf*a*ce, prec*i*p*i*ce, good-
n*e*ss, us*e*less, paral*ysi*s, cert*ai*n, knowledg*e*, orn*a*ment,
orig*i*n*a*l, ph*i*losoph*e*r, rheumat*i*sm, pleas*u*re, countenance, &c.

VIII. AMERICANISMS OF VOWEL SOUND.

110. The Author's opportunities have enabled him to
furnish tolerably complete lists of Anglicisms, Scotticisms,
and Hibernicisms of Vowel Sound.   He cannot pretend
to an equally minute knowledge of American characteristics.   The preceding analysis may be taken as a model
by those who can in a similar manner exhibit the peculiarities of other Dialects.   A few only of the more prominent Americanisms can be noted here.

111. Vowel 3, as a monophthong.

112. Vowel 10,—and the letter R before an articulation,—with a sound which is very peculiar, and cannot
be represented by Roman letters.   It is the " High
Mixed " vowel of Visible Speech.   The effect of R before an articulation is nearly that of Y ; as in *spohyt* for
sport.

113. Vowel 11, before R, with the same sound as the
preceding.

114. Vowels 14 and 15, alike (monophthong.)

115. Diphthong 8–2 as 9–2, with the first element very
long ; as in tah-im for time.

116. Diphthong 8–16 as 5–16; as in deh-oon for down.

117. Diphthong 12–2 as 14–2.

118. Alphabetic U, when not pronounced simply as 17 (as dooty for duty) has the diphthongal sound 1–16; as in nee-oo for new, fee-oo for few, &c.

119. NASAL QUALITY. This is the most marked feature in the American Dialects. A national relaxation of the soft palate seems to prevail, so that the inner ends of the *nares* remain uncovered. Vowels before or after the nasal Articulations M, N, and Ng, are affected in the greatest degree ; but many speakers never utter a purely oral vowel.

IX. DISTINCTION BETWEEN VOWELS AND ARTICU-LATIONS.

120. Before proceeding to illustrate further the Numerical Notation of Vowels, the distinction between VOWELS and ARTICULATIONS, (or Consonants,) must be explained. These primary classes of the elements of speech are united in Y and W, which combine *articulative* quality with the sounds of the closest *vowels* 1, (ee,) and 17, (oo.) Thus : prolong the sounds of y and w, as heard at the beginning of a word, (*yea, way,* &c.) and the Y will then be found identical in sound with Ee, and the w with Oo. Yet that there is a difference between Y and Ee, and between W and Oo,—and one not merely of quantity,—will be evident on pronouncing these vowels twice in succession, in contrast with the words ye and woo—thus ēē-ēē, ōō-ōō. Let these vowels be rapidly or slowly repeated, they will not identify with the words *ye* and *woo.* An experiment will furnish the most simple and convincing illustration of the difference between these utterances, and between Vowels and Articulations generally.

121. Prolong the sound of the First vowel (ee,) and while doing so strike the tongue upwards with the tip of a finger from behind the chin; and the Ee will be changed to YE by each stroke : prolong the seventeenth vowel (oo,) and while doing so, approximate the edges

of the lips, by the action of the finger and thumb, and the Oo will be changed into Woo, by every approximation. In forming the vowels Ee and Oo, the organs are in the closest positions they can assume without influencing the sound by a degree of vibration of the edges of the contracted lingual or labial aperture. In forming Y and W, a compressive action of the tongue and lips creates this oral, articulative effect; while it gives the succeeding vowel a degree of *percussiveness*, arising from previous interception or obstruction.

122. VOWELS, then, are glottal sounds merely *modified* by the shape of the mouth, and having no oral sound ; and ARTICULATIONS are *appulsive* actions of the oral organs, originating a sound *within the mouth*—a puff or hiss of breath, or a flap of the articulating organs.

123. The articulations Y and W often occur in pronunciation, when the letters are not written. The common English digraph qu is sounded kw ; and the alphabetic sound of the letter U is equivalent to Y-17. The sounds of E and I are often contracted into Y, as in *species*, *Asia*, *question*, &c., pronounced speesh-yiz, aish-ya, kwest-yun, &c.

X.—EXERCISES IN VOWEL NOTATION.

124. In the passages which are subjoined for analytic exercise, mark over every *spoken* vowel-letter the *number* of its sound, according to the Scheme at par. 41 ; and indicate the sounds of *y* and *w*, when the letters are not written. Also show when R has its *vowel* quality (No. 10) and *underline* it when it has *both its vowel* and *articulate* effects. Thus :

<pre>
 w 3   6   w 3   y 17   16 10   y 16 1-11   y 17 2
Quake, assuage, use,   your,   curious,   beauty.
</pre>

125. The *indefinite article*, a, is pronounced No. 7. The *definite article*, *the*, is pronounced nearly No. 2 when not emphatic. The pronominal adjectives *my* and *mine* are pronounced No. 2 when they are not accented or emphatic, and 8–2 when under emphasis. The final letters *le*, and often also *el* and *en*, are pronounced *without any vowel sound*,—the *l* and *n* having in themselves

syllabic purity of voice; as in bib*le*, thist*le*, haz*el*, bev*el*, dev*il*, bidd*en*, dead*en*, doz*en*, heav*en*, &c. The letter *m*, also, is similarly syllabic in such words as rhyth*m*, spas*m*,* &c. In all such cases *write a cipher* (⁰) over the l, n, or m, to indicate a SYLLABLE with *no vowel*. Take no notice of *silent letters*, but recognise and note *every sound*. The *plural* termination *es* is pronounced No. 2; and the *verbal* terminations *es, est, eth, ed,* &c., are pronounced No. 4. The final letters *ed* are not syllabically pronounced, except after *t*, or *d*, or for distinctiveness between different parts of speech of the same orthography, as in *learned, blessed,* &c., which are monosyllables, (learn'd, blest, &c.,) when verbs, and dissyllables, (learn-ed, bless-ed, &c.,) when adjectives.

126. Mark the vowels, &c., in the following poem and then compare the marking with the Key at par. 128.

I. Thought and Deed.

Full many a light thought man may cherish,
  Full many an idle deed may do;
Yet not a deed or thought shall perish,
  Not one but he shall bless or rue.

When by the wind the tree is shaken,
  There's not a bough or leaf can fall,
But of its falling heed is taken
  By One that sees and governs all.

The tree may fall and be forgotten,
  And buried in the earth remain;
Yet from its juices rank and rotten
  Springs vegetating life again.

---

* With the syllabic *l* and *n* a *vowel letter* is always written, and the syllable is thus perfect to *the eye*: but such words as *rhythm, prism, &c.*, having no vowel letter, are commonly reckoned monosyllables, though *to the ear* they are perfectly dissyllabic. The words *prism* and *prison*=priz'n, have sound for sound alike, and both are equally therefore dissyllables.

The world is with creation teeming,
And nothing ever wholly dies;
And things that are destroyed in seeming,
In other shapes and forms arise.

And nature still unfolds the tissue
Of unseen works by spirit wrought:
And not a work but hath its issue
With blessings or with evil fraught.

And thou may'st seem to leave behind thee
All memory of the sinful past;
Yet oh, be sure, thy sin shall find thee,
And thou shalt know its fruit at last.

II. Selected Words.

127. Mark the vowels, &c., in the following Selected
Words, and then compare the marking with the Key at
par. 129.

Accli'vous, acquiesce, adver'tisement, ancho'vy, answer,
assure, azure, antipodes, aeronaut, alienable, apophthegm,
apothe'osis, aro'ma, aspi'rant, bandana, banian', battalion, bellows, (s) bowline, breeches, Briton, Britain, brevier', brev'et,
(adj.) brevet', (s) burial, cesu'ra, capuchin', captious, comparable,
chas'tisement, chlorine, colonel, complaisant', con'trary, cor'ol-
lary, curule, coadju'tor, courier, creole, cupboard, deco'rous, des'-
uetude, diabetes, diœresis, dim'issory, duo, duteous, dynasty,
egotism, elegi'ac, ener'vate, equerry, equable, extraordinary,
fabric, facetiæ, fanat'ic, forfeit, fusil, fuchsia, glacier, hallelujah,
height, hypochon'driac, imbecile', impious, indict, invalid', (s)
inval'id, (adj.) issue, lieutenant, million, machinist, Mahomet,
manœuvre, medicinal, me'diocre, met'onymy, mem'oir, minutiæ,

mis'cellany, mischievous, mobile,* national, o'asis, omnipotent,
pique, pacha, panegyr'ic, phrenetic, phrenitis, plethora, ple-
thoric, prolix', puisne, quay, query, quandary, queue, righteous,
recitative', recon'dite, rep'ertory, rule, ref'ragable, rev'enue,
sacerdotal, sali'va, sapphire, satiate, satiety, satrap, stalac'tite,
sub'altern, supernumerary, synecdoche, towards, treasure, ver-
tigo, victuals, women, yacht, zoology, zoological.

Key to Exercises in Vowel Notation.

128. *I. Thought and Deed.*

<pre>
16   5 2 7 8-2   13   6   3   5 2
Full many a light thought man may cherish,
      6 8-2 0   1   3   17
Full many an idle deed may do,
5   12   12 13   6   5 2
Yet not a deed or thought shall perish,
     w-11 11 1   6   5   17
Not one but he shall bless or rue.

5   8-2   2   2   1 2   3 4
When by the wind the tree is shaken,
4   8-16   1   6 13
There's not a bough or leaf can fall,
12 2   13 2   1 2 3 4
But of its falling heed is taken
       6   1   6   11 10   13
By One that sees and governs all.

                12 12 0
The tree may fall and be forgotten,
     5 2 2   10   1 3
And buried in the earth remain;
5   12   17 2   6   12 0
Yet from its juices rank and rotten
   2   5 2 3 2   8-2 7 5
Springs vegetating life again.

  11   2   1-3 11   1   2
The world is with creation teeming,
     11 2   5 10   15 2 8-2
And nothing ever wholly dies;
   2   9   1   12-1   1 2
And things that are destroyed in seeming
11 10   3   12   7 8-2
In other shapes and forms arise.
</pre>

    3 y-16   2   11 ⁕ 15   2   16
And nature still unfolds the tissue
    11   1   11   2 2   13
Of unseen works by spirit wrought;
              6   2 16
And not a work but hath its issue
    5   2   1 2   13
With blessings or with evil fraught.

    8-16   3   1   1 8-2   1
And thou may'st seem to leave behind thee
    13   5 14 2   2 16   8
All memory of the sinful past;
    5 15   1   16   8-2 2   6 8-2   1
Yet oh, be sure, thy sin shall find thee,
    6   8-16   6   15   2   17 6   8
And thou shalt know its fruit at last.

129. For greater clearness the numbers are here printed, not over, *but instead of* the vowel letters. The *articulations* are altered, when necessary, to *represent the sounds* correctly. Italicised *r* shows that the letter has both its vowel and articulate sounds.

II. *Selected Words.*

⁰kl⁸˙²v¹¹s, ⁰kw¹·⁵s, ⁰dv¹⁰rt²zm⁰nt, ⁰ntsh¹⁶v², ⁰ns¹⁰r, ⁶sh¹⁶r, ³zh¹⁶r, ⁰nt²p¹⁵d¹z, ⁴r¹⁵n¹²t, ³ly⁵n⁷bl, ⁶p¹⁵th⁵m, ⁶p¹⁵th¹·¹⁵s²s, ⁷r¹⁵m⁷, ⁶sp⁸·²r⁰nt, b⁶nd⁶n⁷, b⁰ny⁰n, b⁶t⁶ly¹¹n, b⁶l¹¹s, b¹⁶l²n. br²tsh²z, br²t¹¹n, br²t⁰n, br¹v¹r, br⁶v⁶t, br¹v⁶t, b⁶r¹·⁶l, s¹zy¹⁶r⁷, k⁶py¹⁶sh¹n, k⁶psh¹¹s, k¹²mp⁷r⁷b⁰l, tsh⁶st²zm⁶nt, kl¹⁴r⁵n⁶l, k¹¹rn⁶l, k¹²mpl²z⁶nt, k¹²ntr⁴r², k¹²r¹²l⁷r², ky¹⁶r¹⁶l, k¹⁵·⁶dzh¹⁷t¹²r, k¹⁶r²·¹⁰r, kr¹·¹⁶l, k¹¹b¹¹rd, d¹k¹⁴r¹¹s, d⁶sw¹ty¹⁶d, d⁸·²·⁷b¹t¹z, d⁸·²·⁵r²s²s, d²m²s¹²r², dy¹⁷·¹⁵, dy¹⁷ty¹¹s, d²n⁶st², ⁸g¹⁵t²zm, ⁵l¹dzh⁸·²·⁶k, ¹n¹⁰rv³t, ⁵kw⁶r², ⁶kw⁷b⁰l, ⁵kstr¹³rd²n⁷r², f³br²k, f⁷s¹shy¹, f⁷n⁶t²k, f¹²rf²t, fy¹⁶z¹, fy¹¹shy⁷, gl⁶sy¹⁰r, h⁶l¹l¹⁷y⁷, h⁸·²t, h²p¹⁵k¹²ndr²·⁶k, ⁰mb²s¹l, ²mp²·¹¹s, ²nd⁸·²t, ²nv⁷l¹d, ²nv⁶l²d, ²sh¹⁶, l⁶vt⁵n⁶nt, m²ly¹¹n, m¹sh¹n²st, m⁷h¹⁹m⁶t, m⁷n²·v¹⁰r, m¹d²s²n⁶l, m¹d²·¹⁵k¹⁶r, m⁵t¹⁵n²m², m⁵mw¹²r, m²ny¹⁷shy¹, m²s⁶l⁴n², m²stsh²v¹¹s, m¹²b²l, n⁶sh¹¹n⁶l, ¹⁵·⁷s²s, ¹²mn²p¹⁵t⁰nt, p¹k, p⁷sh¹³, p⁸n²dz²r²k, fr¹n⁶t²k, fr¹n⁸·²t²s, pl¹th¹⁴r⁷, pl¹th¹²r²k, pr¹⁵l²ks, py¹⁷n², k¹, kw¹r², kw¹⁶nd⁴r², ky¹⁷, r⁸·²ty¹¹s, r⁶s²t⁷t¹v, r¹k¹²nd²t, r⁸p¹⁰rt¹²r², r¹⁷l. r⁶fr⁷g⁷b⁰l, r⁵v⁰ny¹⁶, s⁶s¹⁰rd¹⁵t⁶l, s⁷l⁸·²v⁷, s⁶f¹⁰r, s⁵sh¹·³t, s⁷t⁸·²·⁵t², s³tr⁶p, st⁷l⁶kt⁶·⁶t, s¹¹b⁷lt¹⁰rn, sy¹¹p¹⁰rny¹⁷m¹⁰r⁷r², s²n⁶kd¹⁶k², t¹⁴rdz, tr⁵zh¹⁶r v¹⁰rt¹g¹⁵, v²t⁶lz, w⁰m⁵n, y¹²t, z¹⁵·¹⁰l¹¹⁵dzh², z¹⁵·¹⁵l¹⁰dzh⁶k⁶i.

XI. THE ASPIRATE, H.

130. The letter H does not represent any fixed formation, but simply an *aspiration of the succeeding element.*
Thus, H before *e* is a whispered *e*, before *a* a whispered
a, &c. ; differing, however, from the simple whispered
vowel by the softer commencement of the aspiration. H
before alphabetic u—which, it will be remembered, represents the combination *y-oo*—denotes a whispered Y, as
in *hue, human,* &c., pronounced *Yhue= Yhyoo,* &c.

131. The vowel aspirate (H) is very irregularly used
in many parts of England ; it is heard when it should be
silent, and silent when it should be sounded ; and that
with such perversity that pure initial vowels are almost
unheard, except in cases where they ought to be aspirated.
The *coup de la glotte* exercise on initial vowels (par. 30)
will correct this habit.

132. A *northern* peculiarity in the formation of H consists in giving a degree of guttural compression to the
breath, which is extremely harsh and grating. This
fault will be avoided by pronouncing the *h* with a softly
sighing effect.

133. Many public speakers have a disagreeable custom
of giving a *vocal* commencement to H, as in *hold, hundred,* &c., pronounced *ŭhold, ŭhundred,* &c. This
tasteless expedient seems to be adopted in the fear that
the delicate effect of *h* would otherwise be inaudible ; but
the succeeding vowel makes it heard.

Silent H.

134. In the following words and their derivatives,
though *h* is written, the vowels are *not aspirated :*—

Heir, heirship, heirloom, &c. ; honest, honesty, &c. ; honour,
honourable, &c. ; hostler ; hour, hour-glass, &c. ; humour, humorous, &c.

XII. ARTICULATIONS.

135. The oral *actions* here denominated ARTICULA-
TIONS, are more commonly called "consonants ;" but as
that term is defined to signify a letter that "cannot be
sounded by itself," and as in fact every element of speech

may be perfectly sounded alone, the name "Articula-tions"—otherwise preferable—is a more appropriate generic term for the oral actions.

136. In par. 120 the line of distinction is drawn be-tween vowels and articulations:—showing the latter to be ORAL sounds arising from *obstruction* or *compression* of the breath behind the conjoined or closely approxi-mated organs.

137. The oral *puff*, or *hiss*, which constitutes the ar-ticulative effect, may be accompanied or not, by a glottal sound. Each articulative action thus produces two dis-tinct elements of speech,—a *breath* form, and a *voice* form,—as in *s*eal and *z*eal, *th*igh and *th*y, *f*ear and *v*eer, *p*ain and *b*ane, *wh*ile and *w*ile, *t*ale and *d*ale, *h*ues and *u*se, *c*all and *g*all, &c. These pairs of articulations have precisely the same oral formation, and differ only in the vocalized breath of the second, and the voiceless aspira-tion of the first of the respective pairs.

138. The articulations are primarily divisible into two classes,—Obstructive and Continuous. In the former class the breath is shut in by perfect contact of the articu-lating organs ; in the latter it escapes through central, lateral, or interstitial apertures ; the organs being either in partial contact or merely in approximation.

139. There are thus *three* MODES of *Articulation :*—I. Complete Contact; II. Partial Contact; III. Approx-imation.

I. Complete Contact.

140. The breath is obstructed at *three* points : (I.) by contact of the lips ; (II.) by contact of the forepart of the tongue with the anterior part of the palate ; (III.) by contact of the back, or root of the tongue, with the pos-terior part of the palate. At the first of these points are formed the articulations P and B ; at the second, T and D ; and at the third, K and G ("hard") ; the former of each of these pairs being the "breath," and the latter the "voice" form of the articulation.

141. While the oral organs are in obstructive contact, the breath or voice may be made to issue *by the nostrils*.

This is the mode of formation of the English elements, M, N, and Ng. For M, the lips are closed as in forming P and B ; for N, the tongue is on the palate as for T and D ; and for Ng, the posterior organs are in contact as in forming K and G.

142. The nine Articulations hitherto described are thus the result of but three actions of the mouth with the modifications of—

BREATH,	VOICE,	NASAL,
P	B	M
T	D	N
K	G	Ng

II. *Partial Contact.*

143. The next mode of articulative action, — partial contact,—produces F and V, Th (thin), and Th (then), the Welsh Ll, the English L, and a Gaelic form of L made with the *middle* instead of the tip of the tongue on the palate.

III. *Approximation.*

144. The remaining mode of articulative action,—organic approximation,—produces Wh and W, S and Z, Sh and Zh, Yh and Y, Rh (Welsh), and R, the soft Spanish sound of B, (bh), and the German, or Scotch guttural Ch, with its vocal form, the SMOOTH *burr*.

145. *Relaxed* approximation gives the trilled R, the ROUGH *burr* and a corresponding vibration of the lips, which is used only interjectionally in English.

146. In the system of "Visible Speech" (see par. 39)—the Alphabet of which is complete for all Languages and Dialects—the Scheme of Articulations includes fifty-two elements. By means of diacritic signs this number is multiplied several fold. The classification cannot be shown by Roman letters. But all the possible hundreds of articulate formations are represented by combinations of only fourteen primary symbols.

147. The following GENERAL SCHEME embraces all the preceding articulations classified according to their *modes* of formation :—

148. *General Scheme of Articulations.*

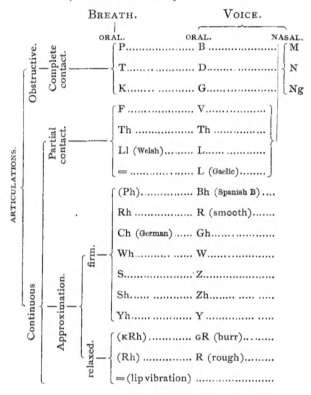

149. The three Nasals, M, N, Ng, are placed on the same line with the Obstructives, to show that their oral mechanism is the same; but as they are continuous in effect (nasally), although orally obstructive, they are connected also with those elements which have Partial Contact.

150. The following Table contains the English Articulations arranged in the order of their formation, commencing with those which have their seat farthest *within the*

mouth, and proceeding to those which have the most anterior formation.

151. *English Articulations.**

BREATH.	VOICE.	
Oral.	Oral.	Nasal.
1 K	2 G	3 Ng
4 H(ew)	5 Y(ew)	
6 Sh	7 Zh	=
=	8 R (rough)	=
=	9 †R (smooth)	=
=	10 L	=
11 T	12 D	13 N
14 S	15 Z	
16 Th(in)	17 Th (en)	=
18 F	19 V	=
20 Wh	21 W	=
22 P	23 B	24 M

152. The student should be able to enounce the *sounds* of these Articulations independently, and exactly as heard in words. The following Table exhibits all the English Articulations in each of the four positions: *initial, final, medial* before a *vowel, medial* before an *articulation*.

---

* For a minute description of each of the English Articulations, the defects to which they are liable, and the means of correcting them, see "Dictionary of English Sounds," in the work referred to in note, par. 69.

† See par. 71.

4

153. Table of Articulations.

P.	....pay	ape	paper	apricot
B.	....bee	glebe	neighbour	ably
M.	....mar	arm	army	arm'd
Wh.	....why	—*	awhile	—*
W.	....way	—*	away	—*
F.	....fed	deaf	definite	deftness
V.	....veal	leave	evil	ev(e)ning
Th,	....third	dearth	ethic	ethnic
Th,	....these	seethe	either	wreathed
S.	....sell	less	essay	estuary
Z.	....zone	nose	rosy	rosebush
R,	....rare	—*	rarity	—*
L.	....left	fell	fellow	fell'd
T,	....tale	late	later	lateness
D,	....day	aid	trader	tradesman
N,	....nave	vain	waning	mainland
Sh.	....shelf	flesh	fisher	fishmonger
Zh,	....giraffe	rouge	pleasure	hedgerow
Y.	....ye	fille (French.)	beyond	—*
K.	....cap	pack	packet	packthread
G,	....gum	mug	sluggard	smuggler
Ng,	....—*	sing	singer	singly

XIII. PRINCIPLE OF DISTINCTNESS.

154. Every ARTICULATION consists of two parts—a *position* and an *action*. The former brings the organs into approximation or contact, and the latter *separates* them, by a smart percussive action of recoil, from the articulative position. This principle is of the utmost importance to all persons whose articulation is imperfect. Distinctness entirely depends on its application. Let it be carefully noted:—audibly percussive organic separation is the necessary action of every articulation.

155. The Breath Obstructives, P-T-K. have no sound in their POSITION. and thus depend, for all their audibility, on the puff that accompanies the organic separation. This therefore must be clearly heard, or the letters are

---

* These articulations do not occur in this position in English.

practically lost. The Voice Obstructives, B-D-G, have a slight audibility in their " positions," from the abrupt murmur of voice which distinguishes them from P, T, and K ; but they are equally imperfect without the organic "action" of separation and its distinctive percussiveness. All the other elements being Continuous, have more or less audibility in their " positions ;" but in every case distinctness and fluency depend on the disjunctive completion of the articulative " action."

XIV. DEFECTS OF ARTICULATION.

156. Various faulty formations of the elements of articulation are extremely common. The Obstructives become mere *stops*, and lack the necessary percussive termination ; the *voice* articulations are deficient in throat-sound, and thus not sufficiently distinguished from their *breath* correspondents ; the Continuous elements are formed by a faulty disposition of the organs, or by the wrong organs ; or their " positions " are not sufficiently firm, and their " actions " altogether wanting or indistinctly languid. The motions of the tongue and the lips are tremulous or indefinite, too feebly or too strongly conjunctive, too rapid or too tardy, &c., &c.

157. LISPING consists in partially obstructing the hissing stream of air, by contact of the point of the tongue with the teeth, or by elevation of the lower lip to the upper teeth.

158. BURRING consists in quivering the uvula instead of the point of the tongue, or approximating the soft palate and back of the tongue instead of raising the tip of the tongue to the anterior rim of the palatal arch.

159. THICKNESS of articulation consists in the action of the *middle* instead of the point of the tongue in the various lingual articulations. This last very common kind of imperfection sometimes arises from congenital inability to raise the tip of the tongue to the palate—removable by a simple operation—but most frequently it is the result merely of a bad *habit*, perfectly removable by energetic and careful application of lingual exercises.

160. In the work referred to in the note, par. 69, the various errors of articulation—including Stuttering and

Stammering—are the subjects of a more elaborate treatment. The following is a summary of the correct—

RELATIVE POSITIONS OF THE ORAL ORGANS.

The Tongue.

161. The TONGUE should be held back from the lower teeth, in order that its actions may be independent of the motion of the jaw : the tip should never be pressed into the bed of the lower jaw ; the tongue should never touch the lips, or be protruded between the teeth : it should be rarely seen, and, when visible, the less the better. The root of the tongue should be depressed as much as possible, to expand the back part of the mouth and give fulness to the vowel sounds :—this is the chief source of the mellow " orotund " quality which distinguishes the voices of well-practised speakers. The tongue should not be *pushed* from point to point without disengagement in passing from word to word : but it should sharply finish the articulations by a perfect recoil of the organ :—this insures *distinctness.*

The Jaw.

162. The lower JAW should not, in speaking, fall behind the upper, but the two ranges of teeth should be kept as nearly in a line as possible. The teeth should never come in contact : even when the lips are closed, the teeth should not clash. The lower jaw should descend freely for every vowel utterance, and, preparatorily, before the commencement of articulation : its motions must be without jerking, equable, easy, and floating.

The Lips.

163. The LIPS should never hang loosely away from the teeth, or be pursed, pouted, or twisted, but they should maintain the form of the dental ranges as nearly as possible, lying equally and unconstrainedly against the teeth. The habits of licking or biting the lips are offensive, and should be carefully guarded against by public speakers. The lips should be used as little as possible in articulation ; the upper lip should remain almost quiescent, safe for *emotive* expression ; the articulative action being confined to the lower lip.

Labial Expressiveness.

164. Habits of speech are so peculiarly operative in giving character to the lips, that an acute observer may generally tell by their aspect whether a person's articulation is good or bad; and there are few stammerers who do not show, to the practised eye, an indication of their infirmity in the lips. The soft and pliant texture of the lips is easily impressed by any habit; and even a passing emotion will mould their plastic substance to express it. Habitual ill-nature everybody looks for and recognizes on the lips; and there sweet temper and cheerfulness have their calm abode. Thus we generally find fixed on these portals of the mouth a legible summary of the man. The lips of the vulgar and ignorant are "arrant tell-tales," which there is no belying; and mental superiority cannot conceal itself from labial disclosure. The lips refuse to screen the lie they may be forced to speak. It may be said, indeed, that falsehood cannot utter itself by these "miraculous organs" of truth; but conscious rectitude, integrity, and virtue shine through the lips, and give irrefragable evidence there, when other testimony is absent or doubtful.

XV. ANGLICISMS OF ARTICULATION.

165. The leading Anglicism of Articulation has been already pointed out in remarks on the letter R (par. 71, *et seq.*) This element is distinctly articulated *only before a vowel;* but less with a trill, than a smooth buzzing vibration of the tongue. In other positions, the letter R is faintly, or not at all articulated. R has a VOWEL sound (No. 10) after any long vowel, before any articulation, and when final.

166. When final R is followed by a word beginning with a vowel, the R is *articulated*, to avoid hiatus between the words. But the Cockney custom of interposing *R* between two vowels, as in the sentences, "*Is Papa r at home?*"—"*What an idea r it is!*" &c., is not to be countenanced. This vulgarism is confined to words ending with the open vowels, Nos. 8, 9, and sometimes 13; the formative apertures of which are of nearly the same expansion as that of the English (R=) 10.

167. English speakers too commonly confound the
Breath with the Voice forms of the articulations Y and
W, and so pronounce alike such words as *hue* and *you*,
which and *witch*, *whale* and *wail*, *whither* and *wither*,
whig and *wig*, &c.

K-G, as in Kind, Guard, &c.

168. In pronouncing such words as *key* and *caw*,
geese and *gauze*, it will be observed that the obstructive
position of the tongue for the initial articulation is not
precisely the same before the open as before the close
vowel ; accommodating itself to the formation of the subsequent vowel, the tongue is much more advanced before
ee than before *aw*. Indeed, the points of contact are not
exactly the same before any two vowels. The closest
lingual vowels are associated with the most anterior consonant positions, and the open and labial vowels with the
most posterior. A peculiar Anglicism arises from *violation* of this principle in certain cases. K and G before
the open vowels, in *card*, *guard*, *kind*, *guile*, *girl*,
&c., are articulated from the *anterior* instead of the
posterior positions ; so that the breath which follows the
articulative " action " has the vowel quality of *ee ;* and
an effect is produced something like that of the articulation *y*. This effect is greatly overdone by those who pronounce *ee* or *y* in such words. " K*ee*-ind," and " k*y*-ard,"
are affected caricatures of this delicate Anglicism. The
following and their derivatives, are the leading words
that partake of this peculiarity :—

card, kind, garden, guard, girl, guide, guile, guise.

XVI. SCOTTICISMS OF ARTICULATION.

169. The leading Scotticism of Articulation consists in
the uniform and rough *trilling* of the tongue for the letter R, in all situations.

170. Another very general Scotch peculiarity consists
in giving a *vowel* sound to the letter L when final, especially when it follows the 5th vowel ; the L. in such words
as *sell*, *bell*, *well*, *swell*, &c., being pronounced nearly like
ul. Thus—" seh-*ul*, beh-*ul*," &c.

171. The articulation *Ng* is pronounced as *n* before *th* —as in *length, strength*, &c. ; and in the final anaccented syllable *ing*,—as in *seeing, believing*, &c. ; pronounced le*n*th, stre*n*th, seei*n*, believi*n*, &c.

172. The Breath Obstructive Articulations, especially the letter T, are, in the West of Scotland, pronounced without any articulative *action*, but with a mere glottal catch after the preceding vowel, as in *better, butter*, &c. ; pronounced bĕ-er, bŭ-er, &c.

173. The Breath form of the articulation Th, is pronounced instead of the Voice form, in the words *th*ough, *th*ither, wi*th*, benea*th*, pa*th*s, &c. A substitution of Breath for Voice forms of articulation is also very generally heard in the words *of, as*, ne*ph*ew, &c., pronounced *off, ass, nefyoo*, &c. ; and the substitution of Voice for Breath forms is likewise common in the words i*f*, u*s*, transact, philo*s*ophic, &c., pronounced, *iv, uz, tranzact, philozophic*, &c.

174. The omission of Y before *ee*, and of W before *oo*, as in *year, yield, wool*, &c., is another northern peculiarity. Ludicrous ambiguities sometimes arise from these omissions ; as when we hear of an old man " bending under the weight of (y)*ears* and infirmities."

175. The addition of a guttural effect to H and Wh is a Celtic peculiarity—harsh and unpleasing to the unaccustomed ear.

176. The pronunciation of *t* before the syllabic sounds of '*l* and '*n* in cas*t*le, apos*t*le, pes*t*le, of*t*en, is a Scotticism almost confined to these words.

XVII. HIBERNICISMS OF ARTICULATION.

177. Irish Articulation is characterized by a general looseness of oral action, which gives a peculiar softness to the transition from an obstructive articulation to the succeeding vowel. The effect is coarsely imitated by interpolating an *h* between the elements, as in p(h)ut for *put*, t(h)ake for *take*, c(h)oat, for *coat*, &c.

178. The sound of *t*, especially at the end of a word, is, from the same cause, but little different from that of *s ;* such words as *bet* and *hat* being pronounced nearly as bess and hass.

179. The sound of *l* final is formed with a convexity
of the middle of the tongue which gives the *l* the effect of
Italian *gl*, as in *well, smile, till*, &c., where the final element has almost the sound of *eel*. This is the converse
of the Scotch peculiarity noticed in par. 170 where *l* has
the open quality of *ul*.

180. The sound of S before an articulation has the effect of Sh; as in *sky, scrape, sleep, snow, star, stripe,
sweet*, &c., pronounced shky, shcrape, shleep, &c.

XVIII. AMERICANISMS OF ARTICULATION.

181. The leading Americanism of Articulation is associated with the letter R. This element has none of the
sharpness of the English R, which, however softly, is
struck from the *tip* of the tongue. The American R has
a very slight vibration, with the tongue almost in the position for the French vowel *e mute*. The high convex
position of the tongue for the American R final or before
an articulation—when the sound is almost that of the
English Y—has been noticed in par. 112.

182. The feeble and indefinite vibration of the American articulate R leads to a habit of *labializing* the sound
when it is between vowels, as in *very, spirit*, &c. This
gives a firmness to the articulation, but altogether changes
its character: the R becomes long and almost syllabic.
Thus: vĕ-wr-y, spĭ-wr-it, &c.

XIX. SYLLABIC QUANTITY.

183. Two degrees of vowel quantity—*long* and *short*,
—are generally recognized, but there are many minuter
degrees arising from the influence of articulations on preceding vowels. Thus all vowels are comparatively short
before Breath articulations, and comparatively long before
Voice articulations; but they are shorter before *another
vowel* than before any articulation. Among vowels
separately considered, there are *three* degrees of quantity;
I. Short monophthongs; II. Long monophthongs; III.
Diphthongs. Among articulations there are *five* degrees;
I. Breath Obstructive; II. Breath Continuous; III.

Voice Obstructive; IV. Voice Close Continuous; V. Voice Open Continuous,—or Liquids.

184. The Open Continuous Articulations, or Liquids, are L, and the Nasals M, N, and Ng. R has been commonly included as a Liquid, but it has none of the coalescent and quantitative characteristics of the Liquid. The term " Liquid " is properly applied only to elements that *flow into*, and seem to be *absorbed* by, the articulation that follows. L, M, N, and Ng are peculiarly affected by the succeeding articulation. Before *Breath* articulations, they are so extremely short as hardly to add any perceptible quantity to the syllables, as in *lap* and *lamp*, *quit* and *quilt*, *flit* and *flint*, *thick* and *think*, &c. : but before *Voice* Articulations they are long and sonorous, and add greatly to the duration of the syllabic utterance ; as in *head* and *held*, *bad* and *band*, *juggle* and *jungle*, &c. R is so softened away as almost to lose all articulative quality before an articulation ; but its sound is not absorbed as that of the Liquids ;—it is rather slurred and omitted.

185. The following Lists contain examples of Monosyllabic Combinations arranged in the order of their quantitative duration,—the shortest first.

186. *Breath Articulations.*

1. Up, sit, black.
2. If, both, gas, wash.
3. Help, felt, elk, tent, lamp, dreamt, bank.
4. Self, health, else, Welsh, ninth, dance, nymph, strength.
5. Apt, act.
6. Steps, depth, feast, eighth (t-th), watch, ox.
7. Left, wasp, fast, ask.
8. Safes, fifth, deaths.
9. Gulped, milked, stamped, inked.
10. Alps, bolts, belch, bulks, prints, inch, imps, tempts, thanks.
11. Gulfs, healths, tenths, nymphs, lengths.
12. Adepts, sects.
13. Shap'st, sat'st, patched, next.
14. Thefts, asps, costs, desks.
15. Fifths.
16. Twelfths.
17. Help'st, halt'st, filched, milk'st, want'st, flinched, limp'st, tempt'st, think'st.
18. Texts.
19. Sixths.

187. *Voice Articulations.*

1. Babe, trade, plague.
2. Leave, bathe, ease, rouge.
3. Ale, lame, own, tongue.
4. Bulb, old, hemmed, end, wronged.
5. Delve, ells, aims, bronze, pangs.
6. Stabbed, begged.
7. Cabs, adge, edge, eggs.
8. Saved, seethed, g r a z e d , rouged.
9. Graves, bathes.
10. Helm.
11. Bulbed.
12. Bulbs, builds, bilge, lands, finds, fringe.
13. Delved, bronzed.
14. Shelves.
15. Helmed.
16. Films.
17. Judged.
18. Bilged, changed.

188. *Mixed Articulations.*

1. Breadth.
2. Stabb'st, add'st, begg'st.
3. Striv'st.
4. Fail'st.
5. Hold'st.
6. Delv'st.
7. Lov'd'st.

XX. DIFFICULT COMBINATIONS.

189. In many of the above combinations there is a difficulty of distinct enunciation which will be readily removed by reference to the principle explained in par. 154. Give to every articulation its appropriate " *action.*"

190. A tendency to indistinctness is especially felt in combinations of the Breath Obstructives—such as *pt* and *kt*, which are of very frequent occurrence. All verbs ending in *p* or *k* have the sounds of *pt* or *kt* in the past tense, as *stopped, walked,* &c. The following is a list of words for exercise. Pronounce the pt and ct like the words " *pit*" and " *kit*" WHISPERED :—

Apt, strapped, kept, slept, whipped, shipped, lopped, cupped, shaped, steeped, piped, hoped, cooped, chapter, styptic, reptile, rapture, captain; act, tact, sect, erect, strict, hacked, shocked, ducked, poked, looked, walked, ached, leaked, liked, cactus, laqteal, affected, lecture, picture, dictate, instructive, octave, doctor.

191. The following words embody similar principles of difficulty. Repeat each word several times—quickly and with firm accentuation :—

Acts, beef, beef-broth, chaise, come, copts, cut, cloud-capt, eighths, (t-ths,) etiquette, faith, fifths, inked, judged, knitting, laurel, literal, literally, literary, literarily, linen, little, litter, memnon, mimic, move, muff, needle, puff, puffed, plural, peacock, quick, quaked, quiet, rail, railroad, raillery, ruler, rural, rivalry, roller, runnel, saith, sash, sashes, search, such, sects, sixths, sooth, soothe, Scotch, slash, sloth, slain, slipped, snail, statist, statistics, shuts, this, thither, thief, thatch, thrash, texts, twelfths, vivid, vivify, vivification, weave, wife, weep, whiff, whip.

192. The following phrases and sentences contain elementary sequences and alternations which are organically difficult. Repeat each sentence two or three times without stopping :—

Very well. Farewell in welfare. Puff up the fop. Fine white wine vinegar with veal. Velvet weaver. Weave the withes. Five wives weave withes. May we vie? Pretty, frisky, playful fellow. A very wilful whimsical fellow. A comic mimic. Move the muse by mute manœuvres. Bring a bit of buttered brown bread. Such pranks Frank's prawns play in the tank. A paltry portly puppy. Portly poultry. A wet white wafer. Beef tea and veal broth. Put the cut pumpkin in a pipkin. Pick pepper peacock. Coop up the cook. A bad big dog. A big mad dog bit bad Bob. Don't attack the cat, Dick. Keep the tippet ticket. Come quickly. Catch the cats. Kate hates tight tapes. Tie tight Dick's kite. Geese cackle, cattle low, crows caw, cocks crow. The tea-caddy key. The key of the tea-caddy. A knapsack strap. Pick up the pips. Take tape and tie the cape. Kate's baked cakes. Quit contact. A school coal-scuttle. Put the pot on the top of the poop. A great big brig's freight. Bid Bob good bye. Pick a pitcher full of pippins. Come and cut the tongue, cook. The bleak breeze blighted the bright broom blossoms. Dick dipped the tippet and dripped it. Fanny flattered foppish Fred. Giddy Kittie's tawdry gewgaws. Kitchen chit-chat. The needy needlewoman needn't wheedle. Fetch the poor fellow's feather pillow. A very watery western vapour. A sloppy, slippery, sleety day. Catch Kate's ten cats. The kitten killed the chicken in the kitchen. Six thick thistle sticks. She says she shall sew a sheet. A sure sign of sunshine. The sun shines on the shop signs. A shocking sottish set of shopmen. Such a sash. A shot-silk sash shop. A short soft shot-silk sash. A silly shatter-brained chatterbox. Shilly-shally, silly Sally. Sickening, stickling, shilly-shally silliness. It is a shame, Sam, these are the same, Sam, 'tis all a sham, Sam, and a shame it is to sham so, Sam. Fetch six chaises. Catch the cats. Pas que je sache. She thrust it through the thatch. Thrice the shrew threw the shoe. The slow snail's slime. A swan swam over the sea, swim, swan, swim, well swam, swan. I snuff shop snuff, do you snuff shop snuff? She sells sea-shells. Some shun sunshine. The sweep's suitably sooty suit. A rural ruler. Truly rural. Rural raillery. A laurel crowned clown. Rob Low's lum reeks. Let reason rule your life. A lump of

raw red liver. Literally literary. Railway literature. A lucent
rubicund rotatory luminary. Robert loudly rebuked Richard,
who ran lustily roar·ng round the lobby. Don't run along the
wrong labyrinth. H.s right leg lagged in the race. Don't run
along the lane in the rain. Lucy likes light literature. Let me
recollect a little. A li⁺tle tittle. A little ninny. A little knitting
needle. Let little Nellie run. A menial million. A million
minions. A million menial minions. We shall be in an inn in
an instant. Don't go on, Ann, in an uninanimated manner.

193. The following phrases and sentences require
careful attention to avoid ambiguity. Reiterate the ambiguous portions without hiatus :—

Laid in the cold ground, (not coal ground.) Half I see the
panting spirit sigh, (not spirit's eye.) Be the same in thine own
act and valour as thou art in desire, (not thy known.) Oh, the
torment of an ever-meddling memory, (not a never meddling.)
All night it lay an ice-drop there, (not a nice drop.) Would that
all difference of sects were at an end, (not sex.) Oh, studied deceit, (not study.) A sad dangler, (not angler.) Goodness centres in the heart, (not enters.) His crime moved me, (not cry.)
Chaste stars, (not chase tars.) She could pain noboby, (not pay.)
Make clean our hearts, (not lean.) His beard descending swept
his aged breast, (not beer.)

XXI. ACCENT OR SYLLABIC STRESS.

194. Every word of more than a single syllable has
one of its syllables made prominent, by superior force
of articulative or vocal effort :—this is called " *accent.*"

195. When the accented syllable of a word is the third,
or any syllable beyond the third, from the beginning, a
slight accentual stress is laid on some former syllable to
support a rhythmical pronunciation. Thus :—
(I.) If the primary accent is on the *third* syllable a
secondary accent is on the *first;* (II.) when the primary
is on the *fourth* syllable, the secondary may be either on
the *first* or *second;* (III.) when the primary accent is
on the *fifth*, the secondary will be on the *second* syllable,
or there may be *two* secondary accents, namely, on the
first and *third* syllables ; and, (IV.) when the primary
accent is on the *sixth* syllable, there will be two second-
aries—distributed either on the *first* and *third*, the *first*
and *fourth*, or the *second* and *fourth* syllables. The
primary accent never falls beyond the sixth syllable.

196. The following table exhibits all the varieties of English accentuation. The asterisks (*) denote the *accent;* the large dots, *secondary accent;* and the small dots, *unaccented* syllables.

197. *Table of Verbal Accents.*

1.	2.	3.	4.
* ·	· *	· · *	· · · *
* · ·	· * ·	· · * ·	· · · * ·
* · · ·	· * · ·	· · * ·	· · · * ·
* · · · ·	· * · · ·	· · * · · ·	· · · *
	· * · · · ·	· · * · · ·	

5.	6.	7.	8.
· · · *	· · · · * ·	· · · * ·	· · · · · * ·
· · · * ·	· · · · * · ·	· · · · * · ·	· · · · · * · ·
· · * · ·			· · · · * · ·
· · · *			

198. *Words Illustrative of the Preceding Table.*

1. Wayward, temperate, temporary, necessariness.
2. Away, remember, contemporal, inveterately, unnecessarily.
3. Recommend, contemplation, anatomical, disingenuously, inconsiderableness.
4. Superintend, epigrammatic, superabundantly.
5. Misunderstand, subordination, extemporaneous, invalitudinary.
6. Personification, impracticability.
7. Antipestilential, indestructibility.
8. Intercolumniation, incommunicability, incomprehensibility.

Principles of Accentuation.

199. The general principles that regulate the position of the accent, are the following:—I. The seat of accent tends to the *penultimate* syllables of *dissyllables,* and to the *ante-penultimate* of *polysyllables,* if no other principle occur to thwart this tendency ; as in aspect, comfort, aggravate, orator, &c.

II. The accent of the primitive word is generally retained in derivatives, as in accept, acceptable, commend, commendable, &c.

III. Words of the *same orthography*, but of *different parts of speech*, (especially nouns and verbs,) are generally distinguished by difference of accent, as in at'tribute, attrib'ute, ac'cent, accent', reb'el, rebel', &c. The *verbs* in such cases have the *lower* accent.

IV. *Prefixes*, terminations, and syllables common to a number of words, are generally without accent; such as *ab, be, con, in, re, mis, ness, less, ly, full, sion, tion, ing, able, ible, ally, ary*, &c.

200. When *three* or more syllables *follow* the accent, a secondary force is generally accorded to one of them for the sake of avoiding, by an agreeable rhythm, the hurrying effect of a long cluster of unaccented syllables. Thus, in such words as the following, the voice will be more or less distinctly poised on the second syllables after the accent:—

Ab''dica'tive, accessoriness, arbitrarily, calculatory, figuratively, gentlewoman, indicator, opinionativeness, secretaryship, temporarily.

201. In all the preceding accentual illustrations, the primary and secondary accents are *separated* by one or two syllables. They may, however, occur in proximate syllables, as in the words A'men'', fare'well''. In pronouncing these words, the *time* of an unaccented syllable intervenes between the accents. Thus, " Amen," and " eighty men," " farewell," and " fare thee well," occupy exactly the same time in utterance.

202. Words are frequently used in poetry with false accentuation. The reader must not sacrifice ordinary prose propriety to suit the casual poetic accent. A compromise may generally be effected by accentuating both the regularly and the rhythmically accented syllables. Thus the words " ravines" and " supreme," in the following lines, may be pronounced rav'ines' and su'preme' :

" Ye ice-falls! ye, that from the mountain's brow
  Adown enormous rav'ines' slope amain!"
" Our su'preme' foe, in time, may much remit."

203. In the pronunciation of sentences, the words are not delivered with separate accentuation, as in a vocabulary, but they are collocated into *accentual groups*, according to grammatical connection and relative value to the sense. Certain classes of words are generally *unaccented*; such as *articles, prepositions, pronouns, auxiliary verbs*, and *conjunctions*. These are primarily accented, only when they are used with ANTITHESIS. The same principles which regulate the *secondary* accentuation of single words, apply also to the grammatical groups, or " oratorical words."

204. When words, the accentual syllables of which are the same, are used in contrast, the primary accent is *transposed to the syllable of difference*, and the regular primary receives a secondary accent ; as in com′prehen″d, pronounced com″prehen′d when opposed to ap″prehend′, lit′erall″y and lit′erar″y, af″fect′ and ef″fect′, in″form′ and re″form′, ex″pel′ and im″pel′, mor″tal′ity and im″-mortal′ity, re″lig′ion and ir″relig′ion, &c. This transposition always takes place in the *second* word of the contrasted pair, but not on the first, unless the contrast is distinctly instituted on its utterance.

205. The same principle of contrast or antithesis, expressed or implied, regulates the accentuation or emphasis of sentences. Any phrase or sentence containing a word or IDEA that has been previously expressed or IMPLIED in the context, will have the primary accent—or the emphasis—on one of the other words, even though of the most subordinate class, conjunction, preposition, pronoun, or article. Much judgement is displayed by a good reader in this accentual recognition of included thoughts or synonymous expressions. Thus in the word " unfeeling " in the following lines, the accent should fall on the negative prefix " *un*," to show that the word " tender," before used, includes the idea of " feeling."

> " To each, his sufferings; all are men,
> Condemn'd alike to groan;
> The tender, for another's pain,
> The *un*feeling, for his own."—*Gray.*

206. The subject of Emphasis will be found separately and fully illustrated in a subsequent section.

PRINCIPLES OF ELOCUTION.

PART SECOND.

INTONATION AND CLAUSING.

I. GENERAL PRINCIPLES.

1. There is an essential difference between the movements of the voice in speech and in song. In singing, the voice dwells monotonously, for a definite time, upon every note, and *leaps* (or sometimes slides) upwards or downwards to the next. In speaking, the end of each note is invariably a slide, and the voice rarely dwells for a measurable space on any part of a note, but is constantly changing its pitch by upward or downward movement, or *inflexion*.

2. The kind and degree of inflexion with which words are pronounced are peculiarly expressive of their relation to the context, or to the feeling of the speaker. Thus the *rising* turns are *connective, referential, dubious, appellatory*, or *tender* in expression; and the *falling* inflexions are *disjunctive, independent, positive, mandatory*, or *harsh*.

3. The vocal expressions constitute a NATURAL LANGUAGE, of the import of which mankind are intuitively conscious. The language of ·tones is most perfectly developed when the *feelings* are excited, and the speaker is free from all restraint. Children, before their utterance has become denaturalized by school-discipline in " reading," speak with the most beautifully expressive intonation; and all persons of sprightly temperament deliver themselves, in animated conversation, with little short of the expressive perfection of infantile oratory.

4. The universally observed difference in the intonations of *reading* and *speaking* arises, in a very great measure, from the manner in which children are allowed to read—in entire ignorance or neglect of the principles of intonation. A natural expressiveness may, and should, be given, even to the A, B, C, or the Multiplication Table.

——

II. MECHANISM OF THE INFLEXIONS.

5. Inflexions are either SIMPLE or COMPOUND in mechanism. Simple inflexions consist of *two* points :—the pitch, accented ; and the termination, unaccented. Thus :—

rising, .˙ (ʹ)   falling, ˙. (ˎ)

Compound inflexions consist of *three* points, by the union of the two simple movements with one accent. Thus :—

rising, ˙ ˙ (ᵛ)   falling, .˙. (ᴧ)

6. The most important fundamental principle of inflexion is primarily a *mechanical* one ; for, if the inflexions are faultily formed, they will be neither pleasing nor expressive, but harsh to the ear, false to the sentiment, and injurious to the voice. An illustrative diagram will best explain this principle.

Simple Inflexions.

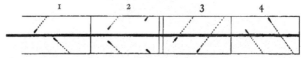

This diagram represents *the speaking voice* divided into an upper and a lower half, the middle line denoting the middle pitch, the upper line the highest, and the lower line the lowest pitch.

7. If inflexions are commenced on the *middle* tone of the voice, as in the first division of the diagram, the speaker, manifestly, has but *half* his vocal compass

through which to range upwards or downwards ; and
the voice will crack, or croak, shrilly or hoarsely, if a
forcible or emphatic inflexion be attempted.

8. Still more limited and powerless will the inflexions
be, if rising turns are pitched above, or falling turns below,
the middle tone, as in the second section of the diagram.

9. Grace and energy are attained by *depressing* the
radical part of the inflexion below the middle tone for a
rise, and by *elevating* it above the middle tone for a *fall*,
as in the third and fourth sections of the diagram ; the
greater or less extent of the accentual elevation or depression of pitch corresponding to the emphasis of the utterance.

10. Thus, the most extensive rising inflexion may not
actually rise higher than a comparatively weak and unimpassioned movement,—but it will *begin lower*, and
with greater radical intensity ; and, on the same principle,
the most extensive falling inflexion will not be that which
falls lowest, but that which, with radical intensity, *begins
highest*.

11. *Unemphatic* inflexions are formed as in the first
and second divisions of the diagram.

12. The tones are capable of great variety, both in radical *pitch*, and also in *extent* of inflexion.   The rise or fall
may be made through any interval, and with an almost
endless diversity of pitch.

13. The mechanism of the compound inflexions exemplifies the same principles of vocal range.   The compound
Rise consists of a simple falling tone finished with upward
inflexion ; and its commencement (the accented part) is
pitched within the lower half of the voice in the less emphatic mode, and in the upper half, in the more emphatic.
The compound Fall consists of a simple rising tone finished by downward inflexion, and its accented commencement is pitched within the upper half of the voice in the
less emphatic mode ; and in the lower half, in the more
emphatic.

14. In the utterance of these compound tones, the following principle is to be noted.   The voice reaches the
turning point in the pronunciation of a *single syllable*.
The termination of the tone may be prolonged through

any number of subsequent syllables. The termination
may extend to the same pitch as the commencement, or
it may stop short of it, or go beyond it.

15. The following diagram illustrates the mechanism
of the compound inflexions. A rising *Double Wave* is
exhibited in the third division of the diagram. This
consists of an ordinary Compound Fall, finished with upward inflexion. The voice reaches the second turning
point in the pronunciation of the accented syllable. A
falling Double Wave is a possible compound tone that is
never used. Its effect is not pleasing. The rising Double
Wave is frequently employed, and its effect is beautifully
expressive.

Compound Inflexions

Compound Rise.   Compound Fall.   Double Wave.

III. NOTATION OF THE INFLEXIONS.

16. The NOTATION of the inflexions* is founded on the
principle of their mechanism. The marks are placed
below the word when the pitch of the accented syllable is
in the lower half of the voice, and *above* the word, when
the inflexion is pitched within the upper half. Thus :—

Well. Ah! Yes. Go! Not I! Beware! You! Oh!

17. The *notation* used in subsequent exercises represents *four degrees*, which, (without any attempt at strict
musical accuracy,) may be taken to correspond generally
with the intervals of the second, third, fifth, and octave.

18. The intervals of the *semitone* and the *minor third*
have a peculiarly *plaintive* effect. The cry of " Fire !"
may be assumed as an appropriate *key-word*, as it is uni-

* See " Expressive Exercises," in a subsequent section.

versally uttered with plaintive intonation. Pronounce
this word with natural expressiveness, and alternate with
it any words of fear or sadness, with similar inflexion,
and the plaintive intervals may be satisfactorily practised
even by the " ear "-less and unmusical student.

Fire! Fire! Alas! Ah! Well-a-day! Farewell! Ah me!

IV. PREPARATORY PITCH.

19. Inflexion is associated with *accent*. The radical
part of the inflexion coincides with the accentual force.
When any syllable or syllables *precede* the accent, they
should be pronounced in the opposite half of the voice—
high when the accent is *low*, and *low* when the accent is
high. Thus :—

What now?   Indeed!   All right.   Away!

Not I!   Take care!   Aha!   Oh really!

20. This principle of opposition of preparatory pitch
gives distinctiveness to two *Modes* of each inflexion ; the
one mode having the accent lower, and the other mode
having the accent higher, than the pre-accentual pitch.
A farther difference in the expressive force of each tone
depends on the *direction* in which the pre-accentual syllables are inflected, *i. e.*, whether *towards* or *from* the
accentual pitch.   The latter is in all cases the more emphatic variety.   (See Diagrams, page 71.)

V. EXPRESSIVENESS OF THE INFLEXIONS.

21. The student, with no other than the mechanical guide
for the formation of the inflexions, would be apt to form
jerking and angular tones instead of the smoothly rounded
transitions of natural intonation.   The following summary of the *expressiveness* of the various vocal movements will assist in giving to the exercises that quality
of *conversational* effect which is, above all, to be cultivated.

I. *Rising Tones* APPEAL :—

1. To bespeak attention to something to follow.
2. For solution of doubt.
3. For an expression of the hearer's will.
4. To question possibility of assertion.

II. *Falling Tones* ASSERT :—

1. To express completion of a statement.
2. To express conviction.
3. To express the speaker's will.
4. To express impossibility of denial.

22. *Compound* tones unite with the ordinary effect of the rising or falling termination, a suggestion of *antithesis*, or reference to something previously understood. Thus :—

Simple Appeal . . . Will you?

Referential Appeal . Will you? (in view of certain circumstances.)

Simple Assertion . . I will

Referential Asssertion. I will, (notwithstanding certain circumstances.)

23. The inflexions have also a sentimental as well as a logical expressiveness. Thus :—
Rising tones express *attractive* sentiments; as pity, admiration, love, &c.
Falling tones express *repulsive* sentiments; as re-proach, contempt, hatred, &c.
24. In practice, always associate some appropriate sentiment or logical formula with the various tones. Thus, in pronouncing words for inflective exercise, associate with—

SIMPLE RISE,	1st mode,	*Inquiry;*	2d mode,	*Surprise.*
SIMPLE FALL,	"	*Assertion;*	"	*Command.*
COMPOUND RISE,	"	*Remonstrance;*	"	*Threatening.*
COMPOUND FALL,	"	*Scorn;*	"	*Sarcasm.*

25. Or prefix, audibly or mentally, to the words to be inflected, the formulas subjoined to the Tones in the following diagrams :—

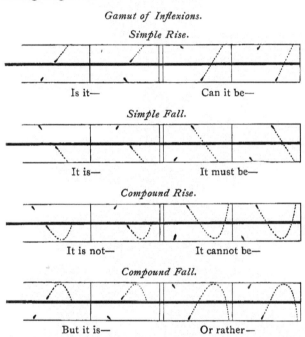

Gamut of Inflexions.

Simple Rise.

Is it—   Can it be—

Simple Fall.

It is—   It must be—

Compound Rise.

It is not—   It cannot be—

Compound Fall.

But it is—   Or rather—

26. In applying the formulas "Is it?" "It is," &c., pronounce them *un*emphatically, and in the *opposite half* of the voice to that in which the word to be inflected is pitched. Thus :—

Ácid?   Can it be   It is   Àcid.

Is it   Acid?   Acid.   It must be

It is not   X̌cid?   Âcid.   Or rather

Acid?   It cannot be   But it is   Acid.

VI. EXERCISES ON THE INFLEXIONS.

27. Pronounce each of the following words with the logical or sentimental expressiveness of the eight varieties of speaking tones. Long monosyllables and words which begin with the accented syllable, being the easiest of inflexion, are put first.

Ah, ay, eh, oh, you, he, she, they, we, me, I, now, so, how, no, see, go, fie, woe, yours, theirs, ours, mine, none, seem, home, here, there, where, all, come, on, gone, shall, her. sir, us, yes, if, off, look, it, that, but, not, out, what, up, stop;—acid, airy, author, blessing, circle, city, dogma, doctrine, easy, gorgeous, greedy, happy, idle, loving, mighty, murder, queenly, rosy, soothing, virtue, welcome;—character, circumstance, calculate, dangerous, enemy, feelingly, finical, hardihood, hideous, liberty, ornament, plausible, roguery, satisfy, somebody, troublesome, victory, yesterday; bibliopole, celibacy, cursorily, despicable, elevated, fascinating, gentlemanly, homicidal, intimately, literally, literary, mannerliness, meditative, missionary, necessary, pettifogger, recreative, serviceable.

28. Pronounce the following words with well-marked preparatory tones in the opposite half of the voice to that in which the accented syllable is pitched :—

Advertisement, away, begone, beware, contemporary, determine, disinterested, forsaken, impossible, impracticable, indeed, intemperate, litigious, opinionative, remember, satanic, subordinate, suspicious, uncompromising, undoubtedly;—acrimonious, bacchanalian, benefactor, detrimental, disagreeableness, epigrammatic, genealogical, hieroglyphic, hypochondriacal, ignominious, liberality, notwithstanding, observation, plenipotentiary, recommendation, understanding.

29. In such words as the following, containing unaccented or secondarily accented syllables before secondary accents, the preparatory tones are susceptible of variety. Thus :—Incomprehensibility or Incomprehensibility.

Artic'ula"tion, cir'cumstan'tial"ity, corrup'tibil"ity, coun'terrev'olu"tion, demo'raliza"tion, disad'vanta"geously, disqual'ifica"tion, eccle'sias"tical, ency'clopæ"dia, enthu'sias"tic, hallu'cina"tion, im'mate'rial"ity, impen'etrabil"ity, imper'spicu"ity, impos'sibil"ity, in'comprehen'sibil"ity, in'commu'nicabil"ity, in'deter'mina"tion, in'tercommu'nica"tion, irrep'arabil"ity, irrep'rehen"sibleness, i'soper'imet"rical, person'ifica"tion.

30. Pronounce the following sentences, &c., with the tones indicated :—

Consultative.	*Communicative.*
Are you góing?	I must, at once.
Cản you not stay?	Unfortunately, I cannot.
Indeéd?	Indeed.

Suggestive.

Don't fǎil! . .	Cêrtainly not.
Well, be sǔre! . . .	Sure? Whỳ?
You will find oǔt! .	Reâlly!
Yes, indeěd! . . .	Indeed!

Passionate.

Do you mǒck me? . . .	Awảy with you!
Hah! .	Begône!
I will not be threǎtened!	There's a hero!

Plaintive.

Ah mé!	Tóo true!	No móre?	No more!

VII. RESUMÉ OF THE PRINCIPLES OF MECHANISM, MELODY AND MEANING OF THE INFLEXIONS.

31. (I.) The beginning, relatively to the end, of a simple *rising* inflection is *low;* of a simple *falling* inflection, *high.*

(II.) The inflection begins on the *accent;* which is thus pitched comparatively low for a rising, high for a falling inflection.

(III.) The rise or fall is continued directly upwards or downwards from the accent, *through whatever number of unaccented or secondarily accented syllables may follow.*

(IV.) Any syllables *before* the accent are pronounced from an *opposite* pitch—high before a low accent, low before a high, to increase the emphasis of the accentual elevation or depression.

(V.) *Rising* tones *appeal; Falling* tones *assert.*

(VI.) The *Compound Rise* consists of a falling or assertive tone, followed by a rising or querulous one, and expresses a QUERY with insinuated assertion.

(VII.) The *Compound Fall* consists of a rising or querulous, followed by a falling or assertive tone, and expresses an ASSERTION with insinuated query.

(VIII.) The rising *Double Wave* has the logical effect of the ordinary compound rise, but with peculiar emphasis.

(IX.) The melody of PREPARATORY pitch is the same for the compound as for the simple movements.

VIII. PRINCIPLES OF VERBAL GROUPING.

32. The principles on which words are phraseologically united furnish a series of exercises of the very highest utility, as affording means of careful application of all the orthoepic and inflective principles. The following STAGES of VERBAL GROUPING should each be separately practised in the reading of varied styles of composition, until facility of spontaneous grouping is attained. The exercise is, besides, valuable as a *grammatical* one.

Stages of Verbal Grouping.

33. 1st STAGE. Pronounce every word with separate accentuation and inflexion, except the ARTICLES *a, an,* and *the.*

WAR.—*H. More.*

O,—war!—the proof—and—scourge—of—man's—fall'n—state!
After—the brightest—conquest—what—appears—
Of—all—thy—glories?—for—the vanquish'd,—chains!
For—the proud—victors,—what?—Alas!—dominion—
O'er—desolated—nations!

---

34. 2d STAGE. Unite PREPOSITIONS (as well as articles) in one accentual group with the words to which

they refer. Include in this stage the sign of the infinitive mood (*to*) and also prepositions used adverbially as accented additions to verbs; as "*to put up*," "*to go by*," &c.

TRUE GREATNESS.

A contemplation—of God's — works,—a voluntary—act—of justice — to our—own—detriment,—a generous—concern — for the good—of mankind,—tears—shed—in silence—for the misery —of others,—a private—desire—of resentment—broken—and—subdued,—an unfeigned—exercise — of humility, — or — any — other—virtue,—are— such —actions — as — denominate — men—great—and—reputable.

_____

35. 3d STAGE. Connect personal or relative PRONOUNS with VERBS; as *the person—who did it—told me—the fact.*" Include also,—as *im*personal pronouns,—the words *there* and *so*, when used as in the sentences, "*there may—there is—there will—do so—I say so.*" When a pronoun is the "antecedent" to a relative, it will be *accented*, (but not necessarily emphatic,) as in the sentence, "His first field against the infidels proved fatal to *him* who, in the English war, had seen seventy battles." Otherwise the pronoun is always *un*accented, except in case of antithesis, when the pronoun becomes *emphatic*.

THE SECRET OF CONTENT.

In whatever—state—I am,—I — first — of all — look up — to heaven,—and—remember—that—the principal—business—here —is,—how—to get—there. I—then—look down—upon the earth,—and—call—to mind—how—small—a portion—I shall—occupy—in it—when—I come—to be—interred;—I—then—look abroad—into the world,—and—observe—the multitudes—who,—in many—respects,—are—more—unhappy—than—myself. Thus —I learn—where—true—happiness—resides,— where — every — care—must—end;—and—I—then—see—how—very—little — reason—I have—to complain.

_____

36. 4th STAGE. Join adjective and relative PRONOUNS to NOUNS; as "*that man, which man*," &c. Include also the NUMERALS *one, two, three*, &c., *first, second, third*, &c., and such words as *such, none, all, both, some*, &c. The compound pronominal adjectives, *my*

own, his own, &c., may be considered as one word. Do
not group words of this class with *verbs;* for the *noun*
must always be *understood* between the pronominal
word, or numeral, and the verb. The pronoun is *unaccented*, except in case of antithesis, or when it is "antecedent" to a relative, as in the sentence :—

> "I clip high climbing thoughts,
>   The wings of swelling pride;
> *Their* fall is worst that from the height
>   Of greatest honour slide."

EVENTFUL EPOCHS.—Emerson.

Real—action—is—in silent—moments.—The epochs—of our
life—are—not—in the visible—facts—of our choice—of a calling,—our marriage,—our acquisition—of an office.—and—the
like; but—in a silent—thought—by the wayside—as—we walk;
in a thought—which revises—our entire—manner—of life,—and—
says,—"Thus—hast thou—done,—but—it were—better—thus."
And—all—our after—years,—like—menials,—do—serve—and—
wait—on this,—and,—according— to their ability,—do—execute
—its will.

37. 5th STAGE. Accentuate into one group AUXILIARY
with PRINCIPAL VERBS when no adverbial word or phrase
intervenes.

THE FINE ARTS.—Emerson.

Because—the soul—is—progressive,—it—never—quite—repeats itself,—but—in every act—attempts—the production—of a
new—and—fairer—whole. Thus—in our Fine—Arts—not—imitation,—but—creation—is—the aim. In landscape,—the painter
—should give—the suggestion—of a fairer—creation—than—we
know. The details—the prose—of Nature,—he should omit,—
and—give us—only—the spirit—and—splendour. Valuing—
more—the expression—of Nature—than—Nature—herself,—he
will exalt—in his copy—the features—that please him. He will
give—the gloom—of gloom,—and—the sunshine—of sunshine.

38. 6th STAGE. Unite ADVERBS with the ADJECTIVES
or ADVERBS which they qualify (not adverbs with *verbs*) ;
and the negatives *no* and *not*, with whatever they refer to.

THE FIRMAMENT.— *Young.*

One sun—by day,—by night—ten thousand—shine;
And—light us—deep—into the Deity;
How boundless—in magnificence—and—might!
Oh,—what a confluence—of ethereal—fire,
From urns—unnumber'd—down the steep—of heaven,
Streams—to a point,—and—centres—in my sight!
Nor—tarries—there;—I feel it—at my heart!
My heart—at once—it humbles,—and—exalts;
Lays it—in dust,—and—calls it—to the skies.

---

39. 7th STAGE. Unite next in the same group or " oratorical word," ADJECTIVES and the NOUNS they qualify. *Two adjectives* cannot be connected, as there is between them a necessary ellipsis of the noun. In this and the following stages, be especially careful to *accentuate* the groups according to the relative value of the words. The noun will generally take the primary accent,[*] but sometimes, the adjective; and, often, both will require an *equal* accentuation—emphatic or unemphatic.

REMEMBRANCE.— *W. E. Aytoun.*

I,—who was—fancy's lord,—am—fancy's slave,
Like—the low murmurs—of the Indian shell,
Ta'en—from its coral bed,—beneath the wave,
Which,—unforgetful—of the ocean's swell,

---

[*] An erroneous rule has been commonly propounded, that the chief accent should be always on the qualifying or limiting word. The primary accent cannot be *always* on either the one or the other, but it is more frequently on the qualifying word. Thus, in Pope's short poem of the " Messiah," 103 adjective clauses occur; in 39 of these the adjectives and nouns are of equal value (equally emphatic or equally subordinate); in 46 the nouns are of superior value to the adjectives; and in only 18 the adjectives require to be primarily accented. In further illustration, the adjective clauses are here collected from two compositions, with which every reader must be familiar :—

" The pathless woods;" " the lonely shore;" " the deep sea;" " thou deep and dark blue ocean;" " ten thousand fleets;" " rock-built cities;" " oak leviathans;" " huge ribs;" " clay creator;" " vain title;" " azure brow;" " glorious mirror;" " funeral note;" " farewell shot;" " struggling moonbeams' misty light;" " useless coffin;" " martial cloak;" " few and short were the prayers;" " narrow bed;" " lonely pillow;" " heavy task;" " distant and random gun;" " cold ashes."

In two-thirds of these adjective phrases the nouns require the primary accent. [See " Emphasis," in a subsequent section.]

Retains,—within its mystic urn,—the hum—
Heard—in the sea-grots,—where—the Nereids—dwell—
Old thoughts—still—haunt me,—unawares,—they come—
Between me—and—my rest,—nor—can I make—
Those aged visitors—of sorrow—dumb.

40. 8th STAGE. COPULATIVE particles may next be
united with the connected word that follows them ; but
if they are not immediately followed by the word or
words which they unite in sense, they must stand apart,
and be separately accented and inflected, as in the following sentence :—

"*I shall call,—and—if possible,—ascertain—the
fact.*"

*Dis*junctives, such as *but, nor,* &c., frequently require
separate pronunciation.

STABILITY OF NATURE.—*Rogers.*

Who—first—beholds—those everlasting clouds,
Seed time—and harvest,—morning,—noon,—and night,
Still—where—they were,—steadfast,—immovable ;
Who—first—beholds—the Alps,—that mighty chain—
Of mountains,—stretching on—from east—to west ;
So massive,—yet—so shadowy,—so ethereal,
As to belong—rather—to heaven—than earth,—
But—instantly—receives—into his soul—
A sense,—a feeling—that he loses not ;
A something—that informs him—'tis—a moment—
Whence—he may date—henceforward—and forever

41. 9th STAGE. The PREDICATE that follows the VERB
to BE, whether it consist of a single word or of a clause,
—may be united with the verb in one accentual group : as,
" *To be thus—is nothing—but—to be safely thus!* "

HUMAN PROGRESS.—*Christian Philosophy.*

Man,—even—in his inglorious—and fallen state,—is eminently
fitted—for progression—in knowledge. There is the eye—to perceive,—the soul—to understand,—the ear—to attend,—and the
judgement—to ponder ;—there are the senses—to supply—material,—and the memory—to store up—the treasures. By deep cau-
sation—man—reasons—on first principles—and chief laws,—and
—by analogy—compares—and contrasts. From the lower steps—
of the intellectual ladder,—he—gradually—ascends—to the high-

est regions—of abstract thought—and reflection. The alphabet—
may be the child's first study,—the heaven—of heavens—the
theme—of his manly contemplations.—As a child—he may whip
—his top—in the street,—or roll—his hoop—on the path;—as a
man,—he measureth—the heavens,—and reckoneth—with mathematical precision—the revolutions—of the planetary worlds.
From the hyssop—he goeth on—to the cedar,—from the wonders
—of nature—to those—of providence,—and—from both,—by a
spiritual flight,—to the higher regions—of grace. With elasticity
—of mind,—in connection—with physical vigour,—and the cultivation—of the moral sense,—none—but God—can tell—where
—man's soarings—will end,—or his discoveries—terminate.

42. 10th STAGE. ADVERBS and adverbial PHRASES
may next be united with the VERBS they qualify; also
interrogative and *conditional* particles,—such as *when,
why, if,* &c. : as in the sentences, " *When I first came
here,—it was far otherwise—than it is now;*" " *If it
must be done—why, then—there is no remedy.*"

SUNSET.—*Alex. Bethune.*

The sun—hath almost reach'd—his journey's close;
The ray—he sheds—is gentle,—softly bright,
Pure—as the pensive light—from woman's eyes—
When kindled up—by retrospective thoughts,
Wandering—to former scenes—of love—and joy.
But yet—there is a melancholy tinge—
In that rich radiance, -and—a passing thought—
Of things departed,—and of days gone by,
At such an hour—insensibly will weave
Itself—into the texture—of the scene.
Nothing—departs alone: the dying day—
Bears—with it—many—to the last repose.
The setting sun,—so gorgeously array'd—
In beams—of light,—and curtain'd round about—
With clouds—steeped—in the rainbow's richest dyes;
So fair,—so full—of light—and living glory,
That—with the ancient Persian,—one might deem
Him—god—of all—he looks upon below,—
His setting—ushers in—a night—to some—
Which—morning—shall not break.

43. 11th STAGE. The word or clause forming the
OBJECT of a *transitive verb* or the COMPLEMENTAL EX-
PRESSION *of a verb*, may next be added to the verb in

the same oratorical group : as "*to love virtue;*" "*to be-come near-sighted;*" "*learn—to do good;*" "*my own tears—have made me blind,*" &c. When the "object" is the grammatical *antecedent* to a relative clause, or when it stands in the relation of *principal* to any dependent sentence immediately following, it should not be grouped with the verb, but with the relative or subordinate to which it stands in closer relationship. When there are two or more " objects " to one verb, the latter should be pronounced by itself, that the equal relation of all the objects to the verb may be manifest. In such cases the objects will generally take the collective form of a SERIES.*

REVELATION.

Should these credulous infidels,—after all,—be in the right,—and—this pretended revelation be all a fable,—from believing it—what harm—could ensue? Would it render princes more tyrannical,—or subjects more ungovernable? the rich more insolent,—or the poor more disorderly? Would it make worse parents,—or children,—husbands—or wives,—masters—or servants;—friends—or neighbors? or—would it not make men more virtuous,—and consequently more happy—in every situation?

---

44. 12th STAGE. COMPLEMENTAL CLAUSES, introduced by prepositions, pronouns, or other parts of speech, may be united with the principal words to which they relate, when they are *necessary* to the expression of sense ; as,

> "*Child of the sun—pursue thy rapturous flight—*
> *Mingling—with her thou lov'st—in fields of light.*"

> "*It was not so much what you said—as your manner of saying it—that struck me.*"

EXERCISE.

It is a universal law of nature—that disuse—diminishes the capability of things,—while exercise—increases it. The seldomer our thoughts are communicated—the less communicable do they become;—the seldomer our sympathies are awakened—the less ready are they to wake;—and—if social affections be not stirred by social intercourse,—like a neglected fire,—they smoulder away,—and consign our hearts to coldness.

---

* See page 102.

IX. PUNCTUATION AND PAUSING.

45. Good clausing is one of the most important qualities in reading. Clausing does not always coincide with
punctuation. Commas are inserted in many cases where
a pause would be inappropriate ; and they are not found
at the boundaries of many clauses where pauses are essential to a clear delivery of the meaning.

46. The *comma* is used to separate words or clauses in
apposition, and to disjoin explanatory or qualifying clauses
from the principal members of a sentence, and from each
other : the *semicolon* is employed at the conclusion of a
dependent sentence ; or of one from which a direct inference is drawn ; or of one of a series of connected sentences ;
or sometimes at the end of an important division of a
complex sentence : the *colon* serves to aggregate into one
period sentences in themselves complete, but more or less
connected in subject ; or it is used after any recurrence of
semicolons, to mark a greater division than they indicate :
and the *period* shows the completion of an independent
sentence, or of a series of collateral sentences. A *paragraph* is a typographical division, which shows the end
of a collection of collateral periods.

47. The shortest pauses are those slight suspensions
which are made at the end of an accentual group or oratorical word ; the next in duration are those which separate subordinate clauses from the principal members,
and from each other ; next are those which separate two
or more subjects, predicates, objects, or complemental
clauses in apposition ; somewhat longer are those which
introduce and conclude parentheses, similes, series, and
important relative or conditional sentences : the conclusion
of a dependent sentence requires a slightly increased hiatus ; of an independent sentence a greater one still ; and
the end of a paragraph, or leading division of a subject,
a more protracted pause. Besides these regular stops,
accidental, expectant, or reflective pauses will occur before or after important words, to render them *emphatic* ;
and longest of all will be those *Expressive Pauses*,
which denote listening, anxious watching, &c.

48. There can be no good reading without frequent and,

6

sometimes, long pauses. They convey an effect of spontaneity, which rivets the attention of the hearer; while
unbroken fluency, especially in the reading of complex
sentences, will never sustain attention, because it is manifestly accompanied with no thought on the part of the
reader. Appropriate clausular pausing will lead the reader to THINK, and it will make him *seem* to do so even
when he does not. For he must always—

"Assume this virtue, if he have it not."

49. The following example illustrates the difference
between oratorical pausing and ordinary punctuation.
As these stanzas are usually printed, commas are inserted
after " night," " storm " and " darkness ;" and no mark
of punctuation is used after " sky," " eye," " along,"
" Jura," " this," " me," " sharer," " tempest," " rain,"
" again," " now," " hills " and " rejoice."

THUNDER-STORM AMONG THE ALPS.*—*Byron.*

The sky—is changed!—and such a change—O—night
And storm and darkness—ye are wondrous strong—
Yet lovely in your strength—as is the light
Of a dark eye—in woman!—Far along—
From peak to peak the rattling crags among--
Leaps the live thunder!—not from one lone cloud—
But every mountain—now hath found a tongue—
And Jura—answers through her misty shroud—
Back to the joyous Alps—who call to her aloud.

And this—is in the night!—Most glorious night!—
Thou wert not sent for slumber!—let me—be
A sharer— in thy fierce and far delight—
A portion—of the tempest and of thee!
How the lit lake shines—a phosphoric sea—
And the big rain—comes dancing to the earth—
And now again—'tis black—and now—the glee
Of the loud hills—shakes with its mountain mirth—
As if they did rejoice—o'er a young earthquake's birth.

X. EMPHATICAL DISJUNCTIONS OF WORDS.

50. Words which in ordinary utterance are collocated
into one group, will be *separated* in EMPHATIC pronun-

* A key to the emphatic words in these stanzas is given in a
subsequent section.

ciation. The hearer's attention is excited, and curiosity awakened, for the word which the speaker stops to introduce; especially when the syntactical construction is such as to admit of no break in ordinary delivery. Thus, between the *pronoun* and the *verb;* the *auxiliary* and the *principal* verb; the *verb* and its *object* or *complement;* the *article, preposition,* or *adjective,* and the *noun,* &c. ; as in the following passages :—

"O, sir, your—honesty—is—remarkable."

"Let me tell you, Cassius, you yourself
Are much condemned to have—an—itching palm !"

"Shall I bend low, and, in a bondsman's key,
With bated breath and—whispering humbleness,
Say this—
'Fair sir ! you—spit on me on Wednesday last;
You—spurned me, such a day; another time
You called me—*dog;* and for these—*courtesies,*
I'll—lend you thus much monies.' "

"If a Jew wrong a Christian, what is his—humility?—Revenge.
If a Christian wrong a Jew, what should his—sufferance be, by—
Christian—example?—Why, revenge ! "

"Hear him, my lord; he's—wondrous condescending;
Mark the—humility—of—shepherd Norval."

————

XI. STACCATO PRONUNCIATION.

51. In strong emotion, each accent, or even every *syllable,* may be separately inflected. This *staccato* pronunciation, is especially used in exclamatory SURPRISE or INTERROGATION; as in the following illustrations :—

"I an itching palm?"

"Gone to be married? Gone to swear a peace?"

"Dost thou stand by the tombs of the glorious dead?"

"And fear not to say that their son hath fled?"

"Away! he is lying by lance and shield!"

"Point me the path to his battle-field!"

52. The Mechanism, and Expressiveness of the vocal
movements or inflexions, and their application to verbal
and clausular accents, have now been explained and illustrated. Let the student perfectly master these principles,
and, by exercise, acquire the power to pronounce spon-
taneously any accentual combination of syllables, in each
of the Modes, both of Simple and Compound inflexion,
before proceeding further. He who is ambitious of excellence in Elocution must thus patiently cultivate his
voice to execute, and his ear to appreciate, *separately*,
the fundamental requisites of correct delivery, before he
attempts to apply them in Expressive Reading.

53. The practice of clausular reading, with proper accentuation and with varied well-defined inflexions accom-
panying every utterance, will be found speedily and perfectly effectual in imparting FLEXIBILITY to the voice,
and in removing habits of MONOTONY, or other inexpressive mannerism in Reading. The following selection of
short passages in Prose and Poetry furnishes *material*
for exercise. These passages should be read in accordance with each of the separate stages of grouping illustrated in this section.

XII. PASSAGES FOR EXERCISE IN THE GRAMMAT-
ICAL GROUPING OF WORDS.

AN ANCIENT TEMPLE.—*Blair.*

See yonder hallowed fane! the pious work
Of names once famed, now dubious or forgot,
And buried midst the wreck of things that were :
There lie interred the more illustrious dead.
The wind is up : hark! how it howls! Methinks,
Till now, I never heard a sound so dreary,
Doors creak, and windows clap, and night's foul bird,
Rook'd in the spire, screams loud; the gloomy aisles,
Black plastered, and hung round with shreds of scutcheons,
And tattered coats of arms, send back the sound,
Laden with heavier airs, from the low vaults,
The mansions of the dead.

ANIMAL ENJOYMENT.—*Cowper.*

The heart is hard in nature, and unfit
For human fellowship, as being void

Of sympathy, and therefore dead alike
To love and friendship both; that is not pleased
With sight of animals enjoying life,
Nor feels their happiness augment his own.

ANGER.

I have remarked that the declamations of angry men make
little impression on those who are not themselves angry. Rea-
sonable men love reason.

CHEERFULNESS.

A cheerful temper, joined with innocence, will make beauty
attractive, knowledge delightful, and wit good-natured; it will
lighten sickness, poverty, and affliction; convert ignorance into
an amiable simplicity, and render deformity itself agreeable.

CONSTANCY IN VIRTUE.

The bird let loose in Eastern skies,
    When hastening fondly home,
Ne'er stoops to earth her wing, or flies
    Where idle wanderers roam;
But high she shoots, through air and light,
    Above all low delay,
Where nothing earthly bounds her flight,
    Or shadow dims her way.
So grant me, God, from every stain
    Of sinful passion free,
Aloft through virtue's purer air,
    To steer my course to Thee!
No sin to cloud, no lure to stay
    My soul, as home she springs;
Thy sunshine on her joyful way,
    Thy freedom on her wings.

CONTENTMENT.

When you are rich, praise God for His abundant bounty; when
poor, thank Him for keeping you from the temptations of pros-
perity; when you are at ease, glorify Him for His merciful kindness; and when beset with affliction and pain, offer thanksgiving
for His merciful remindings that you are approaching your end.

CRITICS.—*Emerson.*

The eye of a critic is often, like a microscope, made so very
fine and nice that it discovers the atoms and minutest particles,
but cannot comprehend the whole, so as to compare the parts,
and perceive at once the general harmony

DESIRE OF DISTINCTION.

The desire of distinction in the world is a commendable quality when it excites men to the performance of illustrious actions; but this ambition is so seldom directed to its proper end, and is so little scrupulous in the choice of the means which it employs for the accomplishment of its purpose, that it frequently ruins the morals of those who are actuated by it; and thus, for the pleasure of being lifted up for a moment above the common level of mankind, many a man has forfeited his character with the wise and good, and inflicted wounds on his conscience, which the balm of flattering dependants can never heal.

DESIRES UNLIMITED.

The desires of man increase with his acquisitions; every step that he advances brings something within his view that he did not see before, and which, as soon as he sees it, he begins to want. Where necessity ends, curiosity begins; and no sooner are we supplied with every thing that nature can demand, than we sit down to contrive artificial appetites.

EMPLOYMENT.—*Baillie.*

The bliss, e'en of a moment, still is bliss,
What! would'st thou, of her dew-drops spill the thorn,
Because her glory cannot last till noon?
Or still the lightsome gambols of the colt,
Whose neck to-morrow's yoke will gall? Fie on't!
If this be wise, 'tis cruel.

FORGIVENESS.—*Lady E. Carew.*

The fairest action of our human life
Is scorning to revenge an injury;
For who forgives, without a further strife,
His adversary's heart to him doth tie.

FORTUNE'S FROLICS.—*Chapman.*

Fortune, the great Commandress of the world,
Hath diverse ways to enrich her followers ;
To some, she honours gives without deserving,
To other some, deserving without honour ;
Some wit, some wealth, and some wit without wealth,
Some wealth without wit ; some nor wit, nor wealth,
But taking faces and appearances,
To make a show without possessing substance.

HASTY ANGER.—*C. Johnson.*

Those hearts that start at once into a blaze,
And open all their rage, like summer storms
At once discharg'd, grow cool again as fast,
And calm.

HUMAN LIFE.—*Emerson.*

The life of man is a self-evolving circle, which, from a ring imperceptibly small, rushes on all sides outwards to new and larger circles, and that without end.

HUMILITY.—*Gill.*

Generally speaking, those who have the most grace, and the greatest gifts, and are of the greatest usefulness, are the most humble, and think the most meanly of themselves. So those boughs and branches of trees which are most richly laden with fruit, bend downward, and hang lowest.

INDUSTRY.—*Emerson.*

Though the wide universe is full of good, no kernel of nourishing corn can come to a man, but through his toil bestowed on that plot of ground which is given him to till.

INNOCENCE.

Whence learned she this? O she was innocent!
And to be innocent is Nature's wisdom!
The fledge-dove knows the prowlers of the air,
Feared soon as seen, and flutters back to shelter.
And the young steed recoils upon his haunches,
The never-yet-seen adder's hiss first heard.
O surer than suspicion's hundred eyes
Is that fine sense which, to the pure in heart,
By mere oppugnancy of their own goodness
Reveals the approach of evil.

LIBERALITY.—*Christian Philosophy.*

What should be the model of the Christian's liberality ? Even the rich perpetual beneficence of God. Observe the many emblems of this spirit which Nature furnishes. How freely does the ocean yield its waters to the empty clouds; and they, again, how richly do they pour their fertilizing drops, to cheer and bless the thirsty earth! The sun, the centre, and the glory of the solar system, the material spirit of its light and joy, how plenteously his golden beams are scattered through our world! The earth, though cursed by man's transgression, yet yieldeth to the sower oftentimes a hundred-fold. The air, the element of life, pervadeth every place, that men may breathe it. The orchard, with its laden boughs of cooling fruits, presents, with yearly constancy, its gifts to men. The avaricious wretch, and sordid selfling, may blush, indeed, to contemplate these emblems of beneficence.

LIBERTY.

'Tis liberty alone that gives the flower
Of fleeting life its lustre and perfume;

And we are weeds without it. All constraint,
Except what wisdom lays on evil men,
Is evil; hurts the faculties, impedes
Their progress in the road to science; blinds
The eyesight of discovery; and begets,
In those that suffer it, a sordid mind,
Bestial, a meagre intellect, unfit
To be the tenant of man's noble form.

LIGHT.—*Christian Philosophy.*

" Let there be light, " is the mandate of Heaven, and all holy intelligences favour its diffusion. Let the light of science, of philosophy, and of letters, exalt to intellectuality every nation of the earth. Let the light of truth disperse the errors of superstition and ignorance from our world. Let the light of revelation illumine with saving rays every nation, and kindred, and people, and tongue. Let the light of celestial favour form the day of hope and rejoicing in every heart of man. Let light be diffused from the printing-press, from the village-school, from the college, from the institutions of science, and from the sanctuary of religion. Let the monarch and the subject, the legislator and the governed, the rich and the poor, all unite for its diffusion.

LIVING MERIT.—*Charles Mackay.*

Who can tell what schemes majestic
Perish in the active brain—
What humanity is robbed of,
Ne'er to be restored again—
What we lose, because we honour
Overmuch the mighty dead?
     And dispirit
     Living merit,
Heaping scorn upon its head?
Or, perchance, when kinder grown,
Leaving it to die alone?

LOVE.

Look how the golden ocean shines above
Its pebbly stones, and magnifies their girth;
So does the bright and blessed light of love
Its own things glorify, and raise their worth.

MIGHT OF MERCY.—*Rowe.*

           The narrow soul
Knows not the God-like glory of forgiving,
Nor can the cold, the ruthless heart conceive
How large the power, how fixed the empire is
Which benefits confer on generous minds.
Goodness prevails on the most stubborn foes,
And conquers more than ever sword subdued.

MISFORTUNES.

The external misfortunes of life, disappointments, poverty, and sickness, are light in comparison with those inward distresses of mind, occasioned by folly, by passion, and by guilt.

MOODINESS.—*Shakespeare.*

O, we are querulous creatures! Little less
Than nothing can suffice to make us happy;
And little less than nothing is enough
To make us wretched.

MUTUAL DEPENDENCE.—*Emerson.*

There is nothing in the universe that stands alone,—nothing solitary. No atom of matter, no drop of water, no vesicle of air, or ray of light, exists in a state of isolation. Everything belongs to some system of society, of which it is a component and necessary part. Just so it is in the moral world.—No man stands alone, nor high angel, nor child. All the beings "lessening down from infinite perfection to the brink of dreary nothing," belong to a system of mutual dependencies. All and each constitute and enjoy a part of the world's sum of happiness. No one liveth to himself. The most obscure individual exerts an influence which must be felt in the great brotherhood of mankind. As the little silvery circular ripple, set in motion by the falling pebble, expands from its inch of radius to the whole compass of the pool, so there is not an infant placed, however softly, in his bulrush-ark upon the sea of time, whose existence does not stir a ripple gyrating outward and on, until it shall have moved across and spanned the whole ocean of God's eternity. "To be, or not to be?" is that the question? No.—We are; and whether we live or die, we are the Lord's; we belong to His eternity, and henceforth His moral universe will be filled with our existence.

NIGHT.—*Blair.*

Night, sable goddess! from her ebon throne,
In rayless majesty, now stretches forth
Her leaden sceptre o'er a slumbering world.
Silence how dead! and darkness how profound!
Nor eye nor listening ear an object finds.
Creation sleeps. 'Tis as the general pulse
Of life stood still, and Nature made a pause,—
An awful pause, prophetic of her end.

OCCUPATION.

Occupation cures at least half of life's troubles, and mitigates the remainder. A manacled slave, working at the galleys, is happier than the self-manacled slave of idleness.

PHILOSOPHY AND RELIGION.

Philosophy may destroy the burden of the body, but religion gives wings to the soul. Philosophy may enable us to look down on the earth with contempt, but religion teaches us to look up to heaven with hope. Philosophy may support to the brink of the grave, but religion conducts beyond it. Philosophy unfolds a rich store of enjoyment, which religion makes eternal.

POTENCY OF COURAGE.—*Rowe.*

The wise and active conquer difficulties
By daring to attempt them; sloth and folly
Shiver and shrink at sight of toil and hazard,
And make the impossibility they fear.

PRAYER AND SUBMISSION.—*Milton.*

If I could hope by prayer to change the will
Of Him who all things can, I would not cease
To weary Him with my assiduous cries;
But prayer against His absolute decree
No more avails than breath against the wind,
Therefore, to His great bidding I submit.

PROGRESS IN GUILT.—*Lillo.*

There's nought so monstrous but the mind of man
In some conditions may be brought to approve;
Theft, sacrilege, treason and parricide,
When flattering opportunity enticed
And desperation drove, have been committed
By those who once would start to hear them named.

SADNESS OF NIGHT.—*Young.*

How, like a widow in her weeds, the night,
Amid her glimmering tapers, silent sits!
How sorrowful, how desolate, she weeps
Perpetual dews, and saddens Nature's scene!

SELF-KNOWLEDGE.—*Emerson.*

Although men are accused of not knowing their own weakness, yet, perhaps, as few know their own strength. It is in men as in soils, where sometimes there is a vein of gold, which the owner knows not of.

SOURCES OF CALAMITY. —*Byron.*

There is an order
Of mortals on the earth who do become
Old in their youth, and die ere middle age;

Some perishing of pleasure, some of study,
Some worn with toil, some of mere weariness,
Some of disease, and some insanity,
And some of withered or of broken hearts :
For this last is a malady which takes
Variety of shapes and names, and slays
More than are numbered in the lists of Fate.

SOURCES OF ERROR.—*Harris.*

Partial views, the imperfections of sense, inattention, idleness, the turbulence of passions, education, local sentiments, opinions, and belief, conspire, in many instances, to furnish us with ideas, some too general, some too partial, and, what is worse than all this, with many that are erroneous, and contrary to truth. These it behoves us to correct, as far as possible, by cool suspense and candid examination.

SUCCESS.—*Thomson.*

It is success that colours all in life;
Success makes fools admired, makes villains honest:
All the proud virtue of this vaunting world
Fawns on success and power, howe'er acquired.

THE COMMON LOT.—*Cowper.*

All flesh is grass, and all its glory fades,
Like the fair flower dishevelled in the wind;
Riches have wings, and Grandeur is a dream;
The man we celebrate must find a tomb,
And we that worship him, ignoble graves.

THE GOSPEL.

There is not an evil incident to human nature, for which the gospel doth not provide a remedy. Are you ignorant of many things which it highly concerns you to know?—The gospel offers you instruction. Have you deviated from the path of duty?—The gospel offers you forgiveness. Do temptations surround you? The gospel offers you the aid of Heaven. Are you exposed to misery?—It consoles you. Are you subject to death?—It offers you immortality.

THE GRAVE.—*Blair.*

When self-esteem, or others' adulation,
Would cunningly persuade us we were something
Above the common level of our kind,
The grave gainsays the smooth-complexion'd flattery,
And with blunt truth acquaints us what we are.

THOUGHTS.—*Christian Philosophy.*

Thoughts are the moving ideas of the mind; the actions of the fancy and imagination. Thoughts are the seeds of words, and the germ of actions. If the mind is in a state of incessant exercise, then how numberless must be the thoughts arising therefrom! Many thoughts are vain and foolish, and therefore of necessity useless. Many thoughts are ungodly and wicked, and therefore injurious to the soul, and hateful to God. A watch over such thoughts is necessary to prevent their intrusion, and holy ejaculations are essential to their expulsion.

TRUTH.—*Christian Philosophy.*

Truth is to fact what the impress is to the seal, the exact transcript. Adherence to truth, the seven-times-heated furnace could not consume, nor the hungry lions destroy. Buy truth at any price: its cost cannot exceed its worth, or surpass its intrinsic value. Whoever possesses truth, holds an inestimable treasure, whose currency is admitted in both worlds.

TYRANNY.—*Brooke.*

Not claim hereditary nor the high
Anointing hand of Heaven can give a law
For lawless power, or to injustice bind
Allegiance. Tyranny absolves all faith;
And who invades our rights can never be
But a usurper.

TYRANNY OF VICE.—*Byron.*

Think'st thou there is no tyranny but that
Of blood and chains? The despotism of vice,
The weakness and the wickedness of luxury,
The negligence of sensual sloth, produces
Ten thousand tyrants who, in cruelty,
Surpass the worst of domineering masters,
However harsh, and hard, and pitiless.

UNCERTAINTY OF TO-MORROW.

In human hearts what bolder thought can rise
Than man's presumption on to-morrow's dawn?
Where is to-morrow? In another world.
For numbers this is certain; the reverse
Is sure to none.

VARIETY OF ENDOWMENTS.—*Wilberforce.*

We have different forms assigned to us in the school of life, different gifts imparted. All is not attractive that is good. Iron is useful, though it does not sparkle like the diamond. Gold has not the fragrance of a flower. So, different persons have different modes of excellence, and we must have an eye to all.

VIRTUE.— *Young.*

Virtue, not rolling suns, the mind matures,
That life is long which answers life's great end.
The time that bears no fruit deserves no name;
The man of wisdom is the man of years.

VIRTUOUS PROMPTITUDE.—*Rowe.*

A virtuous deed should never be delay'd,
The impulse comes from Heav'n and he who strives
A moment to repress it, disobeys
The god within his mind.

VOICES OF NIGHT.—*Baillie.*

How those fallen leaves do rustle on the path,
With whispering noise, as though the earth around me
Did utter secret things!
The distant river, too, bears to mine ear
A dismal wailing. O, mysterious night!
Not silent art thou; many tongues thou hast.

WAR.—*Christian Philosophy.*

War has dinned the world, and crimsoned the earth, and cursed
our species for ages upon ages. What has it effected, and
what are the results which follow in its train? Agricultural ste-
rility, commercial depression, national enthralment, social woe,
physical suffering, the unalleviated agonizing pangs of myriads,
the battle-field strewed with the wounded, the dying, and the
dead: desolated countries, sacked cities, burning dwellings, de-
spairing widows and orphans. The sound of trumpets, the clash
of arms, and the roaring of the cannon, may excite for a season,
but reflection must follow, both to surviving conquerors and to
the conquered. And what a reflection! That they have choked
the avenues of death with myriads of dark and guilty spirits,
crowding in fearful horror into the region of Hades. But a time
is coming, when war shall be hated, reprobated, abhorred, and only
remembered as a woe and a blight that has passed away for ever.

WELL-DOING.— *Young.*

Who does the best his circumstance allows
Does well, acts nobly, angels could no more.

WISDOM.—*Christian Philosophy.*

Wisdom is that faculty which applieth knowledge to its best use
and fitteth means for the best end. It looketh to the future, and
dreameth not of building on the uncertain present. Wisdom
hath its decided preferences, and its fixed antipathies. It avoid-
eth precipitancy in matters of moment, and doeth nothing

rashly. It doth not encourage the whisperer, nor hearken to the tale-bearer, nor attend to idle rumours. It cherisheth openness of demeanour, candour of spirit, and integrity of speech. It decideth not without ample evidence, and it judgeth not without a cause. It sheddeth lustre on every station, age, and condition. It is the brightness of the child's eye, the nobleness of the youth's countenance, and the dignity of the man of years.

WOMAN.—*Charles Mackay.*

A very woman :—full of tears,
Hopes, blushes, tendernesses, fears,
Griefs, laughter, kindness, joys, and sighs,
Loves, likings, friendships, sympathies ;
A heart to feel for every woe,
And pity, if not dole, bestow ;
A hand to give from scanty store ;
A look to wish the offering more.

XIII. APPLICATION OF THE PRINCIPLES OF INFLEX-ION TO SENTENCES.

54. As all inflexions may be resolved into *two* kinds— rising and falling—so, all rules for their application may be resolved into two corresponding, general FUNDA-MENTAL PRINCIPLES.

55. (I.) The *rising* progression CONNECTS what has been said with what is to be uttered, or with what the speaker wishes to be *implied* or *supplied* by the hearer ; and this, with more or less closeness and passion, in proportion to the force and extent of the rise. The *rising* inflexion is thus associated with what is *incomplete* in sense ; or, if apparently complete, *dependent on* or *modified* by what immediately follows ; with whatever is *relative* to something expressed, or implied ; and with what is *doubtful, interrogative, or supplicatory.*

56. (II.) The *falling* progression DISCONNECTS what has been said from what is to follow ; and this with more or less exclusiveness, and passion, in proportion to the force and extent of the fall. The *falling* inflexion is, thus, associated with what is *complete* and *independent* in sense, or intended to be received as such ; and with whatever is *positive, dogmatical, or mandatory.*

57. All sentences belong, constructively, to one or

other of the three classes—ASSERTIVE, INTERROGATIVE, and IMPERATIVE ;—as

(1.) I am coming. (2.) Are you coming? (3.) Come!

The following Principles deduced from conversational usage regulate the closing inflexion of each kind of sentence.

I. *Assertive Sentences.*

58. Assertive sentences have normally a *falling* termination, as predicating facts of which the hearer may be presumed to have been previously uninformed ; but when they cannot be supposed to communicate information they take a *rising* termination, as in appeal to the hearer's consciousness. Thus,

The sun rises in the éast; (implying " does it not? ")

The end of life is déath; (implying " is it not?")

II. *Interrogative Sentences.**

59. Interrogative sentences have normally a *rising* termination ; as relating to facts respecting which the speaker may be presumed to be in doubt or ignorance ; but when they cannot be supposed to ask for information they take a *falling* termination, as in assertion of what the hearer's consciousness must corroborate. Thus,

Is virtue to be commended? (implying " you know it is.")

Does rain fall from the clouds? (implying " you know it does.")

III. *Imperative Sentences.*

60. Imperative sentences have a *falling* termination when they express the *speaker's will* without reference to the will of the hearer, and they have a *rising* termination when they *solicit* rather than enjoin compliance. Thus,

Remember what I have said; (implying "it is my will.")

Remember what I have said; (implying " will you ?")

---

* See " Varieties of Interrogative Sentences," p. 98.

XIV. ANALYSIS OF SENTENCES.

61. Every assertive sentence must consist of at least *two parts:*—(I.) the thing, person, quality, or fact *spoken of*—the SUBJECT;—and (II.) that which is *asserted* of the subject—the PREDICATE. Thus,

John—is speaking.   The event—is doubtful.

62. The subject usually *precedes* the predicate, but this order may be reversed. When both subject and predicate are ACCENTED, the *former* of them, in either order, terminates with a *rising*, and the *latter*, with a *falling* inflexion.

63. When the *subject* has been *previously* expressed or implied, or when it is a pronoun, it is pronounced *without* an accentual inflexion, and if it precedes the predicate, takes merely the preparatory pitch of an unaccented syllable. Thus,

John is silent.   He has finished.

64. When the *predicate* has been previously expressed or implied, the same principle applies, and the subject alone receives accentual inflexion.

65. When the subject or predicate is *antithetic* to any other, either expressed or implied, compound instead of simple tones will be employed.

66. The *predicate* may consist of a *verb only*, or it may include also an *object* or *complement*. The position of the *accent* will vary according to the sense, but the principle of concluding inflexion is the same whether the predicate be simple or compound.

67. An assertive sentence may contain, besides the subject and predicate, a third part—the CIRCUMSTANCE ; which may be either of the adjective class, as qualifying the subject, or of the adverbial class, as qualifying the predicate.

68. The *circumstance* may consist of a *single* word, of a clausular *group* of words, or of a subordinate *sentence*, adverbial, relative, conditional, or participial.

69. The subordinate clause or sentence may be *com-*

plemental of the subject or predicate,—when its accentuation and inflexion must show it to be *a part* of the principal member ;—or it may be merely *explanatory*—when it must be pronounced with independent tones and accents. Thus in the following lines :

> " Behold the emblem of thy state
> In flowers, which bloom and die.''

The principal sentence here terminates with the complementary clause " in flowers ;"

> " Behold the emblem of thy state in flowers !"

and the succeeding relative sentence is an *independent* explanatory addition. Thus :—

> " Behold the emblem of thy state
> In flowers, ⌊which bloom and die.'

70. The *subjects* and *predicates* must always be so pronounced as to strike upon the hearer's mind with unencumbered distinctness among the most multitudinous assemblage of syntactically subordinate clauses or sentences. The subject and predicate are generally the most emphatic parts of a sentence ; they are so always, indeed, except when either of them has been previously expressed or implied ; or when some opposition or contrast of circumstantial clauses or sentences requires *their* comparative elevation.

71. Subordinate clauses or sentences may *precede* the *subject, follow* the *predicate,* or *intervene* between them. In the *first* and *last cases* they will generally terminate with *rising,* and in the *second,* with *falling* inflexions—subject to the same modifications and varieties, from antithesis, previous implication, &c., as the subjects and predicates themselves.

72. The predicate may be either an *absolute* or a *conditional* assertion : in the *former* case it will take the *falling* inflexion, but in the *latter,* it will require a compound *rising* tone to modify its assertiveness and connect it with the conditional member or sentence that follows.

7

Examples.

Conditional Circum- } *stance* . . }	If to *do* were as easy as to know what were *good* to do
Subject . .	*chapels*
Predicate . . .	had been *churches*
Connective	and
Subject	*poor* men's cottages
Predicate	(had been) *princes'* palaces.

Imperative sentence .	*Look*
Circumstance of manner,	how
Subject	the golden ocean
Predicate	*shines*
Circumstance of place .	above its pebbly stones
Connective . . .	and
Predicate	*magnifies*
Object	their girth !
Circumstance of manner,	*So*
Auxiliary to predicate,	does
Subject	the bright and blessed light of *love*
Object	its own things
Predicate . . .	glorify
Connective	and
Predicate . .	raise
Object	their worth.

XV. VARIETIES OF INTERROGATIVE SENTENCES.

73. When we pronounce any sentence in *doubt* or *ig-norance*, and with the desire of assurance or information, we naturally terminate the utterance with a *rising inflexion*, more or less strong, in proportion to the degree of our eagerness to be assured or informed. By the tone of voice we APPEAL to the hearer for a satisfactory response ; and this, without reference to the syntactical form of construction we employ. The declarative, or even the imperative form of composition, may be pronounced with an equally interrogative effect to that which is more commonly associated with the interrogative construction. In reading, we must not be guided by the mere arrangement of the words ; for we often meet with the form of interrogation when the sentence is not interrogative in meaning, but, on the contrary, distinctly assertive ; as when Cassius says to Brutus—

" I said an elder soldier—not a better—

Did I say better ? "

And we frequently find the declarative construction employed when the intention is not assertive, but manifestly
interrogative : as when Cassius further says—

" *You do not love me, Brutus.*"

74. Directly interrogative sentences usually have the
verb preceding the subject ; as, "*will you go?*" " *when
will you go?*" " *went you not with them?*" "*why went
you not with them?*" " *does any one accompany you?*"
" *who accompanies you?*" These questions are of *two
kinds*—VERBAL, and ADVERBIAL or PRONOMINAL. In
the *verbal* class, " *will you? went you?*" &c., the query
has reference to the FACT in the sentence ; and the concluding tone is generally rising, as expressive of doubt or
solicitation. In the *adverbial* or *pronominal* class, the
fact is not called in question, but the query has reference
to some *circumstance* attending it—" WHEN? WHY?
HOW? WHO?" &c., and the concluding tone is generally
falling, as expressive of the assumed certainty as to the
fact.

75. Adverbial and pronominal questions are in fact
assertive or imperative in their nature. Thus, " *When
will you go? who will accompany you?* " imply " *Understanding that you are going, I ask,* (or " tell me")
*when? Expecting that some person will accompany
you, I ask, who?*" But if we are very solicitous to
gain the information, or are in any doubt as to the *fact*
itself, we terminate the question with a rising tone, and
it then strongly *appeals* for a response, or becomes both
a *verbal* and *adverbial* question. Thus, " When will
you go," implies, " Do tell me," or "*Are* you really going, and, if so, *when?*"

76. The rising or falling inflexion may frequently be
used indifferently on a question of this kind which is not
marked by emotional emphasis.

Example.

" How do you do?"			" How do you do?"
" What is it o'clock?"	} *or* {		" What is it o'clock?"

The rising inflection is, however, more deferential than the falling, and is that which would generally be used in addressing a superior, while the falling tone is that which the superior would probably himself employ.

77. It is to be observed also, that when a question of this kind, uttered with a falling inflexion, has not been distinctly apprehended, or, from any cause, is echoed by the person to whom it was addressed, it receives, in this repetition, the rising inflexion.

Example.—" Whence arise these forebodings, but from the consciousness of guilt?"

| " *Whence* arise these forebodings?" |) | (*implying,* " Did you |
| "From the consciousness of *guilt?*" | } | say?") |

This is generally the case also when we have not heard or understood with certainty the answer returned to our question, and consequently repeat the interrogative word.

Example.—" When were you there last?" (*Answer not distinctly apprehended*).

" WHEN?" (*implying,* " Will you oblige me by repeating that?")

But if the feeling of the questioner is not of the apologetic kind, he may throw incredulity or authority into the repeated question.   Thus,

" When?" (*implying,* " Do you really make so improbable a statement?") or

" When?" (*implying,* " Answer directly and without evasion.")

78. In all these illustrations we may trace the working of the two simple fundamental principles of inflexion,— which, among many varieties of application, require no category of Exceptions.

79. In the following sentence, the elliptical questions, "*for whom?*" and "*for thee?*" illustrate the two classes of interrogations,—the former being equivalent to "*for*

whom shall we break it?" and the latter to *" shall we do so for thee?"*

"All this dread order break,—for whom?—for thee?
Vile worm! O madness! Pride! Impiety!"

80. Questions of two parts connected by the conjunctive or *dis*junctive particle *" or,"* importantly illustrate the two classes of interrogation. Thus:—"Are you going to Liverpool or Manchester?"—This, according to the mode in which it is read, will be equivalent to "Are you going to *either* of these places?" or " To *which* of these places are you going?" To convey the former meaning " Liverpool " and " Manchester " will be pronounced with the same or with only one accentual inflexion, or with no accent; and to convey the latter signification they will be pronounced with separate accents and *opposite* inflexions. Questions of this kind, when the *verb* is the subject of inquiry, may be resolved into, *"Is it either?"* and can be answered by *yes* or *no;* and those in which the verb is not called in question may always be resolved into *"which is it?"* and cannot be answered by yes or no.

81. The mark of interrogation (?) is, in English punctuation, placed at the *end* of the grammatical period, but the interrogative sentence frequently terminates with a participial, or other subordinate sentence, or with a simile, and the interrogative inflexion should not be continued in such concluding member. Thus, in the two following passages, the questions virtually close at " esteem " and " presence," and there the interrogative *intonation* must end.

> " Would'st thou have that
> Which thou esteem'st the ornament of life,
> And live a coward in thine own esteem,—
> Letting ' I dare not' wait upon ' I would,'
> Like the poor cat i' the adage ?"—*Shakespeare.*

> " Didst thou not think, such vengeance must await
> The wretch that, with his crimes all fresh about him,
> Rushes irreverent, unprepared, uncalled,
> Into his Maker's presence—throwing back
> With insolent disdain His choicest gift ?"—*Dr. Porteous*

XVI. GOVERNING AND DEPENDENT WORDS.

82. Governing and dependent words should be united ; but when a word is at the same time dependent on what precedes, and governing to what follows, it should be separated from the former, to show its closer relation to the latter.

83. Also, when two or more words have a common relation to some other word, the former should be united among themselves, but separated from the word to which they are equally related.

Examples.

We have done those things.
We have done—those things which we ought not to have done.
We forgive them.
We forgive—them that trespass.
He hath scattered the proud.
He hath scattered—the proud in the imagination of their hearts.
To judge the quick.
To judge – the quick and the dead.
To confess our sins.
To confess—our manifold sins and wickedness.
And am no more worthy.
And am no more—worthy to be called thy son.
Distressed in mind.
Distressed—in mind, body, or estate.

XVII. SERIES.

84. When there are two or more words, clauses, or sentences, *in apposition*—subjects, predicates or circumstances—they may be either compacted into a SERIES—by rising inflexions, *as in counting*—or pronounced with independent inflexions, *as if each stood alone* in the sentence. The former mode of intonation exhibits most emphatically the aggregate value of the serial members, and the latter gives them the greatest amount of individual emphasis. Sequences of words or clauses in apposition are only to be pronounced connectedly, when they seem to require *aggregation* to convey the full import of the passage.

XVIII. RESUMÉ OF THE LEADING PRINCIPLES OF SENTENTIAL INTONATION.

85. The general principles to be attended to in reading are briefly and simply these :—

Does the clause or sentence communicate the *speaker's* will or knowledge? if so, *fall;* if not, rise.

Does the clause or sentence appeal to the *hearer's* will or knowledge? if so, *rise;* if not, fall.

Is the clause or sentence *dependent* on some other to complete the sense? if so, give it connective or referential tones ; if not, pronounce it irrespectively of what follows, and with tones rising or falling in accordance with its own expressiveness.

Is the subordinate sentence a necessary complement of the principal? if so, give it *corresponding* modulative pitch, and connective or referential tones ; if not, read it in a different pitch, and with independent inflexions.

Are the items of the Series *severally* or *collectively* important to the sense? if the former, pronounce them with disjunctive inflexion, and subsequent pause ; if the latter, aggregate them by connective inflexion and correspondence of modulation.

86. Ordinary elocutionary Rules—especially those of the Series—render reading at *sight* impossible ; but, with such guiding Principles as the above, it is perfectly and effectively practicable. The voice has been shown to have a certain definite expressiveness in every movement, which may apply to *any* form of construction, according as the intent of the speaker requires the vocal effect. Rules for natural reading, then, cannot be founded on the grammatical forms of periods, or complete sentences, but on the inherent expressiveness of the vocal movements, and the independent or relative value of clauses.

---

87. *Exercise on Sentential Inflexions.*

The following Exercise, including sentences of every variety, affords a convincing illustration of the governing force of Tones, and the independence of inflexion on grammatical construction. Each of these diverse modes

of delivering the very same words is, under certain circumstances, appropriate and natural.

Will you go. Will you go. Will you go. Will you go.
Will you go. Will you go. Will you go. Will you go.
Were you there. Were you there. Were you there.
Were you there. Were you there. Were you there.
Were you there. Were you there. Were you there.
Were you there.

Is it right. Is it right. Is it right. Is it right. Is it
right. Is it right. Is it right. Is it right. Is it right.

Is it possible. Is it possible. Is it possible. Is it
possible. Is it possible. Is it possible. Is it possible.
Is it possible. Is it possible.

That is all. That is all. That is all. That is all.
That is all. That is all. That is all. That is all.

How do you do. How do you do. How do you do.
How do you do. How do you do. How do you do.
How do you do. How do you do. How do you do.

Gone away. Gone away. Gone away. Gone away.
Gone away. Gone away. Gone away. Gone away.

No more. No more. No more. No more. No more.
No more. No more. No more. No more. No more.

Have patience. Have patience. Have patience. Have
patience. Have patience. Have patience. Have patience. Have
patience. Have patience.

The Christian's hope. The Christian's hope. The

Christian's hope. The Christian's hope. The Christian's hope. The Christian's hope is fixed. The Christian's hope is fixed. The Christian's hope is fixed on heaven. The Christian's hope is fixed on heaven.

He reads correctly. He reads correctly. He reads correctly. He reads correctly. He reads correctly when he likes. He reads correctly when he likes. He reads correctly when he likes. He reads correctly when he likes to pay attention. He reads correctly when he likes to pay attention. He reads correctly when he likes to pay attention.

THE

PRINCIPLES OF ELOCUTION,

PART THIRD.

MODULATION AND EXPRESSIVE DELIVERY.

1. Modulation has reference to the Pitch or "Key" of the voice, and to the expressive variations of Force, Time, and Quality.

PITCH.

2. A change of Pitch is necessary to distinguish:
   I. Questions from answers.
   II. Assertions from proofs or illustrations.
   III. General statements from inferences, &c.
   IV. Quotations.
   V. A new division of a subject.
   VI. Changes of sentiment.
   VII. Explanatory and parenthetic matter.

3. The degree in which the pitch is changed, and, often, even the direction of the change, will depend on the reader's taste, judgement, temperament, &c. As a general rule, low keys are associated with solemnity, awe, fear, humility, and sadness; and high keys with levity, boldness, pride, and joy. Violent passions nearly always take a high modulation.

4. A harmony of modulation must be maintained between syntactically related parts of a sentence—such as subject and predicate, verb and object, &c.—especially when they are separated by intervening clauses.

5. For directive notation in the exercises that follow, five degrees of Pitch are distinguished: a middle or "conversational" key (No. 3); and two keys respec-

tively higher (Nos. 4 and 5) ; and two lower (Nos. 2 and 1).　Thus—

```
5 ——————————————— high
4 ——————————————— above
3 ——————————————— middle
2 ——————————————— below
1 ——————————————— low
```

Besides these numbers for absolute pitch, the following signs for relative pitch are occasionally used :—

```
⌈ .      . . higher
⌊ . . . . lower
```

FORCE.

6. Force is entirely different from Pitch.　All varieties of Pitch may be accompanied by any degree of Force.　Low keys may be vehement, and high keys may be feeble ; and *vice versâ*.　In notation, five degrees of Force are distinguished.　Thus :—

```
V ——————————————— Vehement
E ——————————————— Energetic
M ——————————————— Moderate
W ——————————————— Weak
F ——————————————— Feeble
```

The following signs for relative force are also occasionally employed :—

```
< . . . . . stronger
> . . . . . weaker
```

TIME.

7. A corresponding notation is employed for the Time or *rate* of utterance ; including a " common" or medium degree, and two degrees relatively quicker, and two slower.　Thus :—

```
R ——————————————— Rapid
Q ——————————————— Quick
C ——————————————— Common
S ——————————————— Slow
T ——————————————— Tardy
```

The following additional signs for relative time may sometimes be found convenient :

```
V . . . quicker
Λ . . . slower
```

8. Simple narrative generally requires a medium Force and Time; animated description an increase of energy and speed; violent passions a greater increase; and tender emotions a decrease. Pathos and solemnity require a slow movement. Subordinate clauses and sentences, parentheses, &c., are, generally, but not always, pronounced with less force and in quicker time than principal members.

9. A great deal of pleasing and expressive variety may be produced by slight variations of Pitch, Force, and Time. The musician's consummate delicacy of execution, in keeping the simple *air* running with a separate current in the midst of a river of variations, has its counterpart in the reader's vocal adaptation of sound to sense. The painter's artistic excellence in selecting objects to be " struck out " with varied effects, or " covered down " for contrast, is emulated by the skilful reader, in the due subordination or prominence of every thought and circumstance, according to its relative importance. A Master of Ceremonies is not more punctilious in his arrangements than the voice of a tasteful and judicious reader.

EXPRESSIVE QUALITY.

10. Under this head are comprehended such Expressive Modulations as fundamentally affect the quality of the voice, or the mode of utterance, and enable the reader to " make the sound an echo to the sense."

11. The most finely toned voice, with all the charms of graceful and distinct articulation, will not suffice to make an effective reader, if there be not a constant current of SENTIMENT streaming through the inflexions and articulate utterances. Speech, though chiefly mechanical, and therefore,—so far as articulation, force, time, and musical changes are concerned,—imitable by artificial contrivances, receives a higher and inimitable expressiveness from the feeling of the speaker. There is a Vocal Logic ; a Rhetoric of Inflexion ; a Poetry of Modulation ; a Commentator's explanatoriness of Tone,—and these are combined in effective reading. Reading fails of half its proper effect, and of its highest purpose, if it does not furnish, besides a vocal transcript of the written language,

a commentary upon its sentiment, and a judgement upon its reasoning. The language of Emotion must accompany every utterance that is naturally delivered. Yet how many merely mechanical speakers there are, whose voices know no thrill of feeling, and who throw off their tame monotonous oratory "coldly correct and regularly dull," nerveless, and passionless as automata. Let it be the object of the elocutionary student to awaken in himself a *sympathetic* sensibility with every utterance ;—to "learn to feel ;"—and to keep the fine-strung organs of expressiveness in a state of delicate susceptibility. Let him make the language he reads his own, and always, in its delivery, "be in earnest." A simple system of NOTATION, will be of great assistance in the formation of a habit of discriminating Expressiveness.

12. The following elements of Expressive quality will be found sufficiently to indicate the functional manifestations of nearly all passions. Abbreviations for notation are shown within parentheses.

ELEMENTS OF EXPRESSIVE QUALITY.

Qualities.	*Expressions.*
WHISPER (Wh.) . .	Secrecy, cunning, apprehension of evil, fearful suspense, &c.
HOARSENESS (Ho.) .	Horror, loathing, agony, despair, &c.
OROTUND (Or.) . .	Pomp, sublimity, vastness; also bombast, self-importance, &c.
FALSETTO (Fa.) . .	Puerility, senility; also acute anguish, or overpowering mirth, &c.
MONOTONE (Mo.). .	Reflection, gloom, melancholy, awe, &c.
PLAINTIVE (Pl.) . .	Suffering, sympathy, desire, supplication, &c.
TREMOR (Tr.) . . .	Anxiety, alarm, eagerness, intense emotion.
CHUCKLE (Ch.) . .	Boasting, triumph, delight, sneering, merriment, &c.
STACCATO (St.) . .	Recrimination, reproach, &c.; also distributed emphasis.
SMOOTH (Sm.) . . .	Admiration, tenderness, love, enjoyment, &c.
RHYTHM (Rh.) . .	Regular movement, alternation, suggestion of music.
PROLONGATION (Pr.)—	Scorn, malignity; also admiration, longing, &c.
RESTRAINT (Res.) .	Effect of distance; also subdued passion, choking, &c.

STRAINING (Str.) .   Effect of difficult effort; also violent anger, &c.

PANTING (Pan.) .   Perturbation, flurry, exhaustion, mental suffering, &c.

INSPIRATION (In.) . .   Mental or bodily agony, apprehension of suffering, &c.

EXPIRATION (Ex.)   Sadness, sighing, sympathy in suffering, &c.

PERCUSSION (Per.) .   Intensity of feeling, whether of joy or sorrow.

HEM (Hm.). . .   Impatience, sneering, contempt, &c.

IMITATION (Im.) . .   Analogizing properties of sound or motion, by degrees of Force, Time, &c.. also ridicule.

SYMPATHY (Sym.)   Analogizing sentiments of gaiety, &c., by buoyant inflection; and of solemnity by subdued tones, &c.

APATHY (Ap.) . . .   Inaccordance of expression with sentiment; indifference, &c.

WARMTH (Wa.) .   Admiration, enjoyment, eagerness, anger, &c.

SARCASM (Sar.) . .   Insincerity, double meaning, &c.

BREAK (. . .) .   Reflective, monitory, hesitant, suggestive.

STOP (ᐱ) . . .   Meditation, listening, anxious watchfulness, terror, &c.

13. *Explanatory Notes on the Preceding Expressive Qualities.*

OROTUND :—A deep, full-throated, mellow voice.

FALSETTO :—A thin, shrill voice.

PLAINTIVE :—Inflexions limited to the semitone and minor third.

TREMOR :— ⎱ The quality of tremor is common equally to sentiments of sadness and joy. The inflective intervals are in the minor mode for the
CHUCKLING :— ⎰ former, and in the major mode for the latter.

STACCATO :—Pointed accentuation on every word or every syllable.

SMOOTH :—Soft, flowing, slightly accentuated sound.

RHYTHM :—Equal pulsation of accent and remission.

PROLONGATION :—Either of vowel sound or of consonant effect.

RESTRAINT :—The volume of voice checked at the throat.

STRAINING :—Restrained voice with strong consonant pressure.

PERCUSSION :—Either of voice from the throat or of consonant breath.

HEM :—A kind of snorting utterance.

14. RECAPITULATIVE TABLE OF THE NOTATIONS FOR INFLEXION, PITCH, FORCE, TIME, AND EXPRESSION.

Pitch.		Force.		Time.	
5	. High	V	. Vehemence	R	Rapid
4	. . Above	E	. Energy	Q . .	Quick
3 .	Middle	M	. Moderate	C	Common
2	. Below	W	. Weak	S	Slow
1	. Low	F	. Feeble	T	Tardy
⌈	. Higher	<	. Stronger	V	. . Quicker
⌊	Lower	> .	Weaker	∧	. Slower
⌐	Clause	. . . . .	Break	⌒	. . Pause

Expression.

Wh .	Whisper	St . Staccato	Ex .	Expiration
Ho	Hoarseness	Sm . Smooth	Per .	Percussion
Or .	Orotund	Rh . Rhythm	Hm .	Hem
Fa .	Falsetto	Pr . Prolongation	Im .	Imitation
Mo .	Monotone	Res . Restraint	Sym .	Sympathy
Pl .	Plaintive	Str . Straining	Ap .	Apathy
Tr .	Tremor	Pan . Panting	Wa .	Warmth
Ch .	Chuckle	In . Inspiration	Sar .	Sarcasm

	Inflexion			
	Simple.		Compound.	
	Rise	Fall	Rise	Fall
Middle Pitch	⟋ ⟍	⟍ ⟍ ⟍	⌄ ⌄	⌃
	⟋ ⟍ ⟍	⟍ ⟍	⌄ ⌄	⌃ ⌃

15. The following collection of short expressive passages, carefully marked for exercise, will enable the student to acquire an agreeable flexibility and effective modulation of the voice, and to cultivate the habit of SUITING THE SOUND TO THE SENSE in reading.

16. The marking is to be considered MERELY AS AN EXERCISE. The same passages might be read,—and

perhaps with equal effect—in a variety of ways. The notation simply illustrates one mode, which is at least effective and fully expressive of the sense and sentiment.

17. The preparatory pitch of syllables before the accent is not indicated in the printing. It is always, however, implied. Thus the introductory couplet in the first extract is to be read :—

> Not always   actions show the man;   we find
> Who does   a kindness   is not therefore   kind.

EXERCISES IN EXPRESSIVE READING.

ACTIONS.—*Pope.*

4
> Not always actions show the man; we find   3
>
> Who does a kindness is not therefore kind :
>
> 5 *Ap*
> Perhaps prosperity becalmed his breast;
>
> Perhaps the wind just shifted from the east:
>
> 4
> Not therefore humble he who seeks retreat;
>
> 3 *E*
> Pride guides his steps, and bids him shun the great:
>
> 4
> Who combats bravely is not therefore brave.
>
> 2 *S*
> He dreads a death-bed like the meanest slave :
>
> 4   5
> Who reasons wisely is not therefore wise.
>
> His pride, in reasoning, not in acting lies.

AMBITION.— *Young.*

3
> Ambition, in the truly noble mind,
>
> With sister . . . Virtue, is for ever joined.
>
> In meaner minds, Ambition works alone,
>
> 2   *St*
> But ⌊with sly art, | puts Virtue's aspect on.
>
> 3
> No mask, in basest mind, Ambition wears,
>
> But, [in full light, | pricks up her ass's ears.

8

AMBITION DISSATISFIED.— *Young.*

3
Consult the ambitious,—'tis ambition's cure :
5 F
"And is this all?" cried Cæsar, ⌈in his height,
2 E
Disgusted.

AMBITION REPENTED.—*Brooke.*

4
Oh! that some villager, ⌊whose early toil
Lifts the penurious morsel to his mouth |
              E
Had claimed my birth! ambition had not then
3
Thus stept 'twixt me and heaven.

AMBITIOUS RIVALRY.—*Cowper.*

3
        On the summit | see
4
The seals of office glitter in his eyes ;
3
He climbs, he pants, he grasps them.   At his heels,
Close at his heels, a demagogue ascends,
And | with a dext'rous jerk | soon twists him down,
4 Ch   Ex
And wins them, . . . but to lose them in his turn.

ANCESTRY.—*Alex. Bell.*

3
If we must look to ancestry for fame,
Let us at least deal justly with mankind.
4
Why should we rake the ashes of the dead
For honours only? why conceal their crimes?
3
We snatch our fathers' glories from the dust,
                4 E
And wear them ⌊as our own : | Why should we seek
To cover with oblivion | their shames?
2 S   St
The frailties of our sires ⌈set full in view |
1 F
Might teach their children modesty.

ANGER.—*Baillie.*

Out upon thee, fool! Go, speak thy . . . comforts
To spirits tame and abject as thyself :
They make me . . . mad.

AVARICE.—*Pope.*

Wealth in the gross is death, but life diffused;
⌊As poison heals, in just proportion used :
In heaps, ⌊like ambergris, | a stink it lies,
But, well dispersed, is incense to the skies.

BEAUTY.—*Baillie.*

To make the cunning artless, tame the rude,
Subdue the haughty, shake the undaunted soul;
Yea, put a bridle in the lion's mouth,
⌈And lead him forth as a domestic cur,—
These are the triumphs of all powerful beauty.

BLINDNESS.—*Milton.*

Oh! dark, dark, dark, ⌈amid the blaze of noon, |
Irrevocably dark—total eclipse—
Without all hope of day! |
Oh, first created beam, and thou, great Word.
" Let there be light," ⌈and light was | over all : |
Why am I | thus bereav'd thy prime decree ?

CHARITY.—*Rowe.*

Think not, the good,
The gentle deeds of mercy thou hast done,
Shall die forgotten all : the poor, the prisoner,
The fatherless, the friendless, and the widow,

⌊Who daily own the bounty of thy hand, |
Shall cry to Heaven, and pull a blessing on thee.

CHILDHOOD.

3

The world of a child's imagination is the creation of a far holier spell | than hath been ever wrought ⌊by the pride of learning, or the inspiration of poetic fancy. Innocence that thinketh no evil; ignorance that apprehendeth none; hope that hath experienced no blight: love that suspecteth no guile; these are its ministering angels! these wield a wand of power, making this earth a paradise! ⌒Time, ⌊hard, rigid teacher! | Reality, ⌊rough, stern reality! | World, ⌊cold, heartless world! that ever your sad experience, your sombre truths, your killing cold, your withering success, could scare those gentle spirits from their holy temple! And wherewith do ye replace them? With caution, ⌊that repulses confidence, | with doubt, ⌊that repelleth love; | with reason that dispelleth delusion; with fear, ⌈that poisoneth enjoyment; in a word, with knowledge,—that fatal fruit, the tasting whereof, ⌊at the first onset, | cost us paradise.

COMMENTATORS.— *Young.*

Commentators each dark passage shun,
And hold their . . . farthing candle to the sun.

CONTEMPT.—*Byron.*

4

Patience! Hence,—that word was made
For brutes of burthen, not for birds of prey;—
Preach it to mortals of a dust like thine,
I . . . am not of thine order.

CORRUPTION.—*Cowper.*

Examine well

His . . . milk-white hand ⌒ the palm is hardly clean,

But | here and there, an ugly smutch appears.
1 *Per*   4 *E*   2 *St*
Foh! 'twas a bribe that left it.   He has touched

Corruption.

COURAGE.—*Brown.*

The intent ⌊and not the deed |

Is in our power; and therefore, who dares greatly,

Does greatly.

CONFLICTING PASSIONS.—*Shakespeare.*

I pr'ythee, daughter, do not make me mad!

I will not trouble thee! my child, farewell!

We'll no more meet, no more see one another!
2 *Per*

But yet thou art my flesh, my blood, my daughter,
4 *E*

Or, rather, a disease that's in my flesh—

Which I must needs call mine! thou art ⌒ a boil—

A plague-sore—an embossed carbuncle, ·

In my corrupted blood . . . But ⌒ I'll not ⌒ chide thee :

Let shame come when it will, I do not call it,
Or

I do not bid the thunder-bearer strike,
Tr

Nor tell tales of thee to high-judging Jove : . . .
4 *F*

Mend, when thou canst; be better—at thy leisure!

DEFIANCE.— *Young.*

Torture thou mayst, but . . . thou shalt ne'er despise me.

The blood will follow where the knife is driven,

The flesh will quiver where the pincers tear;

And sighs and cries [by nature | grow on pain:

But these are foreign to the soul : not mine

The groans that issue, or the tears that fall ;

They disobey me ! ⌒ ⌈On the rack | I . . . scorn thee.

DESERT.—*Shakespeare.*

Use every man according to his desert, and who shall escape
whipping? Use them after your own honour and dignity : the
less they deserve, the more merit is in your bounty.

DESPAIR.—*Maturin.*

The fountain of my heart dried up within me,—

With nought that lov'd me, and with nought to love,

I stood upon the desert earth . . . alone ;

And ⌊in that deep and utter agony, |

⌈Though then, ⌊than ever | most unfit to die, |

I fell upon my knees, and prayed for death.

DISCRIMINATION.—*Shakespeare.*

Ye are men?

Ay, in the catalogue ye go for men ;

As hounds and greyhounds, mongrels, spaniels, curs,

Shoughs, water-rugs, and demi-wolves, are cleped

All by the name of dogs : | the valued file

Distinguishes . . . the swift, the slow, the subtle,

The house-keeper, the hunter, every one

According to the gift which bounteous Nature

Hath in him closed ; whereby he doth receive

Particular addition, from the bill

That writes them all alike.

DISTINCTIONS.

Human society requires distinctions of property, diversity of
conditions, subordinations of rank, and a multiplicity of occupations, [in order to advance the general good.

DISTRACTION.—*Shakespeare.*

4 Pl
    You see me here, ye gods, a poor old man,
             Per
    As full of grief as age, wretched in both!
5 Tr   *Pr*
    You think I'll weep; no, I'll not weep:—
2 E   *Per*   4
    I have full cause of weeping; but this heart
        V
    Shall ⌒ burst into a hundred thousand flaws,
          Fa   2 St
    Or ere I'll weep—O Gods, I shall go mad!

DOMINION.—*Milton.*

    Here we may reign secure; and, [in my choice, |
    To reign is worth ambition [though in hell:
4   *Hm*
    Better to reign in hell than . . . serve in heaven.

EMOTIONS.

The emotions pervade every operation of the mind, as the
life-blood circulates through the body; within us and without,
in the corporeal world and in the spiritual, in the past, the present,
and the future, there is no object of thought which they do not
touch; there are few, very few, which they do not colour and
transmute.

ENERGETIC EFFORT.—*Shakespeare.*

3   *Str*
    I saw him . . . beat the surges under him,
    And ride upon their backs; he trod the water,
    [Whose enmity he flung aside, | and breasted

The surge most swollen that met him: his bold head
'Bove the contentious waves he kept, and oared
Himself with his good arms, in lusty strokes,
To the shore, [that [o'er his wave-borne basis] bowed
As stooping to relieve him.

ENVY.—*Byron.*

He who ascends to mountain-tops shall find
The loftiest peaks most wrapt in clouds and snow:
He who surpasses or subdues mankind,
[Must look down on the hate of those below.
Though [high above, | the sun of glory glow,
And [far beneath | the earth and ocean spread,
Round him are icy rocks, | and loudly blow
Contending tempests | on his naked head;
And thus ... reward ... the toils which to those summits led.

EVIL CONSCIENCE.—*Dryden.*

Here, here it lies: a lump ... of lead, | by day: |
And | in my short, distracted nightly slumbers |
The hag ... that rides my dreams.

EXASPERATION.—*Baillie.*

Oh! the side glance of that detested eye!
That conscious smile! that full insulting lip!
It touches every nerve; it makes me ... mad!

EXISTENCE.—*Sewell.*

To be, is better far than not to be,
[Else nature cheated us in our formation.
And when we are, the sweet delusion wears

Such various charms and prospects of delight,

That what we could not will, we make our choice.

⌊Desirous to prolong the life she gave.

EX-OFFICIO ENDOWMENTS.— *Young.*

All soldiers, valour, ⌈all divines have grace,

                     St
⌊As maids of honour, beauty, ⌈by their place.

EXPERIENCE.— *Young.*

3
  'Tis greatly wise to talk with our past hours;
           1 S
And ask them . . . what report they brought to heaven;
2 *Pl*   *Tr*
And how they might have borne . . . more welcome news.
3 *M*
  Their answers form what men Experience call;
2
  If Wisdom's friend, her best, if not, worst foe.

FAITH.

Though faith be above reason, yet is there a reason to be
given of our faith.   He is a fool who believes he neither knows
what nor why.

FAME.— *Young.*

With fame ⌊in just proportion | envy grows;

The man that makes a character makes foes.

FIDELITY.—*Maturin.*

4
  Yea, time hath power upon my hopeless love;
3
  And what a power, I'll tell thee:
2 *S*   *Rh*
  A power to change the pulses of the heart
                Per
  To one ⌒ dull ⌒ throb, of ceaseless agony—
3   *Pr*
  To hush the sigh on the resigned lip

  And lock it in the heart,—freeze the hot tear,
Pl   *Per*
  And bid it on the eyelid hang . . . forever.
4 *M*
  Such power hath time o'er me.

FORTITUDE.—*Byron.*

The torture! you have put me there, already,
Daily [since I was Doge! | but [if you will
Add the corporeal rack | you may : these limbs
Will yield [with age | to crushing iron, but
There's that within my heart shall strain your engines.

FORTUNE.—*Tennyson.*

Turn, Fortune, turn thy wheel and lower the proud;
Turn thy wild wheel ⌈thro' sunshine, storm, and cloud;
Thy wheel and thee | we | neither love nor hate.
Turn, Fortune, turn thy wheel with smile or frown;
With that wild wheel we go not up or down;
Our hoard is little, but our hearts are great.

GREATNESS.—*Young.*

High stations, tumult, [but not bliss | create :
None think the great unhappy but the great.

HEARTS.—*Byron.*

Heads bow, knees bend, eyes watch, [around a throne,—
And hands obey | our hearts . . . are still our own.

HUMAN LIFE.—*Cowper.*

In such a world, [so thorny, and where none
Finds happiness unblighted, ⌈or [if found,
⌈Without some thistly sorrow at its side, ‖
It seems the part of wisdom, and no sin
Against the law of love, to measure lots
With less distinguished than ourselves, that thus
We may, with patience, bear our moderate ills,
And sympathize with others, suffering more.

HUMAN WRETCHEDNESS.—*Southey.*

3 As her bier
4
Went to the grave, a lark sprang up aloft,
Pr   *3*
And soar'd amid the sunshine, caroling
                              Ex
So full of joy, that ⌊to the mourner's ear
More mournfully than dirge or passing bell
                    2 S
His joyful carol came ⌒ and made us feel
That ⌊of the multitude of beings, | none . . .
Ex   *Per*
But man . . . was wretched!

IF.—*Shakespeare.*

4
I knew when seven justices could not take up a quarrel; but
                              5
when the parties were met themselves, one of them thought but
        3   *2 Pr*
of an If, as "If you said so, then I said so." "Oh, ⌒ did you
4 Ch
so?"—and they shook hands and were sworn brothers.

IMITATION.—*Blair.*

3
Nothing is more natural than to imitate, ⌊by the sound of the
voice, | the quality of the sound ⌊or noise | which any external
        4   *3*
object makes, and to form its name accordingly. A certain bird
is termed the CUCKOO, from the sound which it emits. When
                    Im   *Im*
one sort of wind is said to . . . WHISTLE, and another to . . . ROAR;
                    Pr   *Pr*
when a serpent is said to HISS, a fly to BUZZ, and falling timber
Per   *Sm*   *E*
to . . CRASH; when a stream is said to FLOW, and hail to RAT-
4
TLE; the analogy between the word and the thing signified is.
plainly discernible.

INGRATITUDE.—*Shakespeare.*
S Pr
Blow, blow, thou wintry wind,
Pl
Thou art not so unkind
As man's ingratitude;
Thy tooth is not so keen,

⌊Because thou art not seen |

      Although thy breath be rude.

Tr. Pr.

Freeze, freeze, thou bitter sky,

Thou dost not bite so nigh

    As benefits forgot:

Though thou the waters warp

Thy sting is not so sharp

    As—Friend remembered not.

INSECT LIFE.—*American Paper.*

Insects generally must lead a truly jovial life. Think what it must be ⌊to lodge in a lily. Imagine—a palace of ivory and pearl with pillars of silver and capitals of gold, and exhaling such a perfume as never arose from human censer. Fancy again, the fun | of tucking one's-self up for the night in the folds of a rose, rocked to sleep by the gentle sighs of summer air, nothing to do when you wake but to wash yourself in a dew drop, and fall to eat your bedclothes.

INTERROGATION.

"I have something more to ask you," said a young eagle | to a learned, melancholy owl: "Men say | there is a bird, ⌊by name Merops, | who, when he rises in the air, flies with his tail upwards and his head towards the ground. Is that true?"

"Certainly not," answered the owl, "it is only a foolish tradition of man; he is himself a Merops: for he would fly to heaven, without | for a moment | losing sight of the earth."

KINGLY POWER.—*Shakespeare.*

Oh, not a minute, king, thy power can give :
Shorten my days thou can'st ⌊with sullen sorrow ⌋
And pluck nights from me, but not lend a morrow :
Thou can'st help Time to furrow me ⌊with age, ⌋
But stop no wrinkle in his pilgrimage ;
Thy word is current with him, for my death ;
But, ⌈dead, ⌋ thy kingdom cannot buy my breath.

LAZINESS.—*Hall.*

Laziness grows on people ; it begins in cobwebs, and ends in iron chains.   The more business a man has, the more he is able to accomplish ; for he learns to economize his time.

LIFE.—*Madden.*

I have tried this world ⌈in all its changes,
States, and conditions : ⌋ have been great, and happy,
Wretched and low, and passed through all its stages,
And, oh ! believe me, ⌊who have known it best, ⌋
It is not worth the bustle that it costs ;
'Tis but a medley—all—of idle hopes
And abject childish fears.

LIGHTS AND SHADES.

The gloomiest day hath gleams of light ;
  The darkest wave hath white foam near it ;
  And—twinkles through the cloudiest night
    Some solitary star to cheer it.
The gloomiest soul is not all gloom ;
    The saddest heart is not all sadness ;
And sweetly o'er the darkest doom
    There shines some lingering beam of gladness.

LOVERS' STUDIES.

To a lover, the figures, the motions, the words of the beloved
object, are not, ⌊like other images, | written on water, but, ⌊as
Plutarch said | " enameled in fire " and made the study of mid-
night.

LOVERS.—*Sir R. Aytoun.*

Some men seem so distracted of their wits,
    That I would think it but a venial sin,
To take | one of these innocents, that sit
                         Ch
    In Bedlam, | out, and put some lover in.

LUDICROUS DISTRESS.—*Henry Mackenzie.*

I had—a piece—of rich—sweet pudding—on my fork, when Miss
                                Tr
Louisa Friendly begged to ⌢ trouble me for part of a pigeon
        Q
that stood near me.   In my haste ⌊scarce knowing what I did, |
R   *In*
I . . . whipped the pudding into my mouth, ⌢ hot, as a burning
4
coal!   It was impossible to conceal my agony; my eyes were
                          3 S   *Pan*
starting from their sockets!   At last, ⌊in spite | of shame and
resolution, | I was obliged to ⌢ drop ⌢ the cause of my torment
on my plate.

MAN.—*Shakespeare.*

What a piece of work is man! how noble in reason! how
infinite in faculties! in form and moving how express and admirable! in action how like an angel! in apprehension how like
a god!

MARTYRS.—*Hemans.*

3
    Oh! be the memory cherished
Of those ⌊the thousands | that around Truth's throne
                                    E St
Have poured their lives out, ⌈smiling, ⌢ ⌊in that doom
Finding a triumph, if denied a tomb!—

Ay, with their ashes hath the wind been sown,
And [with the wind | their spirit shall be spread,
Filling man's heart with records of the dead.

METHOD.

The man who does not know how to methodize his thoughts
has always [to borrow a phrase from the dispensary, | a barren
superfluity of words.

MURDER.—Dr. Porteous.

One murder made a villain :
Millions a hero.　Princes were privileged
To kill, and numbers sanctified the crime.

MURDER.—Baillie.

Twice it call'd,—so loudly call'd,
With horrid strength, [beyond the pitch of nature ; |
And murder ! murder ! was the dreadful cry. |
A third time it returned, [with feeble strength,
But ... o' the sudden ... ceased, as though the words
Were ... smother'd ... rudely.... in the grappled throat
And all was still again, save the wild blast
Which at distance growl'd—
Oh ! it will never from my mind depart !
That dreadful cry ... all i' the instant stilled.

PARISH COMMON.—Eliza Cook.

It glads the eye - - - it warms the soul
To gaze upon the rugged knoll,
Where tangled brushwood twines across
The struggling brake and sedgy moss.

4
Oh! who would have the grain spring up
Where now we find the daisy's cup?—
Where clumps of dark red heather gleam
With beauty in the summer beam,—
Sym
And yellow furze-bloom ... laughs to scorn
Your ripen'd hopes and bursting corn? ...
2   *E*
God speed the plough! But let us trace
Something of nature's infant face;
3   *St*
Let us behold some spot ⌊where man
Has not yet set his "bar and ban," |
4
Leave us some green wastes, ⌊fresh and wild, |
Tr
For poor man's beast, and poor man's child.

PARTING.

3
The true sadness of parting is not in the pain of separating;
it is the when and the how you are to meet again | with the face
about to vanish from your view. From the passionate farewell,
4
to the friendly good-bye, a chord, stronger or weaker, is snapped
3
asunder in every parting. Meet again you may; but will it be
in the same circumstances? with the same sympathies? with the
2 S
same sentiments? Will the souls now hurrying on in diverse
paths unite once more, as if the interval had been a dream?
Rarely, oh, rarely.

PRAYER.—*N. P. Willis.*
3 S
Oh! when the heart is full—when bitter thoughts
Come crowding thickly up for utterance,—
Per
And the poor common words of courtesy
I   3 E
Are such a very mockery—how much
The bursting heart may pour itself in prayer.

PROSPERITY.

There is ever a certain languor attending the fulness of pros-
perity. When the heart has no more to wish, it . . . yawns over
its possessions, and the energy of the soul goes out, ⌊like a flame
that has no more to devour.

REASONING.—*Dr. Young.*

Bid physicians talk our veins to temper,
And | with an argument | new-set a pulse :—
Then think, ⌊my lord, | of reasoning into love.

REFLECTION.

He that would pass the latter part of his life with honour and
decency, must, when he is young, consider that he shall one day
be old, and remember when he is old, that he has once been
young.

RESULTS.

Scorn not the slightest word or deed,
    Nor deem it void of power;
There's fruit in each wind-wafted seed,
    ⌊Waiting its natal hour : |
No act falls fruitless : none can tell
    How vast its power may be ;
Nor what results infolded, dwell
    Within it | silently.

RIDICULOUS DEFERENCE.—*Cowper.*

He would not, ⌊with a peremptory tone, |
Assert the nose upon his face, his own ;
With . . . hesitation ⌢ admirably . . . slow,
He . . . humbly . . . hopes, ⌢ presumes . . . it . . . may be so.

9

SIGNS OF LOVE.—*Dryden.*

I find she loves him much, ⸢because she hides it. |

Love teaches cunning even to innocence;

And, where he gets possession, his first work

Is to dig deep within the heart, and there

Lie hid | like a miser in the dark,

To feast alone.

SLAVERY.—*Brougham.*

Tell me not of rights—talk not of the property of the planter
in his slaves:—I deny the right, I acknowledge not the property.
The principles, the feelings of our common nature rise in rebellion against it.

SPASMODIC EMOTION.—*Baillie.*

I felt ⌒ a sudden tightness, ⌒ grasp my throat ...

As it would strangle me, ... such as I felt,

⌊I knew it well | some twenty years ago,

When ... my good father ... shed his blessing on me: ...

I hate to weep, and so I came away.

STAIRS TO MARRIAGE.—*Shakespeare.*

Your brother and my sister no sooner met but they ... looked:
no sooner looked but they loved; no sooner loved but they ...
sighed; no sooner sighed but they asked one another the reason;
no sooner knew the reason, but they ... sought the remedy; and
in these degrees they have made a pair of stairs to marriage.

SYMPATHY.—*S. T. Coleridge.*

He that works me good | with unmoved face,

Does it but half: he chills me while he aids,—

My benefactor, ⌊not my brother man.

SYMPATHY.—*Shakespeare.*

3   2
  Thy heart is big: get thee apart and weep.
3 *Sym*
    Passion, ⌊I see | is catching; for mine eyes,

    ⌊Seeing those beads of sorrow stand in thine |
Tr
    Begin . . . to . . . water.

TEARS.—*Byron.*

                 4
            Hide thy tears—
3   4
I do not bid thee | not to shed them; 'twere

Easier to stop Euphrates at its source,
3
Than one tear | of a true and tender heart;—
1   *Tr*
But . . . let me not behold them, ⌢ they . . . unman me.

TEARS.—*W. E. Aytoun.*

3
  Woman's weakness shall not shame me—
2
    Why should I have tears to shed?
4   *Per*
    Could I rain them down like water, |

      O, my hero, on thy head—
3
    Could the cry of lamentation

      Wake thee from thy silent sleep,—
5
    Could it set thy heart a-throbbing ⌢
2   *Pr*
    It were mine to wail and weep.

TIME.—*Carlos Wilcox.*

3
  Time well employed is Satan's deadliest foe:
It leaves no opening for the lurking fiend:
3
  Life it imparts to watchfulness and prayer,—
4
  Statues, without it, | in the form of guards.

TRUE COURAGE.—*Baillie.*

3
The brave man | is not he who feels no fear.

[For that were stupid and irrational; |
4 *St*
But he, whose noble soul its fear subdues,

And bravely dares the danger nature shrinks from,.
2 *Hm*
As for your youth, whom blood and blows delight,
4 *E*
Away with them! there is not in their crew

One valiant spirit.

TEACHERS.

4
Nothing stifles knowledge more than covering every thing
2
with a doctor's robe; and the men who would be for ever
teaching, are great hindrances to learning.

THE FALLING LEAF.—*Hemans.*

As the light leaf, [whose fall, to ruin bears

Some trembling insect's little world of cares, |

Descends in silence, [while around waves on
E
The mighty forest . . . reckless what is gone!—
2 *St*   3
| Such is man's doom | and, [ere an hour be flown, |
1   3
Reflect, thou trifler such may be thine own!

WISDOM OF THE DEITY.—*Dr. Dick.*

The astonishing multiplicity of created beings, the wonderful
laws of nature, the beautiful arrangement of the heavenly
bodies, the elegance of the vegetable world, the operations of
4
animal life, and the amazing harmony of the whole creation,.
loudly proclaim | the wisdom | of the Deity.

WIT.—*Cowper.*

Is sparkling wit the world's exclusive right—
⌊The fix'd fee-simple of the vain and light?
Can hopes of heaven, ⌊bright prospects of an hour,
⌈That come to waft us out of sorrow's power, |
Obscure, or quench . . . a faculty, that finds
Its happiest soil in the serenest minds?
Religion curbs indeed its wanton way,
And brings the trifles under rigorous sway;
But gives it usefulness ⌈unknown before, |
And ⌊purifying | makes it shine the more.
A Christian's wit is inoffensive light,
A beam that aids, but never grieves the sight;
Vigorous | in age, as in the flush of youth,
'Tis always, | active on the side of truth;
Temperance and peace insure its healthful state,
And make it brightest at its latest date.

WOMAN.—*Barrett.*

Ask the poor pilgrim, ⌊on this convex cast,—
⌊His grizzled locks distorted in the blast, | —
Ask him . . . what accent soothes, what hand bestows
The cordial beverage, garment and repose?
O, he will dart a spark of ancient flame,
And clasp his tremulous hands, . . . and . . . woman name!
Peruse the sacred volume: Him who died
Her kiss betrayed not, nor her tongue denied.
While even the apostle left Him to His doom,
She lingered round His cross, and watched His tomb.

PRINCIPLES OF ELOCUTION.

PART FOURTH.

EMPHASIS.

I. GENERAL PRINCIPLES.

1. As every word of more than one syllable has an accented syllable, and every grammatical group of words has an accented word, so every sentence or association of grammatical groups has an accented or emphatic *idea*. Emphasis is to verbal and clausular accents what the accents themselves are to unaccented syllables.

2. Accent gives prominence to the leading syllables in words, or words in clauses; emphasis gives prominence to the leading Idea, although it may be expressed by the most subordinate word in the sentence.

3. The leading idea in a sentence is almost invariably the *new* idea, and on the word expressive of this, whatever its grammatical value, the accent or emphasis falls.

4. The primary words in sentences are the *noun* (the subject) and the *verb* (the predicate); and were clauses containing nouns and verbs with their adjuncts, separated from their sentential context, and pronounced as in a vocabulary, the clausular accents would fall on these parts of speech. Thus,

A funeral note,	Eagerly wished.
A farewell shot,	Distinctly remembered.
The struggling moonbeam,	Greatly marvelled.
No useless coffin,	No longer hesitating.

If the noun or verb *preceded* the qualifying word, the accent would probably be required by the latter, as it would then be directly suggestive of antithesis. Thus,

| The moonbeam struggling, | Wished eagerly. |
| No coffin useless, | Remembered distinctly. |

5. Nouns and verbs are the essential elements of sentences. A sentence may be complete with these alone, while no other parts of speech could make a sentence.

6. Next in grammatical value to nouns and verbs, are those words which *qualify* nouns and verbs, called adjectives and adverbs ; and next to these latter are those words which qualify adjectives and adverbs, called also adverbs, although they are adjuncts of an inferior class to ad*verbs* proper.

7. Of the other parts of speech the article is of the same nature as the Adjective ; the Pronoun of the same nature as the Noun ; the Preposition of the same nature as the Adverb ; and the Interjection and Conjunction of the same nature as the Verb.

8. "We never speak but we say something" is an adage that is not merely sarcastic in its application. Every sentence says (or asserts) something, or asks something, or enjoins something ; but in connection with that something, much more is frequently added of an explanatory or complemental nature. In conversation we *feel* what we wish to say, and we instinctively give prominence to the leading thought and subordinate the accessory parts of our sentences. On the printed page we have the whole of a sentence before the eye at once, principal and accessory parts alike ; and in accordance with our view of the sense, we can, by varying the emphatic relation of the accents, make the sentence express any one of half a dozen different thoughts as the principal idea. As in extemporary delivery our perfect knowledge of our own intention dictates the emphasis that best expresses our meaning ; so, in reading, a clear perception of the author's *aim*, and recollection of what *has been said*, suggests the emphasis that is expressive of the intended meaning.

9. In extemporary delivery we do not pronounce whole sentences at a time, but clauses only ; and each clause, as it is pronounced, receives such a modification of stress, inflexion, and modulation, as marks its relation to the dominant idea. We must apply the same principle to

reading. Each clause contains a distinct idea, which might take the form of a separate grammatical sentence, and which is not so expressed only because its idea is subordinate to the principal thought with which it is associated in the grammatical period. Clauses, then, should be considered as distinct assertions, appeals or injunctions ; and each SHOULD BE PRONOUNCED WITH TONES ACCORDANT WITH ITS OWN NATURE, merely modified as to pitch, force, time, and stress, in reference to the leading idea in the sentence.

10. Antithesis or contrast is involved in emphasis. We have seen that words, having a common accented syllable, as expulsive and *r*epulsive, have the accent shifted to the syllable of difference when the words are used in contrast. So in sentences : the most important grammatical words will be pronounced without emphasis if the same words, or any words involving the same idea, have occurred in the context ; and the leading emphasis will be given, perhaps, to some words of the most subordinate grammatical class which, but for the previous implication of the more important words, would have been pronounced entirely without accent.

11. The strongest emphasis is given to words that are suggestive of unexpressed antithesis. When antithesis is fully expressed, the first of the contrasted words will be emphatic only when it is new or antithetically suggestive in relation to the *preceding* context ; it is not emphatic merely because an antithetic word follows. The second of the contrasted words *must* be emphatic, because opposed to the preceding term.

12. To make the mode of applying the principle of Emphasis perfectly clear, the best way will be to analyse a familiar piece of composition.

II. EXAMPLE OF EMPHATIC ANALYSIS.

LINES ON THE BURIAL OF SIR JOHN MOORE.— *Wolfe.*

13. At the commencement of a Composition everything is, of course, new ; and the first subject and predicate will be emphatic unless either is in the nature of things implied in the other.

> " Not a *drum* | was heard, | not a funeral *note* |
> As | his corpse | to the *rampart* | we hurried."

The subject " drum" will be accented and the predicate " was heard" unaccented, because the mention of a " drum " involves, in the nature of things, recognition by the sense of hearing.   To accentuate " heard " would involve one of the false antitheses,

> " Not a drum was heard, " (because we were deaf) ;
>
> or,
>
> " Not a drum was heard, (but only seen or felt.)

The second subject " note " will be *emphatic* because it is contrasted with " drum," and suggests the antithesis " not a note " (of any instrument.)   " Funeral " is unaccented because pre-understood from the Title of the Poem.   In the next line " as " will be separately accented, because it has no reference to the words immediately following, but to the verb " we hurried. "   " His corpse" will be unaccented, because a funeral implies a corpse, and there is no mention in the context of any other than " his. "   The principal accent of the line may be given to " rampart" or " hurried ; " the former would perhaps be the better word, as it involves the antithesis,—

> " To the rampart, " (and not to a cemetery.)

14. In the next two lines,

> " Not a soldier | discharged his farewell *shot* |
> O'er the grave | where | our hero | we buried,"

" Soldier " is implied in connection with " drum " and " rampart, " and the emphasis will fall on " shot, " " discharged " being involved in the idea of " shot, " and " farewell" being involved in the occasion to which " shot" refers—a funeral.   In the next line no word is emphatic, as a " grave " is of course implied.   " O'er " is implied in the nature of things, as the shot could not be discharged *under* the grave ; " our hero " is the same as " his corpse ;" and " we buried" is involved in the mention of " corpse" and " grave."

15. In the next lines,

> " We buried him | darkly | at dead of *night*, |
> The sods | with our *bayonets* | turning, "

the first clause will be unemphatic, as the fact has been already stated. To emphasize " buried " would suggest the false antithesis

" We buried him " (instead of leaving him on the battle-field.)

" Darkly " and " at dead of night " convey the same idea ; the latter being the stronger expression will receive the principal accent—on " night ; "—and " darkly " will be pronounced parenthetically. " Turning the sods " is. of course, implied in the act of burying ; the word " bayonets, " therefore, takes the principal accent of the line, because involving the antithesis

" With our bayonets, " (and not with spades.)

16.   " By the struggling *moon*beam's misty light.
And the *lantern* | dimly burning. "

In the first clause, " moonbeam's " will be accented, and " misty light" unaccented, because implied in " the *struggling* moonbeam's. " " Lantern " in the second line will take the superior accent of the sentence because, of the two sources of light spoken of, it is the more immediately serviceable on the occasion ; and " dimly burning " will be unaccented, unless the forced antithesis be suggested,—

" Dimly burning,"(as with shrouded light, to escape observation.)

17.   " No useless *coffin* | enclosed his breast;
Not in sheet | nor in *shroud* | we wound him. "

Emphasis on " coffin, " because the word not only conveys a new idea, but is suggestive of contrast :—

"No coffin, " (as at ordinary interments.)

No accent on " useless, " because it would suggest the false antithesis.

" No *useless* coffin, " (but only one of the least dispensable kind.)

" Enclosed his breast " without emphasis, because implied in the mention of "coffin. " Emphasis on "breast " would convey the false antithesis,

(Not) " his breast, " (but merely some other part of his body.)

" Sheet" and "shroud" in the second line express the same idea ; the latter being the stronger term, takes

the leading accent. " We wound him " unaccented, because implied in the idea of " shroud. " The tones in
these lines should be *rising*, to carry on the attention to
the leading fact of the sentence predicated in the next
lines.

18.   " But | he lay | like a warrior taking his *rest*,
       With his martial *cloak* | around him."

" But " separately accented, because it does not refer to
" he lay, " which is of course implied in the idea of the
dead warrior. To connect " but " with " he lay" would
indicate the opposition to be,

   " But he lay, " (instead of being in some other attitude.)

The reference is rather

   (In " no coffin " or " shroud. ") " but " in "his martial cloak."

In the simile that follows, no accent on " warrior, " because he *was* a warrior, and not merely was " like " one.
The principal emphasis of the whole stanza lies on "rest,"
which suggests the antithesis,

   (As if) " taking his rest" (and not with the aspect of death.)

In the next line, the principal accent on " cloak; "
" martial " being implied, unless intended contrast could
be supposed between his " martial " and some other
cloak; and " around him " being included in the idea of
a warrior taking rest in his cloak.

19.   " *Few* | and *short* | were the *prayers* | we said,
       And we spoke not | a word of *sorrow*. "

The principal accent in the first line will be on the *subject* " prayers," but the two *predicates* " were few, and
short, " are also accented, because all the ideas are new ;
the predicates are subordinate to the subject only because
the latter is placed last. Had the arrangement been reversed, the principal accent would have fallen on the second predicate " short." Thus :—

   " The prayers we said were few and *short*. "

No accent on " we said, " because implied in the nature
of " prayers, " unless intended contrast could be supposed
between " said " and *chanted*, or otherwise uttered. In

the next line " spoke " being involved in " said, " will be unaccented, unless the antithesis be suggested,

" We spoke not " (though we had the feeling) " of sorrow ; "

and " word " being involved in " spoke, " will be unaccented, unless the antithesis be suggested,

(So far from making an oration) " we spoke not (even) a word."

" Not" must be united accentually with the word " spoke, " as the negation refers to the verb, and not to the *object* " a word. " To say

" We spoke | not a word,"

would be nonsense. " Sorrow, " will be accented, unless either of the preceding words is emphasized ; in the latter case " sorrow," would be unemphatic, because " spoke not (even) a *word* " would imply " of sorrow " as the feeling natural to the occasion.

20.   "But | we | steadfastly | *gazed* | on the face of the dead,
And | we *bitterly* thought | of the *morrow.* "

The first four words will be separately pronounced, with the emphatic force on " gazed, " which should have a falling turn because it completes the sense. "But " is separated from " we " because it does not connect that with any other pronoun, but joins " spoke" with " gazed." The pronoun, adverb, and verb, might be united in one accentual group, but such an utterance of this clause would be too light and flippant for the solemnity of the sentiment. " On the face " without emphasis, as no contrast can be intended between face and any other part of the body ; " of the dead " unemphatic, because implied. In the next line " and " should have a separate accent ; " we bitterly thought" may be united, with the accent on the adverb ; " thought" being implied in the " steadfast gazing " of thinking beings. In the last clause " morrow " will be accented, because it introduces a new idea.

21.   "We thought | as we hollowed his narrow bed,
And smoothed down his lonely pillow, |
That the foe | and the stranger | would *tread* o'er his head,
And *we* | far *away* | on the billow, "

No emphasis in the first two lines, "we thought" having been already stated, and "as we hollowed and smoothed," &c., being implied in the making of a grave. The grammatical sentence is, "we thought that the foe," &c. "Foe" and "stranger" are accented, but not emphatic, as there can be no antithesis. Treading on the grave, whether by friend or foe, would be equally repugnant to the speaker's feelings. The emphasis of the sentence therefore lies on "tread." The next clause must be unemphatic, as there can be no antithesis intended to "o'er" or "his" or between "head" and any other part of the body. "And we" will have the pronoun accented, because opposed to "foe," &c.; "far away" will have the adverb accented because suggesting

"Far away" (and not here to prevent the indignity.)

The meaning is not "away on the billow" but "away" no matter where; and "on the billow" is merely expletive.

22. "But *half* | of our heavy task | was done |
When the clock | struck the hour | for *retiring*."

Accent on "half" to suggest

"But half" (and not the whole.)

"Heavy" and "done" may be accented but not emphatic. In the second line the emphatic force must fall on the expressive complement of the predicate, "for retiring," because suggesting the antithesis,

"For retiring" (and not indulging longer in our reverie.)

23. "And we heard | the distant | and random *gun*—
That the *foe* | was sullenly firing."

The first clauses unemphatic, because implied in "the clock struck," which of course was also "heard." The emphasis of this line lies on "gun," which is antithetic to "clock." In the last line "foe" is emphatic, because antithetic to *friend*, understood as giving the signal for "retiring."

24. "*Slowly* | and *sadly* | we laid him down
From the field of his fame | fresh | and *gory*."

In this sentence the subject "we," the predicate "laid him down," and the expletive clause "from the field of his fame," are all implied in the occasion, and the accents fall on "slowly" and "sadly," and on "fresh and gory," which latter are complements of the object "him." The principal accent is on "gory" as the stronger of the two adjectives. The predicate includes all the words "laid him down from the field of his fame," which must be connectively read. A falling termination is necessary to disconnect the last clause from "fresh and gory," which would otherwise seem to refer to "field" or "fame."

25. "We carved not | a *line,* | and we raised not | a *stone,*
     But | we left him | *alone* | with his *glory.*"

The accents in the first line will fall on "line" and "stone." The negatives must not be united with the objects but with the verbs. To read,

"We carved | not a line"

would be nonsense. In the second line "but" should be separately pronounced, because it does not refer to "we left him" which is implied as a matter of course, for even if they had raised a monument to mark the spot, they would equally have "left him." The meaning is equivalent to

"We left him" (with no monumental tablet or cairn, *but)* "alone with his glory."

The last are therefore the new and accented words.

26. "*Lightly* | they'll talk | of the spirit that's gone,
     And | o'er his cold ashes | *upbraid* him;
     But | *nothing* | *he'll* reck | if they let him sleep on |
     In the grave | where | a *Briton* | has laid him."

The emphasis in the first line falls on "lightly"—the expressive complement of the common-place predicate "will talk,"—antithesis being implied. Thus,

"Lightly" (and not reverently as he deserves.)

The subject "they" is used in the general sense of "people" and is unaccented ; "of the spirit that's gone" is implied in connection with the subject of the poem. "And" in the second line, must be separate, to disconnect it from the expletive clause that follows ; "upbraid " will be emphatic, as contrasted with the previous predicate,

> (Not only) "talk lightly" (but even) "upbraid."

" But " in the third line, must be separate, to show the sense " notwithstanding " (these facts.) " Nothing he'll reck, " the first word accented, but the principal emphasis on " he'll " to suggest the antithesis,

> " *He*'ll reck nothing" (although we shall.)

The only other emphasis is on " Briton, " which is suggestive of an inference of pride in the nation whose chivalry will defend the hero's name and mortal remains from insult.

III. REPETITIONS.

27. The only exception to the rule that the emphatic is always the new idea, is to be found in sentences which contain a repetition of an idea previously expressed. But the exception is more apparent than real, for the repeated word will generally be found to be suggestive of an antithesis between the ordinary meaning and some *special* acceptation of the word or phrase.

28. When the repetition includes a clause or a sentence, and not a word merely, the emphasis will be shifted to a different syllable at each repetition, or as often as may be practicable. Thus in the following lines from Dryden's Ode, " Alexander's Feast,"

> Happy, happy, happy pair!
> None but the brave,
> None but the brave,
> None but the brave
> Deserves the fair.

In such cases as " happy, happy," &c., the accents cannot be shifted, and variety must be given by change of tone. Either of the following arrangements would be effective.

> " happy happy happy pair;" or

> " happy happy happy pair."

In such cases as " none but the brave," &c., where a

clause is repeated, the accent may be shifted to a different syllable at each repetition. Thus,

> None but the brave,
>
> None but the brave,
>
> None but the brave
>
> Deserves the fair.

29. In the following series of short extracts the emphatic words are indicated to the eye in further illustration of the Principle of Emphasis. [The student should exercise himself in discovering the contextual reasons for the selection of the emphasized words, and also for the non-selection of the other words.] Notations for Pitch and Clause are introduced in these Exercises.

IV. READING EXERCISES.

MARKED FOR EMPHASIS, CLAUSE, AND PITCH.

ADULATION.—*Pope.*

²At this—*entranced*—he lifts his hands and eyes—
Squeaks like a high-stretched *lute* string—and replies :—
⁵"O, 'tis the *sweetest*—of *all* earthly things—
To gaze on *princes*—and to talk of *kings !*"—
³*Then*—happy man who shows the *tombs !*—said I—
⁴He dwells *amidst* the royal family;—
He—every *day*—from king to *king* can walk—
Of *all* our Harrys—all our Edwards talk—
And get—²by speaking *truth* of monarchs dead—
⁴What few can of the *living*—³*ease*—and *bread.*

AGE'S SORROW.—*Byron.*

⁴What is the *worst*—of woes that wait on *age ?*—
³What stamps the wrinkle *deeper* on the brow?—
²To view each *loved* one—*blotted* from life's page—
³And be *alone* on earth—¹as *I* am now.

ANTIQUARIAN RAPTURE.—*Young.*

⁴How his eyes *languish*—how his thoughts *adore* . . .
That painted *coat*—which Joseph *never* wore!
³He shows—on holidays—a sacred *pin*—
⁴That touched the *ruff*—⁵ that touched Queen *Bess's* chin!

10

BATTLE ALARM.--*Byron.*

³Did ye not *hear* it?—²No—'twas but the *wind*—
Or the *car* rattling o'er the stony street;—
⁴*On* with the dance!—let joy be unconfined;—
³No sleep till *morn*—when youth and pleasure meet—
To chase the glowing hours with flying feet—
²But *hark!*—that heavy sound breaks in once *more*—
⁴As if the clouds its *echo* would repeat—
³And *nearer*,—clearer,—*deadlier* than before!
⁵*Arm!*—arm!—it *is*—it is the *cannon's* opening roar!

BATTLE ARRAY.—*Byron.*

—⁴It is a *splendid* sight—²to see—
²For one who hath no friend, no *brother* there—
³Their rival *scarfs* of mixed embroidery—
Their various *arms* that glitter in the air!—
⁴What *gallant* war-hounds—rouse them from their lair,
And gnash their fangs—loud yelling for the prey!—
³*All* join the chase-but *few*—the *triumph* share;—
²The *grave*—shall bear the *chiefest* prize away—
³And Havoc—⁴scarce for joy can *number* their array.

BEAUTY.—*Hunt.*

⁴What is *beauty?*—²not the show
Of shapely limbs and *features;*—no;—
²These are but *flowers* –
That have their dated *hours*—
To breathe their transitory sweets—then *go.*
⁴'Tis the stainless *soul* within—
That outshines the *fairest* skin—
And yields delights *outlasting* beauty's glow.

BEREAVEMENT.—*Campbell.*

²*Hushed* were his Gertrude's lips;—but still—their bland
And beautiful *expression*—⁴seemed to melt
With love that *could* not die!—³and still—his hand
She *presses*—to the heart no more that felt.
⁴Ah! heart—where once each *fond* affection dwelt—
And features—yet that spoke a *soul*—*more* fair!—
³Mute—gazing—⁴*agonising* as he knelt.
³Of them that stood encircling his despair—
He . . . *heard* some friendly words—but—²*knew* not what they
were.

CLAIMS OF KINDRED.—*Scott.*

³The *slow*-hound—wakes the *fox's* lair—
The *grey*-hound—presses on the *hare*—
The *eagle*—pounces on the *lamb*—
The *wolf*—devours the fleecy *dam;*

¹Even *tiger* fell—and sullen *bear*—
Their likeness and their *lineage—spare:—*
Man only—*mars* kind Nature's plan—
And turns *his* fierce pursuits—*on* man.

CONSTANCY.—*Campbell.*

³Thought ye—your iron hands of *pride*—
Could *break*—the knot that *love* had tied?
No—⁴let the *eagle* change his plume—
The *leaf* its hue—the *flower* its bloom;
⁵But—ties around this *heart* were spun—
⁴That *could* not—*would* not be undone.

CONTEMPTUOUS FORTITUDE.—*Byron.*

²Have I not had my brain *seared*—my *heart* riven—
Hopes sapped—*name* blighted—life's *life*—*lied* away!
³And only not to *desperation* driven—
Because—⁴not altogether of *such* clay—
As *rots*—into the souls of those whom I survey!

COURAGEOUS DEFEAT.—*Moore.*

³The minstrel *fell*—⁴but—the foeman's chain—
Could not bring his proud *soul* under;—
³The *harp* he loved—*ne'er* spoke again—
For—⁴he *tore* its chords asunder—
³And said—" ⁴*No* chains—shall sully *thee*—
³Thou soul of *love* and bravery!—
Thy songs were made for the pure and *free*—
⁴They shall *never*—sound in *slavery!*"

COURTIERS.— *Wolcot.*

²Low at his feet—the *spaniel* courtiers cower—
Curl—wheedle—whine—paw—*lick* his shoe—for *power:*
³Prepared for *every* insult—servile train—
⁴To take a *kicking*—and to fawn *again.*

COWARDLY SURRENDER.—*Butler.*

³'Tis not the *least* disparagement—
To be defeated by the *event*—
Nor to be beaten by main *force*—
⁴*That* does not make a man the worse :—
But—to ³turn tail and run *away*—
⁴And *without* blows give up the day—
Or to surrender *ere* the assault—.
⁵That's no man's *fortune*—⁴but his *fault.*

DEFIANCE.—*Scott.*

³His back—against a *rock* he bore—
And—firmly placed his foot before :—
⁴"Come one,—come *all!*—⁵this *rock*—shall fly
From its firm base—as soon as *I.*"

DESPAIR.—*Byron.*

³Loud sung the *wind* above—and doubly loud—
Shook o'er his turret-cell the *thunder* cloud—
⁴And *flashed* the lightning by the latticed bar—
To *him*—more genial than the midnight *star.*
²*Close* to the glimmering grate—he dragged his chain—
³And *hoped*—*that* peril—*might* not prove in vain.
⁴He raised his ironed hand to heaven—and *prayed*
One pitying flash—to *mar* the form it made :—
²His chains and impious prayer—attract alike—
³The storm rolled *onward*—and disdained to strike ;—
²Its peal waxed fainter⌢¹ceased—²he felt *alone,*
³As if some faithless *friend* had spurned his groan !

DESPERATE CONFLICT.—*Byron.*

⁴"*One* effort—one—to *break* the circling host !"
³They form—unite—⁵*charge*⌢²waver⌢¹all is lost !
⁴Within a *narrower* ring compressed—beset—
³Hopeless—not heartless—⁴strive and struggle *yet !*
²Ah !—*now* they fight in firmest file no more—
Hemmed in—cut off—cleft down—and *trampled* o'er ;—
⁴But—each strikes singly—silently—and *home*—
³And sinks *outwearied*—rather than o'ercome :—
²His last—faint quittance—rendering with his breath—
³Till⌢the blade glimmers in the grasp of *death.*

ERROR.—*Prior.*

³When people once are in the *wrong*—
⁴Each *line* they add—is much too *long ;*
³Who *fastest* walks—but walks astray—
⁴Is only *farthest* from his way.

FAME.—*Byron.*

⁴What is the *end*—of *fame ?*—²'tis but—to fill
A certain portion of uncertain *paper :*—
³Some—liken it to climbing up a *hill*—
Whose summit—like all hills—is lost in *vapour.*
⁴For this—men write—speak—*preach*—and heroes *kill*—
And *bards*—burn what they call their "midnight taper"—
³To have—when the original is dust—
A *name*—a wretched *picture*—and worse *bust.*

GREED OF PRAISE.—*Goldsmith.*

³Of praise a mere *glutton*—he swallowed what came—
⁴And—the puff of a *dunce*—he miscounted for fame—
³Till—his relish grown callous almost to disease—
⁴Who *peppered* the highest—was surest to please.

HOPE PERSONIFIED.—*Collins.*

⁴But thou—O *Hope*—with eyes so fair—
What was *thy* delighted measure? —
³Still—it whispered *promised* pleasure—
And bade the lovely scenes—at *distance* hail!
²Still would her touch the strain *prolong*—
And—from the rocks—the woods—the vale—
⁴She called on *Echo*—still—through all her song—
³And—where her sweetest theme she chose—
A soft responsive voice ⌒ was *heard*—at every close—
⁴And Hope *enchanted*—smiled—and waved her golden hair.

HUMAN ENJOYMENTS.—*Pope.*

³Behold the *child*—by Nature's kindly law
Pleased with a *rattle*—tickled with a *straw;*—
⁴Some *livelier* plaything—gives his *youth* delight—
³A little louder—but *as* empty quite;—
⁴*Scarfs*—garters—*gold*—amuse his *riper* stage;
²And beads and *prayer*-books—are the toys of *age;*—
³Pleased with *this* bauble still—as *that* before—
Till—tired—he *sleeps* ⌒ and life's poor *play*—is o'er.

HUMAN KNOWLEDGE.—*Pope.*

³When the proud *steed*—shall *know*—²*why*—man *restrains*
His fiery course—or *drives* him o'er the plains;—
³When the dull *ox*—²why now he breaks the clod—
Is now a victim—and now—Egypt's *god;*—
⁴*Then*—shall *man's* pride and dulness—comprehend
His actions'—passions'—*being's*—use and end;
³Why doing—suffering;—checked - impelled;—⁴and why—
This hour a *slave*—the next—a *deity.*

HUNTING.—*Gay.*

³The jocund thunder - wakes the enlivened *hounds*—
They rouse from sleep—⁴and *answer*—sounds for sounds;—
⁵The tuneful noise the sprightly *courser* hears—
⁴*Paws* the green turf—and pricks his trembling ears:—
⁵The *slackened* rein—now gives him all his speed—
⁴*Back* flies the rapid ground beneath the steed;—
Hills—dales—and forests—*far* behind remain—
³While the warm scent—draws on the deep-mouthed train.

INDIGNATION.— *Wolcot.*

⁴*Ungrateful* scoundrels!—³eat my rolls and butter—
⁴And *daring* thus their insolences mutter!—
³Swallow my turtle and my beef by pounds—
And tear my ven'son like a pack of *hounds*—
⁴ *Yet* have the impudence—the brazen face—
To say—I am not *fitted* for the place!

KING LEAR.— *Hood.*

³A *poor—old*—king,—with *sorrow* for my crown,—
Throned upon *straw*—and mantled with the *wind*—
For pity—my own tears have made me *blind*—
⁴That I might never see—my *children's* frown;
³And maybe—*madness*—like a friend—has thrown
A folded fillet over my dark *mind*—
²So that unkindly speech—may *sound*—for *kind*:—
³Albeit—I *know* not.—I am *childish* grown—
And have not gold—to *purchase* wit withal—
⁴I—that have once maintained *most* royal state—
A very *bankrupt* now—²that may not call
My *child*—my child!—⁴*all* beggared—³*save* in tears—
²Wherewith I *daily* weep an old man's fate—
Foolish—and blind—and *overcome* with years.

LANDING OF AN ARMY. — *Scott.*

³It was a dread—yet *spirit*-stirring sight!—
⁴The billows—*foamed* beneath a thousand oars;—
³Fast as they land—the red-cross ranks *unite*—
Legions on *legions* brightening all the shores.
⁴Then *banners* rise—and *cannon*-signal roars;—
Then peals the warlike thunder of the *drum*—
Thrills the loud *fife*—the *trumpet* · flourish pours—
⁵And patriot *hopes* awake—and *doubts*—are *dumb*—
For—bold in *Freedom's* cause—the bands of Ocean—come.

LAW.— *Pope.*

³Once—²says an author—*where* I need not say—
³Two *travellers*—found an *oyster* in their way:
⁴Both fierce—both hungry—the *dispute* grew strong—
³While—scale in hand—Dame *Justice*—passed along.
Before her—⁴*each* with clamour pleads the laws—
Explained the matter—and would win the cause.
³Dame Justice—*weighing* long the doubtful right—
Takes—opens ⌒ ⁴*swallows* it before their sight.⌒
³The *cause* of strife—removed so rarely well—
" There—·*take*—" says Justice—" take you each—a *shell*;—
⁴We thrive at *Westminster*—on fools like you—
³"'Twas a *fat* oyster—⁴live in *peace*—*adieu*."

LEADERSHIP.—*Byron.*

³What is that *spell*—that—with commanding art—
Still dazzles—leads—yet *chills* the vulgar heart?
What should it be—that thus men's *faith* can bind? ⌐
⁴The power of *thought*—the magic of the *mind!*
³This—with *success*—assumed and kept with skill—
⁴Moulds *ever*—human weakness to its will.
³Such *hath* it been—*shall* be—beneath the sun :—
⁴The *many*—still must labour for the *one!*
'Tis *Nature's* doom :⌐but—let the wretch who toils—
Accuse not—*hate* not—him who wears the spoils!
²Oh!—if he *knew*—the *weight* of splendid chains—
³How *light*—the balance of *his* humbler pains!

MISDIRECTED EFFORTS.—*Swift.*

·⁴*Brutes*—find out where their *talents* lie :—
³A *bear*—will not attempt to *fly ;*—
A foundered *horse*—will oft debate
Before he tries a five-barred *gate ;*
A *dog*—by instinct turns aside—
Who sees the *ditch* too deep and wide :—
⁴But *man*—we find the only creature—
Who—led by folly—*combats* nature—
And—⁴where his genius *least* inclines—
³*Absurdly*—bends his whole designs.

MISFORTUNES.—*Young.*

³Oh! mortals—*short* of sight—who think—the past
O'erblown misfortune—still shall prove the *last :*—
²Alas!—misfortunes travel in a *train*—
And oft in life form one *perpetual* chain.
³*Fear* buries fear—and ills *on* ills attend—
Till—⁴*life* and sorrow—meet one *common* end.

MUSIC AND LANGUAGE.—*Moore.*

⁴*Music !* ⌐ oh!—³how faint—how weak—
Language—*fades* before thy spell!—
⁴Why should feeling *ever* speak—
⁴When *thou* canst breathe her soul so well?
³*Friendship's* balmy words—may *feign*—
⁴*Love's*—are even *more* false than they ;—
²Oh!—'tis only—⁴*music's* strain—
³Can sweetly soothe—⁴and *not* betray!

OUTCRY.—*Pope.*

⁴Then flashed the living *lightning* from her eyes—
⁵And *screams* of horror rend the affrighted skies—

³Not louder shrieks to pitying heaven are cast—
⁴When *husbands*—⁵or when *lap-dogs* breathe their last—
Or—when rich *china* vessels—fallen from high—
²In glittering dust and painted *fragments* lie.

PATRIOTIC RESOLVE.—*Campbell.*

⁴Oh ! *Heaven!*—he cried—my bleeding country *save!*
Is there *no* hand on high—to shield the brave? ⌢
³Yet—though destruction sweep these lovely plains—
⁴*Rise*—fellow *men!*—our *country* yet remains !—
³By *that* dread name—we wave the sword on high—
⁴And *swear* ⌢ for *her* to live—*with* her—to *die.*

PEASANT LIFE.—*Goldsmith.*

⁴*Ill* fares the land—to *hastening* ills a prey—
³Where *wealth* accumulates—³and *men*—*decay;*—
³Princes and *lords*—may flourish or may *fade*—
A *breath* can make them—as a breath hath made ;—
⁴But—a bold *peasantry*—³their country's pride—
When once destroyed—⁴can *never* be supplied.

POWER OF MUSIC.—*Pope.*

³By *music*—minds—an *equal* temper know—
Nor swell too high—nor sink too low :
⁴If—in the breast—*tumultuous* joys arise—
²Music—her soft *assuasive* voice applies ;—
³Or—when the soul is pressed with *cares*—
Exalts her—in enlivening airs.
⁴*Warriors*—she *fires* with animated sounds—
²Pours *balm* - into the bleeding *lover's* wounds :—
³*Melancholy*—lifts her head—
Morpheus—rouses from his bed—
Sloth—unfolds her arms and wakes—
⁴Listening *Envy*—*drops* her snakes.
²Intestine wars—no *more*—our passions wage—
And giddy factions—hear *away* their rage.

PRECEDENTS.—*Cowper.*

⁴To follow foolish *precedents*—and *wink*
With both our eyes—²is *easier*—than to *think.*

RETROSPECTION.—*Moore.*

³*As*—slow—our ship—her foamy track
Against the *wind* was cleaving—
Her trembling pennant—still looked *back*—
To that dear land 'twas leaving—

⁴*So*—loath *we* part from all we love—
From all the links that bind us—
So turn our hearts—*where'er* we rove—
⁵To those we've left behind us.

SECOND-HAND FAME.—*Young*.

³He stands for *fame*—on his *forefathers'* feet--
By . . . ⁴*heraldry*—proved valiant or discreet!

SEPARATION. —*Moore*.

³A *boat*—²at midnight sent alone—
To drift upon the moonless sea—
³A *lute*—²whose leading chord is *gone*—
³A wounded *bird*—²that hath but *one*
Imperfect wing—to soar upon—
⁴Are *like* ⌒ ²what *I* am—²without *thee*.

SHIPWRECK.—*Byron*.

⁴Then rose from sea to sky—the wild farewell—
⁵Then *shrieked* the timid—and stood still—the *brave*—
⁴Then some leaped *overboard*—with dreadful yell—
²As eager to anticipate their grave—
³And the sea *yawned* around her—like a hell—
And *down* she sucked with her the whirling wave—
⁴Like one who *grapples* with his enemy—
And strives to *strangle* him—before . . he die.

³And first—⁵one *universal* shriek there rushed—
²Louder than the loud *ocean* —like a crash
Of echoing *thunder*—²and then ⌒ all ⌒ ¹was *hushed*—
³Save the wild wind—and the remorseless dash
Of billows ;—⁴but ⌒ at intervals ⌒ there gushed—
Accompanied with a convulsive *splash*—
³A *solitary* shriek—the bubbling cry
Of some *strong* swimmer—in his agony.

SLEEP.—*Byron*.

³There lie—*love's* feverish hope—and *cunning's* guile—
Hate's working brain—and lulled *ambition's* wile ;—
²O'er each vain eye—⁴*oblivion's* pinions wave—
And quenched existence—crouches in a *grave*.
³What *better* name—may slumber's bed become?
Night's *sepulchre* —the universal *home* --
²Where weakness – strength--vice –virtue—sunk supine—
³*Alike*—in naked helplessness recline ; --
⁴*Glad*—for awhile to heave unconscious breath—
⁵Yet wake—to wrestle with the *dread* of death.--
⁴And *shun*—though day but dawn on ills *increased*—
That sleep—the *loveliest* since it *dreams* the least.

SOLITUDE.—*Byron.*

³To sit on *rocks*—to muse o'er flood and fell—
To slowly trace the *forest's* shady scene—
Where things that own not *man's* dominion—dwell—
And mortal foot hath ne'er—or *rarely* been;—
⁴To climb the trackless *mountain*—all unseen—
³With the wild flock that never needs a fold; –
Alone—o'er steeps and foaming *falls* to lean;—
⁴*This* -is not *solitude ;*—³'tis but to hold
Converse with nature's charms—and view her stores unrolled.

⁴But—midst the *crowd*—the hum—the shock of men—
To hear—to see—to feel—and to possess—
³And roam along - the world's *tired* denizen—
²With *none* who bless us - none whom *we* can bless –
⁴Minions of *splendour—shrinking* from distress !
³None—that—with kindred consciousness endued—
⁴If we were *not*—would seem to *smile* the less –
²Of *all*—that *flattered*—followed –sought and sued—
⁴*This*—is to be *alone;*—this—this—*is* solitude.

SOUNDS OF AN ARMY.—*Moore.*

³Hearken !—what *discords* now,—of every kind——
⁴*Shouts,* laughs, and screams –are revelling in the wind !—
³The *neigh* of cavalry—the tinkling throngs
Of laden *camels*—and their drivers' *songs;* –
⁴Ringing of *arms*—and flapping in the breeze—
Of streamers from ten *thousand* canopies;—
³War-*music*—bursting out from time to time—
⁴With gong and tymbalon's tremendous chime;—
²Or—in the pause,—when harsher sounds are mute—
³The mellow breathings of some *horn*—or flute --
That—far off--⁴broken by the eagle note
Of the directing *trumpet*—³ swell and float.

SOUNDS OF MORNING.—*Beattie.*

⁴The *melodies*—of *morning*—who can *tell?*⌒
³The wild *brook*—babbling down the mountain's side—
The lowing *herd*—the sheepfold's simple *bell*—
The *pipe* of early shepherd—dim descried
In the lone valley;—⁴echoing far and wide—
The clamorous *horn*—along the cliffs above;—
²The hollow murmur—of the *ocean* tide;—
The hum—of *bees*—³the *linnet's* lay of love—
⁴And the *full* choir—that wakes the universal grove.

STANDARDS OF CHARACTER.—*Pope.*

⁴'Tis from *high* life—high *characters* are drawn :—
³A *saint*—in *crape*—is *twice* a saint—in *lawn;*—

A *judge*—is *just ;*—a *chancellor*—juster *still ;*—
A *gownman*—*learn'd ;*—⁴a *bishop*—what you *will;*⌢
³*Wise*—if a *minister;*—but—⁴if a *king*—
More wise—more learn'd—more just—⁵more . . . *everything.*

STILLNESS.— *Scott.*

⁹The wind—breathed soft as *lover's* sigh—
²And—oft renewed—seemed oft—to *die*—
    With breathless pause between.
²O,—*who*—with speech of war and woes—
Would wish to *break*—the soft repose—
    ⁴Of such *enchanting* scene !

THE HUNTED DEER.— *Scott.*

²As *chief*—who hears his warder call—
⁵" To *arms!*—the foemen storm the wall !"—
³The *antlered* monarch of the waste—
⁴*Sprung* from his heathery couch in haste.
. ⁹But—ere his fleet career he took—
The *dew*-drops from his flanks he shook—
²A moment *gazed* —adown the vale—
A moment—snuffed the tainted gale—
A moment *listened* ⌢ ³to the cry
That thickened as the chace drew *nigh*—
⁴Then—as the headmost foes *appeared*—
⁵With one brave *bound*—the copse he cleared.

THE PASSING CHACE.— *Scott.*

⁴Their peal—the merry *horns* rung out—
⁵A hundred *voices*—joined the shout;—
³With hark and whoop and wild hailoo—
⁴No *rest*—the mountain echoes knew.
³*Far* from the tumult—fled the roe—
²*Close* in her covert—cowered the doe ;—
⁴The *falcon*—from her cairn on high
Cast on the rout a *wondering* eye—
Till—far *beyond* her piercing ken—
The hurricane had swept the glen.
³*Faint*—and more faint—its failing din—
²*Returned*—from cavern, cliff, and linn;—
¹And silence ⌢ ²settled—wide and still—
³On the lone wood and mighty hill.

WISEACRES.— *Byron.*

⁴Of all the *horrid,*—hideous notes of woe—
²Sadder than *owl* songs on the midnight blast—
⁸Is that portentous phrase—⁴" I *told* you so "—
⁵Uttered by . . . *friends*—those prophets of the *past*—

Who—'stead of saying what you *now* should do—
   ⁴'Own—they *foresaw*—that you would fall at last—
   ³And solace your slight lapse 'gainst " bonos mores "—
With a long memorandum of *old* stories.

                    YOUTH.—*Gray.*

³Fair—laughs the *morn*—and *soft*—the zephyr blows—
While—*proudly* riding o'er the azure realm—
In gallant trim—the gilded vessel goes—
⁴*Youth* on the prow—and *Pleasure* at the helm;—
³*Regardless*—of the sweeping *whirlwind's* sway—
²That—hushed in grim repose—expects his *evening* prey.

V. RESUMÉ OF THE PRINCIPLES OF SENTENTIAL ACCENT OR EMPHASIS.

44. I. All words expressive of ideas *new* to the context, are emphatic.   II. Words used in contrast to a *preceding* term are emphatic in a stronger degree.   III.
All words suggestive of *unexpressed* antithesis are emphatic in the strongest degree.   IV. Words which are of
necessity *implied*, or the idea conveyed by which has
been included in former expressions, explanatory terms,
and repeated words—not suggesting a *special*, in opposition to their ordinary, acceptation—are unemphatic.

45. The following passages which have been selected
for their unusual difficulty of emphasizing,—should be
carefully studied.   Read each extract three times ; at the
first reading insert a pencil *dot* below the accented syllable of the words selected for emphasis ; at the second
reading, draw a short *line* below the emphatic syllables ;
and at the third reading underline the *whole* of each emphatic word.   An examination can then be made of the
differences of marking at the various readings, and the
reasons revolved on which words have been rejected or
approved.   Afterwards, but not before, compare with
the KEY, appended to the Extracts.

VI. PASSAGES FOR EXERCISE IN THE SELECTION OF EMPHATIC WORDS.

ANECDOTE.—*Fuller.*

The Sidonian servants agreed amongst themselves to choose him to be their king who that morning should first see the sun. Whilst all others were gazing on the east, one alone looked on the west; some admired, more mocked him, as if he looked on the feet to find the eye of the face. But he first of all discovered the light of the sun shining on the tops of the houses. God is seen sooner, easier, clearer, in his operations than in his essence; best beheld by reflection in his creatures.

BLINDNESS.—*Milton.*

When I consider how my light is spent
  Ere half my days, in this dark world and wide,
  And that one talent which is death to hide
Lodged with me useless, though my soul more bent
To serve therewith my Maker, and present
  My true account, lest He, returning, chide;—
  " Doth God exact day-labour, light denied?"
I fondly ask: but Patience to prevent
  That murmur, soon replies, " God doth not need
Either man's work, or His own gifts; who best
Bear His mild yoke, they serve Him best; His state
  Is kingly; thousands at His bidding speed,
And post o'er land and ocean without rest ;
They also serve who only stand and wait."

CHEERFUL PIETY.—" *Private Life.*"

The cultivation of cheerfulness is not sufficiently considered as forming part of the duty of a Christian; but it forms a very material part. It recommends religion to the world in general, and gives a brightness and charm to domestic life. Piety, with her skull and cross-bones, her haircloth, scourges, and tearful countenance, is a very repulsive personage; but Piety with her gentle silver tones of kindness, her hand of helpfulness, her glad smile, and eyes full of grateful hope fixed on Heaven, is attractive and beautiful. Cheerfulness ought to be one of the unfailing attributes of Christian Piety.

CONSOLATION IN MISFORTUNE.—*Lord North.*

Voltaire gives an account of an unfortunate man, who had lost a leg and an arm in one place; had his nose cut off and his eyes put out, in another; had been hung up and cut down, in a third; had been imprisoned by the Inquisition, and condemned to be burnt, and at last found himself chained to the oar as a galley-slave; and who, nevertheless, consoled himself with saying, " Thank God for all I have suffered! I should not otherwise have known the luxury of eating orange-chips and pistachio nuts in the harbour of Constantinople."

CONTENTMENT.— *Warwick.*

There is no estate of life so happy in this world as to yield a Christian the perfection of content, and yet there is no state of life so wretched in this world, but a Christian must be content with it.   Though I have nothing that may give me a true content, yet I will learn to be truly contented herewith what I have. What care I, though I have not much?   I have as much as I desire, if I have as much as I want; I have as much as the most, if I have as much as I desire.

COURTEOUSNESS.—*Leighton.*

The roots of plants are hid under the ground, so that themselves are not seen, but they appear in their branches, and flowers, and fruits, which argue there is a root and life in them : thus the graces of the Spirit planted in the soul, though themselves invisible, yet discover their being and life, in the tract of a Christian's life, his words and actions, and the whole frame of his carriage.

EQUALITY OF MEN.—*Bishop Horne.*

The different ranks and orders of mankind may be compared to so many streams and rivers of running water.   All proceed from an original, small and obscure; some spread wider, travel over more countries, and make more noise in their passage than others; but all tend alike to an ocean, where distinction ceases, and where the largest and most celebrated rivers are equally lost, and absorbed with the smallest and most unknown streams.

ERROR AND IGNORANCE.

It is almost as difficult to make a man unlearn his errors as his knowledge.   Mal-information is more hopeless than non-information; for error is always more busy than ignorance.   Ignorance is a blank sheet, on which we may write; but error is a scribbled one, from which we must first erase.   Ignorance is contented to stand still with her back to the truth; but error is more presumptuous, and proceeds in the backward direction. Ignorance has no light, but error follows a false one : the consequence is, that error, when she retraces her footsteps, has farther to go before she can arrive at the truth than ignorance.

EVIL SPEAKING.— *Warwick.*

It is not good to speak evil of all whom we know bad; it is worse to judge evil of any who may prove good.   To speak ill upon knowledge shows a want of charity; to speak ill upon suspicion shows a want of honesty.   To know evil of others, and not speak it, is sometimes discretion; to speak evil of others, and not know it, is always dishonesty. He may be evil himself who speaks good of others upon knowledge, but he can never be good himself who speaks evil of others upon suspicion.

FAITHFUL PRAYER.

Friend, thou must trust in Him who trod before
The desolate path of life :
Must bear in meekness, as He meekly bore,
Sorrow, and pain, and strife.
Think how the Son of God
These thorny paths hath trod ;
Think how He longed to go,
Yet tarried out for thee, the appointed woe.
Think of His weariness in places dim,
Where no man comforted, or cared for Him.
Think of the blood-like sweat
With which His brow was wet,
Yet how He prayed, unaided and alone,
In that great agony—"Thy will be done !"
Friend! do not thou despair,
Christ, from His heaven of heavens, will hear thy prayer.

FIGURATIVE LANGUAGE.—*Berkeley.*

Nothing is more natural than to make the things we know, a step towards those we do not know; and to explain, or represent things less familiar by others which are more so. We imagine before we reflect, and we perceive by sense before we imagine; and of all our senses sight is the most clear, distinct, various, agreeable, and comprehensive. Hence it is natural to assist the intellect by the imagination, the imagination by sense, and the other senses by sight. Hence figures, metaphors, and types. We illustrate spiritual things by corporeal ; we substitute sounds for thoughts, and written letters for sounds ; emblems, symbols and hieroglyphics, for things too obscure to strike, and too various or too fleeting to be retained. We substitute things imaginable for things intelligible; sensible things for imaginable, smaller things for those that are too great to comprehend easily, and greater things for such as are too small to be discerned distinctly; present things for absent, permanent for perishing, and visible for invisible.

FLOWERS.—*Mary Howitt.*

God might have bade the earth bring forth enough for great
    and small,
The oak tree and the cedar tree, without a flower at all.
The ore within the mountain mine requireth none to grow ;
Nor doth it need the lotus flower to make the river flow.
The clouds might give abundant rain, the nightly dews might fall,
And the herb that keepeth life in man might yet have drunk
    them all ;

Our outward life requires them not : then wherefore had they
    birth ?
To minister delight to man,—to beautify the earth,—
To whisper hope, to comfort man whene'er his faith is dim :
For who so careth for the flowers, will care much more for him.

FORGIVING DISPOSITION.—*Sterne.*

The brave only know how to forgive ; it is the most refined
and generous pitch of virtue human nature can arrive at.   Cowards have done good and kind actions ; cowards have even
fought, nay, sometimes even conquered : but a coward never for-
gave ; it is not in his nature ; the power of doing it flows only
from a strength and greatness of soul, conscious of its own force
and security, and above the little temptations of resenting every
fruitless attempt to interrupt its happiness.

FRUITLESS RESOLUTIONS.— *Young.*

At thirty, man suspects himself a fool ;
Knows it at forty, and reforms his plan ;
At fifty, chides his infamous delay,—
Pushes his prudent purpose to resolve ;
In all the magnanimity of thought,
Resolves, and re-resolves, then dies the same.

GRATEFUL RECOGNITION—ARGUS.—*Pope.*

When wise Ulysses,—from his native coast,
Long kept by wars, and long by tempest tossed,—
Arrived at last, poor, old, disguised, alone,
To all his friends, and e'en his queen, unknown ;—
Changed as he was, with age, and toils, and cares,
Furrowed his reverend face, and white his hairs,
In his own palace forced to ask his bread.
Scorned by those slaves his former bounty fed ;
Forgot of all his own domestic crew ;—
The faithful dog alone his rightful master knew.
Unfed, unhoused, neglected, on the clay,
Like an old servant now cashiered he lay ;
Touched with resentment of ungrateful man,
And longing to behold his ancient lord again.
Him, when he saw, he rose, and crawled to meet,—
'Twas all he could—and fawned and kissed his feet—
Seized with dumb joy—then falling by his side,
Owned his returning lord, looked up, and died !

KNOWLEDGE AND WISDOM.

Knowledge and wisdom, far from being one,
Have oft-times no connection.   Knowledge dwells
In heads replete with thoughts of other men ;
Wisdom, in minds attentive to their own.

Knowledge—a rude unprofitable mass,
The mere materials with which wisdom builds,—
Till smoothed, and squared, and fitted to its place,
Does but encumber whom it seems to enrich :
Knowledge is proud, that he has learned so much ;
Wisdom is humble, that he knows no more.

MAN.—*King.*

Like to the falling of a star,
Or as the flights of eagles are,
Or like the fresh spring's gaudy hue,
Or silver drops of morning dew ;
Or like a wind that chafes the flood,
Or bubbles which on water stood :
Even such is man, whose borrowed light
Is straight called in, and paid to night :—
The wind blows out, the bubble dies,
The Spring entombed in Autumn lies,—
The dew's dried up, the star is shot,
The flight is past, and man forgot.

ON LITERARY EXTRACTS.—*Willmott.*

Johnson condemns the belief that a poet can be introduced to
a just reputation by select quotations ; and compares a critic
who should make the attempt, to the famous pedant in Hierocles, who, when he wished to sell his house, carried a specimen
brick in his pocket. Such a sentiment was natural and appropriate upon the lips of an editor of a great dramatic poet ; but
that it did not extend to literary extracts, we know from Boswell, to whom Johnson often expressed his love of those little
volumes of " Beauties, " by which celebrated authors have been
recommended to the vulgar. A thousand persons will read a
page, who would never open a folio. A single flower may in-
duce a wanderer to visit the garden ; a single bunch of grapes
may allure him into a land of promise.

POLITENESS.—*Lord Chatham.*

As to politeness, many have attempted its definition. I believe
it is best to be known by description ; definition not being able
to comprise it. I would, however, venture to call it benevolence in trifles, or the preference of others to ourselves, in little,
daily, hourly occurrences in the commerce of life. A better
place, a more commodious seat, priority in being helped at table ;
what is it but sacrificing ourselves in such trifles to the convenience and pleasure of others ? And this constitutes true politeness. Bowing, ceremonies, formal compliments, stiff civilities.
will never be politeness ; that must be easy, natural, unstudied,
manly, noble. And what will give this—but a mind benevolent
and perpetually attentive to exert that amiable disposition
towards all you converse and live with ? Benevolence in great
matters takes a higher name, and is the Queen of Virtue.

11

SELF-SATISFACTION.—*Hare.*

Thorwaldsen being found by a friend one day somewhat out of spirits, was asked whether anything had occurred to distress him; he answered: " My genius is decaying. " " What do you mean?" said the visitor. " Why, here is my statue of Christ; it is the first of my works that I have ever felt satisfied with. Till now, my idea has always been far beyond what I could execute; but it is no longer so; I shall never have a great idea again."

TEMPER.—*" Private Life."*

There are persons who, on the subject of temper, plead a sort of prescriptive right to indulgence, on the ground of constitutional infirmity, or hereditary entailment; but before such pleas can be considered valid in the court of Conscience, let such persons ask themselves, whether there are no circumstances sufficiently powerful, whether there is no presence sufficiently august, to awe them into self-control; whether in certain moments of their lives they have not found the most indignant feelings controllable, the fiercest blaze of passion repressible? If this be the case—and experience will generally attest that it is so—the plea of necessity falls to the ground; for we should never forget that, in every moment of our lives, we are in a Presence the most august, under the vigilant observation of a Being, compared to whose glance the gaze of an assembled world is powerless and insignificant.

TO THE BUTTERFLY.—*Rogers.*

Child of the sun! pursue thy rapturous flight,
Mingling with her thou lov'st in fields of light.
And where the flowers of paradise unfold,
Quaff fragrant nectar from their cups of gold:
There shall thy wings, rich as an evening sky,
Expand and shut with silent ecstasy.
Yet, wert thou once a worm,—a thing that crept
On the bare earth, then wrought a tomb, and slept.
And such is man! soon from his cell of clay
To burst, a seraph, in the blaze of day.

TIME.

Time moveth not! our being 'tis that moves;
And we, swift gliding down life's rapid stream,
Dream of swift ages, and revolving years,
Ordained to chronicle our passing days;
So the young sailor, in the gallant bark
Scudding before the wind, beholds the coast
Receding from his eyes, and thinks the while,
Struck with amaze, that he is motionless,
And that the land is sailing.

VEGETATION.

Say what impels, amidst surrounding snow
Congealed, the crocus' flaming bud to glow?
Say what retards, amidst the summer's blaze,
The autumnal bulb, till pale declining days?
The God of Seasons, whose pervading power
Controls the sun, or sheds the fleecy shower;
He bids each flower his quickening word obey,
Or to each lingering bloom enjoins delay.

WIT.—*Pope.*

True wit is Nature to advantage dressed,
What oft was thought, but ne'er so well expressed;
Something whose truth, convinced at sight, we find,
That gives us back the image of our mind.
As shades more sweetly recommend the light,
So modest plainness sets off sprightly wit,
For works may have more wit than does them good,
As bodies perish through excess of blood.

46.   KEY.

To the Emphatic Words in the Foregoing Extracts.

1. Sidonian, agreed, King, Sun, one, west, mocked, feet, face, he, houses, God, his, reflection.

2. Light, half, hide, more, account, labour, Patience, need, bear, they, kingly, thousands, ocean, also, stand.

3. Cheerfulness, duty, very, recommends, world, domestic, cross, tearful, repulsive, kindness, hand, hope, beautiful, unfailing.

4. Voltaire, leg, arm, nose, eyes, up, Inquisition, burnt, galley, consoled, thank, otherwise, pistachio, Constantinople.

5. No, happy, content, yet, wretched, must, give, learn, have, much, desire, want, most.

6. Roots, hid, branches, flowers, fruits, is, Spirit, discover, their, whole.

7. Orders, streams, all, obscure, noise, alike, ceases, celebrated, equally, un(known).

8. Almost, errors, hopeless, non-(information), busy, blank, scribbled, erase, still, proceeds, no, false, consequence, farther, ignorance.

9. Speak, know, judge, good, knowledge, charity, suspicion, honesty, not, discretion, know, always, evil, never, suspicion.

10. Trust, before, bear, He, sorrow, God, longed, thee, weariness, no, Him, blood, prayed, Thy, despair, hear.

11. Natural, know, not, less, more, imagine, reflect, sense, sight, comprehensive, intellect, imagination, sense, other, sight, figures, spiritual, corporeal, sounds, letters, hieroglyphics, ob-

scure, retained, imaginable, intelligible, sensible, smaller, easily, greater, distinctly, present, permanent, in-(visible).

12. Might, enough, flower, ore, river, dews, herb, all, outward, not, wherefore, delight, beautify, hope, faith, so, more, him.

13. Brave, forgive, can, cowards, kind, fought, conquered, never, nature, greatness, conscious, above, interrupt.

14. Thirty, suspects, fool, knows, forty, plan, fifty, chides, resolve, thought, re-(resolves), dies.

15. Ulysses, long, tempest, arrived, queen, unknown, was, bread, scorned, forgot, dog, knew, clay, resentment, longing, when, crawled, kissed, falling, died.

16. One, connexion, knowledge, other, wisdom, own, knowledge, materials, encumber, proud, wisdom, humble, more.

17. Star, eagles, spring's, dew, wind, bubbles, even, man, in, night, out, bubble, autumn, dew's, star, flight, forgot.

18. Johnson, condemns, poet, just, quotations, attempt, Hierocles, house, brick, appropriate, editor, not, Boswell, love, beauties, recommended, thousand, page, folio, flower, garden, grapes, land.

19. Politeness, many, definition, description, able, benevolence, trifles, others, place, commodious, helped, sacrificing, constitutes, never, easy, manly, give, perpetually, all, great, Queen.

20. Thorwaldsen, spirits, occurred, genius, mean, Christ, first, satisfied, far, never.

21. Temper, indulgence, constitutional, valid, ask, no, control, indignant, fiercest, if, is, ground, never, every, are, most, world, insignificant.

22. Sun, pursue, lov'st, paradise, nectar, sky, ecstasy, worm, earth, man, his, seraph.

23. Time, not, being, dream, chronicle, sailor, receding, he, motionless, land.

24. What, snow, crocus, retards, autumnal, God, controls, shower, He, lingering.

25. Wit, advantage, well, sight, our, shades, light, plainness, good, blood.

KEY TO THE EMPHATIC WORDS IN "*Thunderstorm among the Alps*," p. 82.

1. Such, night, wondrous, lovely, eye, far, thunder, one, every, Jura, Alps.

2. Night, glorious, slumber, me, sharer, portion, shines, phosphoric, rain, black, glee, shakes, earthquake's.

PRINCIPLES OF ELOCUTION.

PART FIFTH.

LOOKS AND GESTURES.

I. GENERAL PRINCIPLES.

1. VOCAL Expression, however perfect, fails to give delivery its full impressiveness, if the face and whole body do not sympathetically manifest the feeling which vibrates in the tones. Nothing can be more spiritless and unnatural than rigid stillness on the part of an orator. But the tendency to gesticulate is so natural, that instruction will generally be needed rather to subdue and chasten, than to *create* gesticulation. To a speaker of any animation, the greatest difficulty is to stand still.

2. In the natural order of passionate expression, LOOKS are first, GESTURES second, and WORDS last. " The strongfelt passion bolts into the face " before it moves the massier muscles of the trunk and limbs ; and its tardiest expression is in the artificial and conventional form of articulate language. Gesture which, thus, in strong emotion *precedes* the words, in calmer feeling accompanies them ; but it must never lag behind the utterance it illustrates.

II. EXPRESSIVENESS OF THE DIFFERENT FACIAL AND BODILY MOTIONS.

3. THE FEATURES expand in pleasure and contract in pain.

They are elongated in melancholy.

They are smooth in placidity, and variously furrowed in emotion.

They grin in folly.

4. The Eyebrows are lifted in surprise, in inquiry,
and in hope.

They are depressed in conviction, in authority, and
in despair.

They are knitted in sorrow, in solicitude, and in
anger.

They droop in weakness.

5. The Eyes beam in love, they sparkle in mirth, they
flash and roll in anger, they melt in grief.

They are raised in hope, and dejected in despond-
ency.

They measure their object from head to foot in
contempt.

They stare in wonder, and wink in cunning.

They are levelled in modesty, and cast downward
in shame.

They are restless in terror, in anxiety, and in idiocy.

They are fixed in confidence, in boldness, and in
energy.

They look askance in suspicion, and secrecy.

They are cast on vacancy in thought.

6. The Nostrils are relaxed in equanimity.

They are expanded and rigid in violent passions.

They quiver in excitement.

They are twitched up in disgust and contempt.

7. The Lips are drawn back and raised in delight and
mirth.

They are depressed and projected in pain, in sadness,
and grief.

The corners of the lips are curled upward in contempt, and downward in disgust.

The lips are loose and sprawling in mental vacuity.

They are muscular and mobile in intellectuality.

They are firm in decision and energy.

They are relaxed in weakness and irresolution.

They are pouted in boasting, and in pettishness.

They are bitten in vexation and discomfiture.

They are compressed in agony.

8. THE MOUTH is open in fear, in wonder, in listening, in languor, and in desire.
   It is shut in apathy, in pride, in boldness, and in sullenness.
   The jaw falls in melancholy.
   The teeth are gnashed in anger.
   The tongue is protruded in imbecility.
9. THE HEAD is erect in courage and confidence.
   It is crouched in fear.
   It is thrown back in pride and self-conceit.
   It hangs forward in humility.
   It is protruded in curiosity, and in short-sightedness.
   It lies to one side in bashfulness, in languor, or in indolence.
   It rolls or tosses in anger.
   It shakes in denial, and in sadness.
   It is jerked backward in invitation, forward in assent, and to one side in boasting, in threatening, or in dogmatism.
10. THE ARMS hang easily from the shoulders in grace.
    They droop listlessly in weakness and in humility.
    They are rigid in anger.
    They are folded across the chest or placed a-kimbo in self-complacence.
    They are held forward in entreaty.
    They are extended in welcome and in admiration.
    They are raised in appeal or in expectancy.
    They fall suddenly in disappointment.
    They are drawn back in aversion.
    They shrink and bend in terror.
11. THE HANDS are open and relaxed in graceful calmness.
    They are rigidly expanded in fear or horror.
    They are locked or clasped in emotion.
    They are wrung in anguish and clenched in anger.
    They are raised in supplication.
    They descend slowly in blessing.
    They fall with quiet vehemence in malediction or threatening.
    They are moved towards the body in invitation or in egotism.

They are pushed from the body in rejection or dis-
missal.

They start in astonishment.

They wave or clap in joy or approbation.

The palms are turned upwards in candour or sin-
cerity, and downwards in concealment or cunning.

They are turned outwards in defence, in apprehension, or in aversion, and inwards in boldness or
confidence.

The hand on the forehead indicates pain, confusion,
or mental distress ; on the crown of the head, gid-
diness or delirium ; on the side of the head, stupor ;
on the eyes, shame or grief.

Both hands similarly applied intensify the expression.

The hand supporting the cheek expresses languor or
weariness ; supporting the chin, meditation.

The hand laid on the breast appeals to conscience, or
indicates desire.

The hands crossed on the breast express meekness or
resignation.

The hand pressed on the upper part of the chest, or
beating it, expresses remorse, or acute bodily distress.

The hand on the lower part of the chest indicates
boldness or pride.

The back of one hand laid in the palm of the other
shows determination or obduracy.

The hands applied palm to palm express supplica-
tion.

The hands crossed palm to palm express resignation.

12. THE FINGERS are relaxed and slightly separated in
placidity.

They are rigidly separated in fear.

They are firmly bent in anger.

The forefinger directs attention to any object by
pointing ; with a falling motion of the hand it
reproves or warns ; applied successively to the
finger tips of the other hand, it enumerates.

Laid in the palm of the other hand, it specifies dog-
matically.

The fingers of both hands loosely applied tips to tips express accumulation or adjustment.

13. THE BODY held easily erect expresses courage and resolution.

Held stiffly erect, it denotes pride, haughtiness, or the assumption of dignity.

Thrown back, it indicates defiance.

Stooping forward, it denotes condescension, compassion, or humility.

Bending, it expresses respect, reverence, or salutation.

Prostrated, it denotes moral degradation or self-loathing.

14. THE LOWER LIMBS held straight and rigid indicate self-conceit or obstinacy.

Relaxed and bent, they show timidity, awkwardness, or frailty.

One limb slightly bent and the other straight, denote graceful ease.

The limbs shake in terror.

They kneel in prayer.

15. THE FEET pointing directly forward indicate boorishness.

Turned inward, they suggest deformity.

Close together, they denote timidity or awkwardness.

Separated by about the breadth of the foot, and with one heel in advance of, and pointing towards, the other heel, they show graceful ease.

The weight of the body supported on the retired foot denotes dignity, dislike, or carelessness ; on the advanced foot, familiarity, attention, or sympathy.

Separated by about the length of the foot, with the weight on the advanced foot, listening, appeal, or attack ; with the weight on the retired foot, disgust, horror, or defence ; with the weight supported equally on both feet, pomposity or bluster.

Frequent change denotes mental disturbance.

Starting, sudden apprehension or violent surprise.

Stamping, harsh authority, impatience or determination.

Advancing steps show energy or boldness ; retiring, alarm or fearfulness.

Light tiptoe steps express caution or secret intrusion ; heavy, striding steps, boasting or bravado.

III. SUMMARY OF THE GENERAL PRINCIPLES OF GESTICULATIVE EXPRESSION.

16. Motions towards the body indicate self-esteem, egotism, or invitation ; from the body, command or repulsion.

Expanding gestures express liberality, distribution, acquiescence, or candour ; contracting gestures, frugality, reserve or collection.

Rising motions denote suspension, climax or appeal ; falling motions, completion, declaration, or response.

A sudden stop in gesture expresses doubt, meditation or listening ; a sudden movement, decision or discovery.

A broad and sweeping range of gesture illustrates a general statement, or expresses boldness, freedom, and self-possession ; a limited range denotes diffidence or constraint or illustrates a subordinate point.

Rigidity of muscles denotes firmness, strength, or effort ; laxity, languor, or weakness ; slow motions are expressive of gentleness, caution, or deliberation ; quick motions, of harshness or temerity.

IV. PRINCIPLES OF GRACE.

17. The eye should generally accompany the motions of the hand ; but, in directing attention to any object, the eye will first merely glance towards it, and then fix itself on the person addressed, while the finger continues to point.

18. The head must not lean from side to side, as the gesture points ; nor must it rise and fall with the inflexions of the voice ; it should be kept moderately, but not rigidly, erect.

19. The motions of the arm must commence at the shoulder joint, not at the elbow ; the upper part of the arm should never rest in contact with the side.

20. The motions of the arms should not be accompanied by any action of the shoulders, or swaying of the body. Thus, in projecting forward one arm, the opposite shoulder must not retire ; or in raising one arm, the opposite shoulder must not be depressed. The shoulders should be kept square to the eye of the auditor, or to the centre of the auditors. The habit of shrugging the shoulders is ungraceful, and should be avoided.

21. A harmonious accompaniment of arm to arm, is essential to graceful motion. When only one arm is used in the gesture, the other should be brought into action less prominently, and at a lower elevation. When the gesticulating arm comes in front of, or across the body, the retired arm falls a little behind ; and when the gesture is backwards, the subordinate arm advances. When the gesture is under the horizontal elevation, the other arm may hang laxly by the side.

22. Every action of the arm should be terminated by an accentual motion of the hand, from the wrist. In calm and unimpassioned speaking, the accentual beat of the gesture will coincide with the vocal accent ; in strong emotion, the gesture will precede the words. The motions of the hand must be made entirely from the wrist joint, which must therefore be held perfectly slack.

23. Every accentual motion must have a preparatory movement in the opposite direction, more or less sweeping, according to the nature and emphasis of the accentual motion. A direct rise, fall, or lateral movement would be ungraceful and unnatural. As we first bend the body in order to leap up, and raise the hammer in order to strike the nail, so we must carry the hand towards the left, before a gesture to the right; raise it before a downward motion, and *vice versa*.

24. The line described by the hand in any motion must be a curve—except in violent passion, when the rigidity of the joints renders the line of motion straight and angular. The graceful curve is obtained by turning the hand freely upon its joint, keeping the wrist slack, and the elbow detached from the side.

25. The fingers should always be somewhat apart,

and the thumb considerably separated from the forefinger. The joints should be slack, and the fingers slightly
bent, but not beyond a gentle curve—except for particular expressiveness.

26. The weight of the body should generally be sustained entirely by one foot; and it should be shifted from
one to the other at every change of style or of subject.
The limb that does not support the weight of the body
should be slightly bent, and its foot should rest lightly,
or only partially, on the floor.

27. Gesture is most graceful with the right hand and
arm when the left foot is in advance, and with the left
hand when the right foot is in front.   This preserves the
square of the body.

28. The feet should be generally separated about as
much as the breadth of the foot—the one in advance of
the other, with its heel pointing to the heel of the retired
foot.   More extended positions will be occasionally required in expressive action. The angle at which the feet
stand should be about 75 degrees, unless in very extended
separations,—as in longeing,—when it may be increased
to 90 degrees. With ordinary extension, the angle of
grace and stability cannot exceed 75°.

29. The feet must not cross each other in any movement.   Their motions should always be in outward diag-
onal lines.   A direct lateral or front extension of the feet
would be ungraceful.   Even in walking, the left foot
must be moved towards the left, and the right towards
the right side.

30. In turning to one side, the body must not be twisted ;
but the motion should commence with the feet; and
the feet should not be lifted from the floor.   The weight
of the body being on the forepart of the feet, a turn of
45° may be made by merely sliding the heels round ; and
the weight being on the heels, a turn of 90° may be made
by sliding round the forepart of the feet.   These turns
can only be made to the side corresponding with the *retired* foot.   Thus :—when the right foot is in front,
turn to the left, and *vice versa*.   In order to turn to the
other side, the advanced foot must first be drawn back, or
the retired foot advanced.

31. In kneeling, bring that knee to the floor first which is next to the spectator; in rising, bring up the knee which is farthest from him.

32. In making a bow, do not shuffle one foot backwards, or jerk the head forwards, but extend one foot slightly to the side—the right foot to the right, or the left to the left—and draw (not lift) the other in the same direction, while you gracefully bend the body. The arms must not adhere to the side, but depend freely from the shoulders, limber as ropes.

33. In standing before a bar, or rail, or in a pulpit, do not lounge on the frame, or even keep the hand on it habitually; but stand back sufficiently far to allow the arm to rise and fall without touching the rail.

34. In holding a book, endeavour to do so with *one* hand—generally the left; but if the volume is too large for one hand, let both hands sustain it equally by the corners. In either case, let the plane of the book be as nearly as possible horizontal—and do not hold it up between your face and your auditor's line of vision.

35. In sitting, do not draw the feet backwards under the chair, but advance them, and keep the soles on the floor, with as much variety of position as may be consistent with grace and with the subject in hand.

V. RELATIVE POSITIONS OF THE HAND AND ARM IN MOTION.

36. The following illustrations exemplify a Principle of the utmost simplicity and comprehensiveness; one which in fact includes all that can be needed to secure mechanical excellence in any movements of Hand and Arm. The Principle is:—THE HAND INVARIABLY POINTS IN THE OPPOSITE DIRECTION TO THAT OF THE ARM'S MOTION.

37. The Hand, in RISING or FALLING, must be always in one of two positions; namely, with the edge, or with the flat presented to the eye of the spectator. Thus:—

No. I.

Arm rising—Hand hangs downward.

Edge presented.   Flat presented.

No. II.

Arm falling—Hand points upwards.

Edge presented.   Flat presented.

38. Any movement to right or left with the hand on *edge* is ungraceful ; therefore :—The hand, in moving to RIGHT or LEFT, must always have either the *palm* or the *back* turned upwards. Thus :—

No. III.

Arm moving to right—Hand points to left.

Palm upwards.   Back upwards.

No. IV.

Arm moving to left—Hand points to right.

Palm upwards.   Back upwards.

39. The principle exemplified in these illustrations should be practised until its application becomes a habit and requires no thought. The student is recommended, at first, to divide each motion into two parts—stopping at the end of the arm's motion before commencing that of the hand. Thus :—

Rising Motion.

1. Raise arm from position No. 1 towards position No. 2, while the hand remains pendent as in No. 1.
2. Raise hand into position No. 2.

Falling Motion.

1. Depress arm from position No. 2 towards position No. 1, while the hand continues to point upward.
2. Bring hand into position No. 1.

Motion to Right.

1. Move arm from position No. 3 towards position No. 4, while the hand continues pointing to left.
2. Move hand into position No. 4.

Motion to Left.

1. Move arm from position No. 4 towards position No. 3, while the hand continues pointing to right.
2. Move hand into position No. 3.

40. After a few repetitions of these exercises, the *knack* will be acquired of moving arm and hand separately—which is the essence of the Principle. The whole of each movement should then be performed without a break. Practise with each hand, alternately, and with both hands, simultaneously, until facility is attained.

VI. APPLICATION OF GESTURE.

41. INEXPRESSIVE motions should always be avoided. No gesture should be made without a reason for it; and when any position has been assumed, there should be no change from it without a reason. The habit of allowing the hands to fall to the side immediately after every gesture, produces an ungracefully restless effect. The speaker seems

> " Awkward, embarrassed, stiff, without the skill
> Of moving gracefully, or standing still.—
> Blessed with all other requisites to please,
> He wants the striking elegance of ease."

42. A speaker must not be constantly in motion. REPOSE is a chief element of gesticulative effect. Some orators accompany every vocal accent by a bodily motion; but the consequence is, that, gesticulate ever so well, and be energetic as they may, they can produce no effect—but that of mesmeric drowsiness. The monotonous manipulations fatigue the eye, and rock the brain to

slumber. A gesture that illustrates nothing is worse than useless. It destroys the effect of really appropriate movements. Perhaps the most difficult part of gesture is gracefully to STAND STILL. Let the speaker study this.

43. The FREQUENCY of gesture will depend on the variety of ideas, and moods that occur in the language. A uniform strain will require little gesture ; and a variable, flighty, passionate strain will demand many gestures.

44. Gestures should not be used to picture ideas which are sufficiently expressed—or implied—in language. For example :—

> " The moon was shining bright and high,
> The torches gleamed below."

> '· Cannon to right of them,
> Cannon to left of them.
> Cannon in front of them
> Volleyed and thundered."

In these cases, the relations of "high," "low," "right," "left," &c., are fully understood from the utterance of the words, and gestic illustration of the same facts would be tautology.

45. Gestures are either DIRECTIVE, ILLUSTRATIVE, or EMOTIVE. DIRECTIVE gestures carry the eye of the spectator to the objects spoken of, which are either visible, supposed to be visible, or figuratively presented to the " mind's eye." Directive gestures are most appropriate with language in the present tense. They are *necessary* when the demonstrative words, *Lo ! yon, this, that, behold !* &c., are used.

46. Directive gestures must be arranged with pictorial accuracy. Thus, the hand and eye must be elevated in pointing to the firmament, to mountains, and to near objects above the speaker ; and depressed below the horizontal elevation for rivers, and for near objects below the level of the speaker's eye. They must be horizontal in addressing persons around us, and in pointing to objects at a distance.

47. Directive gestures must be " suited " to the language. Thus, in the following lines :—

> " 'Tis morn but scarce yon level sun
> Can pierce the war-clouds rolling dun, " &c.

12

"The sun has almost reached his journey's close," &c.

we must not point upwards to the sun; for at "morn," and at his "journey's close," the sun must be near the horizon. Thus, too, in the following:—

> "His setting ushers-in a night to some,
> Which morning shall not break."

Suppose the setting sun located on the speaker's *right*, then "night" must be ushered in from his *left;* and "morning" must not "break" on the right, but—opposite to where the sun set,—on the left.

48. Having located any fixed object by a directive gesture, we must recur to the same point in again speaking of it, or of any object associated with it without change of scene. Thus in the following lines:

> "Scaling yonder peak,
> I saw an eagle wheeling near its brow
> O'er the abyss;—his broad, expanded wings
> Lay calm and motionless upon the air.
> As if he floated there without their aid,
> By the sole act of his unlorded will
> That buoyed him proudly up. Instinctively
> I bent my bow," &c.

If the "peak" be supposed on the speaker's left side, the action of bending the bow must not be directed to the right, but—towards the peak—to the left.

49. ILLUSTRATIVE gestures must be "suited" to the idea or action they illustrate. Thus in the following lines:—

> ' By torch and trumpet-sound arrayed.
> Each horseman drew his battle blade,
> And furious every charger neighed
> To join the dreadful revelry;"

the idea "arrayed" should be illustrated by a slow, horizontal expansion of the arm, the hand flat and pointing outwards, as if to the serried rank of soldiers; at the words "drew his battle blade," there may be an imitative action, but if indulged in it must be *correctly* imitative; the right arm, in drawing the sword, must not be curved backwards across the body, but drawn straight up, as if it had a yard of steel behind it. The hand must be reversed in taking hold of the hilt, and turned round when the act of drawing the blade is completed, as if to elevate the point in the air. The *left* hand—the " horseman's" bridle-hand,—must take no part in the action. In drawing an *infantry*-sword the left hand grasps the scabbard ; but a cavalry-sword has a heavy scabbard to resist the pull.

50. SHAKESPEARE'S admirable compendium of the principles of gestic application—

" Suit the action to the word, the word to the action, with this special observance, that you o'erstep not the modesty of nature !"

must not be so interpreted as to lead the speaker to aim at illustrating individual words. " To THE WORD," must be understood to mean, " TO THE UTTERANCE." The sort of imitative gesture, in which many orators indulge at the mere mention of any word which is susceptible of imitative illustration, is to be condemned, and must not be allowed to plead a misinterpretation of Shakespeare's rule as a justifying authority. Some speakers carry the principle of suiting the action to the " word " so far, that, if they would not imitate the sounding of a trumpet, and the neighing of a charger, in the lines quoted in the last paragraph, they do perform actions equally ridiculous in every sentence of their oratory.

51. EMOTIVE EXPRESSION will be, in a greater or less degree, associated with ALL GESTICULATION. The speaker's feelings, with respect to the object spoken of, should invariably find expression in his delivery. If the orator is thoroughly conversant with the expressiveness of the different varieties of gesture, and well exercised in the mechanical principles of graceful motion, he may trust to the spontaneous development of Emotive Gesture in his delivery, without fear of its being inappropriate.

52. All the parts of the body must blend in HARMONIOUS ACCOMPANIMENT to the Gesticulating member. Isolated motions are ungraceful and unnatural. The impulse that moves the hand will not be unfelt by every muscle in the frame. If gesture were practised merely as a mechanical art, this united expression might not be attained ; but the Mechanics of Action should be studied

chiefly for the sake of grace, and as a means to keep in
check the energy that might else run wild.   For

> "In the very tempest, torrent and. as I may say, whirlwind of
> your passion, you must acquire and beget a temperance that may
> give it smoothness."

A speaker who loses command over himself either in
language, intonation, or gesture, must not be surprised if
he preserve none over his audience.

    53. Gestures may be divided into COLLOQUIAL AND
ORATORICAL.   The difference between the two classes
arises only from the comparative proximity or distance of
speaker and hearer.   In the former class the arm is bent,
and held near the side,—although not in contact with it,
and the action is chiefly confined to the *hand;* in the
latter class, the arm—the "oratorical weapon,"—is fully
unfolded, advanced from the body, and moved directly
from the shoulder.

    54. With reference to the application of Gesture, the
following is a grand precept :—

> "To this one standard make your just appeal,
>   Here lies the golden secret,—*Learn to feel!*"

VII. EXAMPLES OF THE APPLICATION OF GESTURE.

    55. The following Examples are added as Illustrations
of the mode of applying Gesture.   The aim of the prescribed actions is simply to realize the scene.   This indeed is the principle of all oratorical action.   The Shake-
sperian precept, "Suit the action to the word," being—
as we have shown—liable to a serious misapplication, its
true meaning will be unambiguously conveyed by the
equally laconic direction, REALIZE THE SCENE.

LOCHINVAR.—*Scott.*

    I. ¹O young Lochinvar is come out of the west!   Through all
the wide Border his steed was the best; and, save his good broad-
sword, he weapon had none; he rode all unarmed. and he rode
all alone!   So faithful in love, and so dauntless in war, there
never was knight like the young Lochinvar!
    ²He staid not for brake. and he stopped not for stone; he swam
the Esk river where ford there was none ;—but, ³ere he alighted at
Netherby gate, the bride had consented !—the gallant came late :

for ⁴a laggard in love, and a dastard in war, was to wed ⁵the fair Ellen of brave Lochinvar!

⁶So boldly he entered the Netherby Hall, ⁷'mong bride's-men, and kinsmen, and brothers, and all: II. ⁶Then spoke the bride's father, his hand on his §word— ⁷for the poor, craven bridegroom said never a word— ⁹ "O, come ye in peace here, or come ye in war?—¹⁰or to dance at our bridal,—young Lord Lochinvar?"

¹¹ "I long wooed your daughter, my suit you denied: love swells like the Solway, but ¹²ebbs like its tide! And now am I come, ¹³with this lost love of mine, to lead but one measure, drink one cup of wine!—There are maidens in Scotland ¹⁴more lovely by far, ⁶that would gladly be bride to the young Lochinvar!"¹⁵

¹⁶The bride kissed the goblet! the knight took it up; he quaffed off the wine, and he·threw down the cup! She looked down to blush, and she looked up to sigh—with a smile on her lip, and a tear in her eye. ¹⁷He took her soft hand, ¹⁸ere her mother could bar,—⁸ "Now tread we a measure!" ¹⁹said young Lochinvar.

²⁰ So stately his form, and so lovely her face, that never a hall such a galliard did grace! While her mother ²¹did fret, and her father ²²did fume, ²³and the bridegroom stood ²⁴dangling his bonnet and plume; ²⁵and the bride-maidens whispered, ²⁶ "'Twere better by far to have matched our fair cousin with ²⁷young Lochinvar!"

²⁸One touch to her hand, and one word in her ear, when they reached ²⁹the hall-door, ³⁰and the charger stood near;—³¹so light to the croupe the fair lady he swung, so light to the saddle before her he sprung! ³² "She is won! ³³we are gone, over bank, bush, and scaur! they'll have ³⁵fleet steeds that follow!" ¹⁹quoth young Lochinvar.

³⁴There was mounting 'mong Græmes of the Netherby clan; Fosters, Fenwicks, and Musgraves, they rode and they ran; there was racing and chasing ³⁵on Cannobie Lea—but the lost bride of Netherby ne'er did they see. ³⁶So daring in love, and so dauntless in war, ³⁷have ye e'er heard of gallant ³⁸like young Lochinvar?³⁹

Pictorial Arrangement.—I. Lochinvar on the left—Netherby on the right. II. The father on Lochinvar's right—the bridegroom on the left—the bride and the mother in front.

Details of action, &c.—¹Looking with admiration to left alternately with speaking to front. ²energetic tone with accentual swaying of the head. ³quiet undertone to front—indicating the position of Netherby by a motion of the head to the right. ⁴strong tone of denunciation. ⁵clasping the hands, or otherwise expressing disappointment and determination. ⁶to right. ⁷alternately to left and right. ⁸to left. ⁹turn and speak to left. ¹⁰with mocking courtesy. ¹¹turn and speak to right. ¹²pointing to the breast. ¹³carelessly tossing the head to left. ¹⁴looking askance to left. ¹⁵a contemptuous nod, then turn to left. ¹⁶look to left alternately with speaking to front, as if describing to the audience what is taking place. ¹⁷turning to left · nd extending left hand. ¹⁸looking smilingly to right. ¹⁹to front. ²⁰stepping backwards, as if to make room, and carrying the eye from left to right, as if following the motion of the dancers. ²¹imitative sound of vexation. ²²panting with anger, and grasping the scabbard with left hand, while repeatedly opening and closing the right hand. ²³pointing with the thumb to the left, and looking in

the opposite direction. [24]imitative—supporting the right arm in the left hand and
dang'ng the right hand from the wrist, keeping time to the action with a motion
of the head. [25]pointing and looking to front with face averted. [26]applying the back
of right hand to the left corner of the mouth, and speaking in an undertone. [27]in-
dicating his position by looking askance to left, and nodding the head in that direction. [28]speaking to front in a semi-whisper [29]pointing and looking askance
to left. [30]to front with look of eager surprise. [31]quick utterance in undertone progressively intensified. [32]loud tone, with action as if drawing the bridle in the left
hand. [33]backward action of right hand, as if urging the steed with a whip. [34]in-
dicate commotion on all sides by alternately moving the right hand to the right and
the left hand to the left. [35]both hands pointing to front. [36]looking to front and
pointing left hand to left. [37]right hand extended open to front. [38]both hands
pointing to left. [39]bow.

HAMLET'S MEDITATION ON DEATH.—*Shakespeare.*

[1]To be, or not to be? [2]that [3]is the question : [4]whether 'tis nobler
in the mind to suffer the stings and arrows of outrageous fortune,
or to take arms against a sea of troubles, and by opposing, [5]end
them ;[6]—To die?—[2]to sleep—no more ;—and, by a sleep, to say we
end the heart-ache, and the thousand natural shocks that flesh is
heir to—'tis a consummation [7]devoutly to be wished. [8]To die?
—[9]to sleep :—[9]to sleep?—[10]perchance to dream—[3]Ay, [2]there's the
rub! For [11]in that sleep of death [12]what dreams may come, when
we have shuffled off this mortal coil, [3]must give us pause ; [13]there's
the respect that makes calamity of so long life : [6]for who would
bear the whips and scorns of time, the oppressor's wrong, the
proud man's contumely, the pangs of despised love, the law's
delay, the insolence of office, and the spurns that patient merit
of the unworthy takes, when [14]he himself might his quietus make
with a bare [15]bodkin?[3] Who would fardels bear, to groan and
sweat under a weary life ; but that the dread of something [16]after
death—[3]that undiscovered country, from whose bourn no travel-
ler returns—[2]puzzles the will, and makes us [17]rather bear those
ills we have, [18]than fly to others [19]that we know not of?[3] Thus
conscience does make cowards of us all ; and thus the native hue
of resolution is [20]sicklied o'er with the pale cast of [21]thought, and
enterprises of great pith and moment; [16]with this regard, their
currents turn awry, [22]and lose [23]the name[6] of action.[24]

[1]Standing for some seconds before speaking, with the right elbow supported in
the left hand, the forefinger and thumb of the right hand supporting the chin,—or
in any attitude of meditation—with the eyes fixed on vacancy. [2]an accentual nod
of the head. [3]shaking the head. [4]letting the right hand fall on the left arm.
[5]extend the arms with the accent—palms downwards. [6]rest. [7]look upwards
with desire. [8]meditative attitude—the arms extended downward—palms downwards and fingers interlaced, the head lying to one side. [9]head quickly erected.
[10]looking uneasily forward, with raised eyebrows and open mouth. [11]head depressed, eyes raised. [12]raising the head progressively. [13]pointing demonstra-
tively upwards. [14]extending the right hand in front. [15]an accentual stroke of the
right hand towards the left side, as if pointing to a dagger or sword. [16]slowly raising the head and eyes. [17]extending both arms—hands open. [18]turning the hands
round and elevating them from the wrist. [19]raising the arms to the level of the
head, and dropping them to rest with an accentual sigh. [20]moving the right hand
to and fro in front—palm downward. [21]throwing out the right hand obliquely, and
shaking the head. [22]extending both arms and raising the hands—palm outward.
[23]a gentle accentual stroke of the hands forwards. [24]bow.

THE DEATH OF MARMION.—*Sir Walter Scott.*

(I.) 'With fruitless labour, Clara bound, ²and strove to staunch, the gushing wound: ³the monk, ⁴with unavailing cares. ⁵exhausted all the Church's prayers; ⁶Ever, he said, that, ⁷close and near, a lady's voice was in his ear, and that the priest⁸ he could not hear, for that she ever sung—⁹ "In the lost battle, borne down by the flying, where mingles war's rattle, with groans ¹⁰of the dying!" ¹¹so the notes rung.

¹² "Avoid thee, Fiend!—with cruel hand, shake not the dying sinner's sand! ¹³Oh, look, my son, upon yon sign of the Redeemer's grace divine! ¹⁴oh, think on faith, and bliss! ¹⁵By many a death-bed I have been, and many a sinner's parting seen, but never aught ¹⁶like this."

(II.) ¹⁷The war, that for a ´space did fail, now trebly thundering, swell'd the gale, and ¹⁸" Stanley!" was the cry: ¹⁹A light on Marmion's visage spread, and fir'd his glazing eye; with dying hand, above his head he shook the fragment of his blade, and shouted, ²⁰" Victory! ²¹Charge! Chester!—Charge! ²²On! Stanley! on!"²³ ²⁴were the last words of Marmion.²⁵

Pictorial Arrangement.—I. Marmion lying on the ground in the centre—facing the speaker—Clara kneeling by his side to the right—the monk standing beside him, to the left.   II. The battlefield to the extreme left.

Details of action, &c.—¹Pointing downwards with right forefinger to Clara, on right of centre. ²open the hand. ³pointing horizontally with left forefinger to left of centre. ⁴r ising the hand and looking downwards sympathetically to centre. ⁵the hand falling to rest with the accent—the head shaking. ⁶pointing downwards to centre with right hand. ⁷the eyes fixed on vacancy. ⁸shaking the head. ⁹slow utterance—muffled voice—listening attitude. ¹⁰feebly nodding the head. ¹¹looking around at the audience. ¹²the left arm extended in front—palm downward—as if shielding the prostrate man; the right arm extended backward—the palm outward—as in repulsion. ¹³looking to Marmion and raising the right forefinger. ¹⁴clasping the hands. ¹⁵averting the head—to right. ¹⁶drawing back the head and looking fearfully askance at Marmion. ¹⁷look suddenly with raised eyebrows to the extreme left. ¹⁸pointing with left hand in the same direction. ¹⁹pointing abruptly with right hand to Marmion. ²⁰with the action previously described—shaking the sword. ²¹the left hand downwards as if supporting the body—panting utterance. ²²raise both hands eagerly. ²³drop both arms suddenly—rest—²⁴point with both hands to Marmion, and shake the head mournfully while speaking. ²⁵bow.

AN ORATOR'S FIRST SPEECH IN PARLIAMENT.—*Alex. Bell.*

¹The virgin Member ²takes his honoured place, ³while beams of modest wisdom light his face : multum in parvo in the man you see; he represents—³the people's majesty! 'Behold their choice! the pledged, 'midst many a cheer, to give free ⁴trade! ⁵free votes! ⁶free bread and beer! Blest times!—⁷He sits at last within the walls of famed St. Stephen's venerated halls! ⁸O, shades of Pitt and Fox! ⁹is he within the House of Commons? ⁹How his senses spin! Proud man! ¹⁰has he then caught the Speaker's eye? ¹¹no, not just yet—but he will, by-and-by. 'I wonder if there are reporters here? ¹²Ay, that there are, and hard at work they appear. ¹³O happy man! By the next post shall reach your loved constituents, ¹⁴the maiden speech! The Press (great tell tale!) will to all reveal, ¹⁵how you have—spoken

for your Country's weal! In gaping wonder will the words be read, [14]"The new M. P., Lord Noodle, rose, and said."

This pillar of "ten-pounders" rises now, and towards the Speaker [16]makes profoundest bow. [17]Unused to so much honour, his weak knees bend with the weight of senate-dignities. [18]He staggers—almost falls-—stares—[19]strokes his chin—clears out his throat, and ventures to begin. [19]"Sir, I am sensible"[20] (some titter near him)—[19]"I am, Sir, sensible" [21]"Hear, hear!" [22](they cheer him!) [23]Now bolder grown, for praise mistaking pother, [6]tea-pots one arm, and spouts out with the other. "I am, Sir, sensible—I am, indeed—that, though—I should—want—words— [24]I must proceed; and, for the first time in my life [25]I think—I think—that—no great orator—[26]should shrink:—and, therefore, —Mr. Speaker—I for one—[27]will speak out freely. [28]Sir—I've not yet done. [29]Sir, in the name of those enlightened men who sent me here to [30]speak for them-—why then, to do my duty—as I said before—to my constituency—[31]I'll say no more."

Pictorial Arrangement.—The House of Commons. The "Virgin Member" on the right—the "Speaker" in front—reporters' gallery to left of centre—the interrupting members on the left side.

Details of action, &c.—[1]Look and point with right forefinger to the "virgin member," then speak to front. [2]open the hand. [3]expand both arms. [4]upward wave to right. [5]upward wave to left. [6]a confidential communication—the hand covering the mouth. [7]look around with pride. [8]clasping the hands. [9]hand on forehead. [10]a quiet undertone to front. [11]look to right and centre, and right again before speaking. [12]look upwards to left. [13]swaying the head rapturously. [14]point with the open right hand as if at a paper in the left hand. [15]point to the speech with the right forefinger. [16]imitative. [17]point to right, and speak to front jocularly. [18]look to right before speaking to front. [19]to centre, with obeisance. [20]look annoyed to left side then speak smilingly to front. [21]look amused to left. [22]point to left, and speak mirthfully to front. [23]look archly to front. [24]look with a contemptuous shrug to left before speaking. [25]look bewildered and glance with an air of annoyance to left before speaking. [26]frowning to left. [27]with a determined side jerk of the head. [28]look to left with an air of triumph, then speak to front. [29]proudly. [30]hesitating. [31]look disconcertedly to left, then speak lugubriously.

RUSTIC LOGIC.—*Anonymous.*

(I.) [1]Hodge, a poor honest country lout, not over-stocked with learning, chanced on a summer's eve [2]to meet the Vicar, home returning. [3]"Ah! Master Hodge," the Vicar cried, "what, still as wise as ever? [4]the people in the village say that you are wondrous clever." [5]"Why, Measter Parson, as to that I beg you'll right conceive me. [6]I do na brag, but yet 'I knaw a thing or two, believe me." [7]"We'll try your skill," [8]the Parson cried, [9]"for learning what digestion : and this you'll prove or right or wrong, by solving me a question. [10]Noah, of old, three babies had, or grown-up children rather; [11]Shem, Ham, and Japhet they were called;—now [12]who was Japhet's father?"

[13]"Rat it!" cried Hodge, and scratched his head; " that does my wits belabour : but howsomde'er I'll [14]homeward run, and ax old Giles my neighbour."

[15]To Giles he went, and put the case with circumspect intention : (II.) [16]"Thou fool," cried Giles, " I'll make it clear to thy

dull comprehension. Three children has Tom Long, the smith,
or cattle-doctor rather; Tom, Dick, and Harry, they are called;
[6]"now, who is Harry's father?"
    [17]"Adzooks, I have it," Hodge replied, "right well I know
your lingo; who's Harry's father?[18]—stop—[17]here goes,—why
Tom Long, smith, by jingo."
    (III.) [19]Away he ran to find the priest, with all his might and
main; who with good humour instant put the question once again.
[10]"Noah, of old, three babies had, or grown-up children rather;
[11]Shem, Ham, and Japhet they were called: now [20]who was
Japhet's father?"
    [21]"I have it now," [22]Hodge grinning cried, [23]"I'll answer like
a proctor: [24]who's Japhet's father? [25]now I know; why, Long
Tom, smith, the doctor."[26]

Pictorial Arrangement.—I. Hodge coming from left meets the Vicar coming from
    right. II. Giles stands on Hodge's right. III. Hodge runs towards the
    Vicar on the right.

Details of action, &c.—[1]Look and point to left, then speak to front. [2]giving
a rustic salute to right. [3]turn and speak to left with raised eyebrows. [4]pout the
lips, depress the eyebrows, and shake the head. [5]turn and speak smilingly to
right. [6]with raised eyebrows. [7]smiling and jerking the head to one side. [8]speak
to front without turning the body. [9]speak to left. [10]very deliberately. [11]striking
the thumb, fore and middle fingers of left hand with right forefinger, in pronouncing the names. [12]repeating the last stroke and accentually nodding the head.
[13]turn and speak to right with puzzled expression and "scratching" action.
[14]point backwards over the shoulder with the thumb of left hand. [15]pointing to
left, and speaking amusedly to front. [16]to left with knitted brow and giving Hodge
a dig with the thumb. [17]slapping the leg or otherwise expressing vulgar triumph.
[18]chuckle, then change to a wandering silent look of serious stupidity. [19]point to
right, and speak smilingly to front. [20]repeatedly strike the middle finger while
speaking, [21]chuckling and rubbing the legs, or otherwise expressing vulgar delight.
[22]jerk the head to one side triumphantly, then speak to front. [23]panting, as if
from quick running. [24]with the head lying knowingly to one side. [25]with a nod
of pride. [26]a chuckle of self satisfaction suddenly changed to a look of puzzled
disappointment—then look to the audience while you point laughingly to Hodge,
and make your bow.

VIII. NOTATION OF GESTURE.

56. A system of Notation for Attitude and Motion is
presented in the following pages.   By this means a
speaker can record for practice any position or movement
which, in Oratory, in Painting, or in Sculpture, strikes
him as effective.   By this, also, an artist can jot for re-
production any attitude of which he may have obtained
a momentary glimpse.   To teachers of Gesture the system of Notation will be of great service, in furnishing a
nomenclature for the mechanics of action; and to students it will be found of considerable assistance in the acquisition of variety and precision of movement.

57.   *Positions of the Feet.*

The following diagram illustrates the positions and
shifts of the feet:—

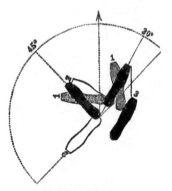

Explanation.

No. 1. A turn on the ball of the foot from the position indicated by the black feet.

No. 2. A turn on the heel from the same position.

No. 3. Preparatory shift for turning to the opposite side.

58. When the right foot is in front, these turns can only be made to the left; and when the left foot is in front the turns can only be made to the right. A circle may be traversed, as an exercise, by shifting one foot after each turn. The circle will be completed in four turns on the heel, or eight turns on the ball of the foot.

When the feet are separated by the breadth of a foot the positions are noted:

Right foot in front.	Left foot in front.
R 1	L 1
R 2	L 2

When the feet are separated by the length of a foot the positions are noted :—

R 3	L 3
R 4	L 4

When the feet are more widely separated the positions are noted :—

R 5	L 5
R 6	L 6

In these notations the weight of the body is on the retired foot for the odd numbers (1, 3, 5) and on the advanced foot for the even numbers (2, 4, 6).

Vertical and Transverse Motions of the Arms.

59. Either arm may move with grace to the extent of a SEMI-CIRCLE, both vertically and horizontally. For NOTATION, five points are selected—the *extremities* of the semi-circle, the *middle*, and a point *intermediate* to the middle and each extreme.

60. The extremities of the *vertical* semi-circle are the *zenith* and the *nadir* (marked *z* and *n*) ; the middle point is the *horizontal* (*h*) ; and the other intermediate points are :—*elevated* half-way to the zenith (*e*), and *downwards* half-way to the nadir (*d*). When the arm hangs at *rest*, it is of course directed to the nadir. The notation N is used to distinguish the rest position from the *gesture*, *n*.

61. The extremities of the *transverse* semi-circle are :—the arm *across the body* (*c*), and *backward* about 30 degrees (*b*) : the other points are :—the arm *extended* in a line with the shoulders (*x*) ; projected in *front* of the body (*f*), and directed *obliquely* between the front and the extended positions (*q*). The diagram illustrates these notations :

Graceful and Passionate Transitions.

62. Gestures would be disagreeably angular if the most direct line of transition from point to point were followed by the arms.   A preparatory movement is therefore made, in the opposite direction, before any important gesture.

63. In unimpassioned delivery the preparatory movement may be sweeping and varied, for graceful effect.

64. In strong passion the preparatory movement will be direct and simple, but extensive, and the lines of the accentual gesture bold and straight.

IX. GENERAL SCHEME OF NOTATION FOR ATTITUDE AND MOTION.

65.   I. *The Feet, Lower Limbs, and Trunk.*
(Notation placed below the line).

R 1;   R 2;   R 3;   R 4;   R 5;   R 6; ⎫
L 1;   L 2;   L 3;   L 4;   L 5;   L 6. ⎬ See p. 186.
                                                 ⎭

ad...advancing	sh .. shaking	+...standing with one
re...retiring	wk...walking	foot across the other
r.....stepping to right	kn.. kneeling	up...b o d y drawn up,
l.....stepping to left	bw...bowing	as in pride
st...starting	crt...curtseying	dn...body sunk down,
sp ...stamping		as in languor

NOTE.—I. The right foot is *in front* for the R series, and the left, f r the L series. The weight of the body rests *on the foot in front* for all the *even* numbers, and on the *retired* foot for the *odd* numbers.

II. A small *number* should be prefixed to the notation for *advancing, retiring,* stepping to the *right,* or to the *left,* when more than one step is to be made. Thus ²ad, *advancing two* steps, ³re, *retiring three* steps.

66.   *The Arms.*

(All the subsequent notations placed above the line.)

z ...pointing to the zenith	c...directed across the body
e...elevated 45° above the horizon	f... " forwards
h...horizontal	q... " obliquely 45°from f
d...downwards 45 ° below the	x...extended in the line of the
horizon	shoulders
n...pointing to the nadir	b...directed backwards

N (nadir) . the arm hanging at rest.

---

pp....preparatory movement	de.....descending
con...the arm contracted	r ......moving to the right
exp... " " expanded	l.......moving to the left
as ....ascending	pj.....the arm projected

bk....the arm drawn back
rb ....rebound from any position to the same again
dr.....the arms drooping
fd......the arms folded
kim...à kimbo
shr....shrinking
tr......tremulous

wv....waving
w......lying close to the waist
sl......slow motion
qk.....quick motion
⌒(or oc) over curve
⌣(or uc) under curve
ouc or uoc...serpentine

67.   III.— *The Hands.*

nt ...naturally opened
s ....supine, (palm upwards)
p.....prone, (palm downwards)
o.....palm outwards
i.....palm inwards
v.....raised vertically
do...turned downwards
ix....indexing or pointing
rv ...hands revolving

sh....shaking
ch....clinched
str...striking
gr....grasping
in....moved inwards, as in invitation
ou....moved outwards (from the wrist)

---

ap ...both hands applied palm to palm
tip...fingers of both hands spread and applied tip to tip
en...enumerating (the r i g h t forefinger touching successively the left finger tips)

pal...striking the left palm with the right forefinger or hand
cr....hands crossed
cl....hands clasped
wr....hands wrung
clp...clapping

NOTE.—I. When the *left* hand or arm is meant, a *line is prefixed* to the symbolic letter. Thus:—d q signifies LEFT HAND, *downwards, oblique.*

II. A *colon* is placed between any two sets of letters that refer to the different hands. Thus—d q : z, signifies LEFT HAND, *downwards, oblique,* and RIGHT HAND *pointing to the zenith:* d q :—N signifies RIGHT HAND *downwards, oblique,* LEFT HAND *falling to rest.* The several symbols are separated from each other by spaces or points.

III. A small ² prefixed to the notation will indicate that BOTH HANDS perform the same motion.

IV. *Alternation* is denoted by the letter a. A number prefixed shows how often the alternation is repeated. Thus h c⌒q ²a, signifies *right hand horizontal, across the body,* whence *overcurved to the oblique position ;*—the *left hand alternately with the right, performing the same motion twice* to the opposite side. The notation a a may be used for *again and again.*

V. *Imitative* gestures are expressed by the general symbol im.

68. IV.—*Parts of the Body on which the Hands may be placed.*

He ...hand on head
Fo.... " forehead
Te.... " temple
Ey.... " eyes
Mo... " mouth
Li....finger on lip

Ck....hand supporting cheek
Cn ... " " chin
Br.... " on hreast
Bbr... " beating the breast
Bk.... " behind the back

NOTE.—A small ² prefixed to either of these will denote both hands. Thus :—
²Ey signifies *both hands on the eyes;* ²Bk, *both hands behind the back.*

69.   V.—*The Head and Face.*

B......head thrown back	Ts....head tossing
Cr..... " crouched	Sh ... " shaking
I....... " inclined to one side	Nd... " nodding
Il...... " " to left	Av... " averted from the di-
Ir...... " " to right	rection of the gesture
H...... " hanging down	Sm..a smiling countenance
Fr.....frowning	F.....eyes looking in front
Lu....lugubrious	Ar ... " around
Lau ..laughing	As ... " askance
Lf.....eyebrows lifted	St....staring
Dp.... " depressed	We...weeping
Kn ... " knitted	Wi...winking
R......eyes looking to the right	V.....eyes fixed on vacancy
L...... " " left	Cl.... " closed
U...... " " upwards	Mr... " measuring (See par. 5)
D...... " " downwards	No...nostrils turned up
Pt.....lips pouted	O....mouth open
Bt..... " bitten	Gn...teeth gnashed
Cp.... " compressed	

X. ORDER OF SYMBOLIC ARRANGEMENT.

70. The symbolic letters being in all cases different, no confusion could arise whatever order of notation might be adopted; but when several letters have to be employed, the following order should be observed, as more convenient than a random arrangement.

71. Place *first* the notation of the *vertical* situation of the *arm* (z e h d n); then of its *transverse* direction (c f q x b); next of the manner of presentation or motion of the *hand;* and the other symbols in the most convenient order.

72. The notations of the " Parts of the Body on which the Hands may be placed," and of the Expressions of the " Head and Face," are in CAPITAL letters; all the others (written above the line) are in *small* letters.

73. The compound symbols will be easily remembered, as they generally suggest at once the words of which they are contractions; but the *single letters* directly tax the memory. For convenience of reference, all the symbols written above the line are collected in the following

Recapitulative Table of Symbolic Letters:

a.........alternation	ad......advancing
aa.......again and again	ap......applied

as......ascending
b.......backward
bk......drawn back
bw.....bowing
c........across
ch .....clinched
cl.......clasped
clp ....clapping
con ....contracted
cr ......crossed
crt.....curtseying
d.......downward
de .....descending
dn .....sunk down
do .....turned downwards
dr......drooping
e........elevated
en......enumerating
exp....expanded
f........forward
fd ......folded
gr......grasping
h.......horizontal
i........inward
in......moved inwards
ix ......indexing
kim....a kimbo
kn .....kneeling
l........to left
n.......to nadir
nt .....naturally
o.......outward

oc .....over-curve
ou......moved outwards
ouc ....over and under-curve
p ....prone
pal ....striking palm
pj ......projected
pp......preparatory
q ....oblique
qk......quick
r........to right
rb......rebound
rv......revolving
s........supine
sh......shaking
shr ....shrinking
sl.......slow
sp .....stamping
st.......starting
str.....striking
tip.....tip to tip
tr.......tremulous
uc .....under-curve
uoc ...under and over-curve
up......drawn up
v ....vertical
w.......to waist
wk ....walking
wr .....wringing
wv ....waving
x ....extended
z........zenith

Ar.....looking around
As..... " askance
Av.....eyes averted
B.......head back
Bbr ...beating breast
Bk ....hands behind back
Br..... " on breast
Bt.....biting lips
Ck ....hand on cheek
Cl.....eyes closed
Cn.....hand on chin
Cp.....lips compressed
Cr.....head crouched
D .....eyes down
Dp.....eyebrows depressed
Ey ....hand on eyes

F ......looking in front
Fo.....hand on forehead
Fr......frowning
Gn.....gnashing teeth
H ......head hanging
He ....hand on head
I........head inclined
Il....... " " to left
Ir ......head inclined to right
Kn.....brows knitted
L.......looking to left
Lau ...laughing
Lif.....eyebrows lifted
Li......hand on lip
Lu ....lugubrious
Mo ....hand on mouth

Mr ....eyes measuring	St .....staring
No ....nostrils lifted	Te.....hand on temple
Nd.....nodding	Ts......tossing head
O ......mouth open	U.......looking upward
Pt.....pouting	V.......vacant aspect
R ......looking to right	We ....weeping
Sh.....shaking head	Wi ....winking
Sm ....smiling	

74. The following passages are *marked*, as Exercises in the Notation. The subject does not require lengthened illustration. Gesture should not be made too studied, or rigidly systematical ; FREEDOM—the chief characteristic of grace—would be destroyed in the attempt to follow a minutely directive notation. Let every motion be in itself expressive and graceful, and scope may be left for *spontaneity* of application.

XI. ILLUSTRATIONS OF THE NOTATION OF GESTURE.

MACBETH TO THE DAGGER-VISION.—*Shakespeare.*

h q p shr
Is this a dagger ⌊which I see before me ?—
st R3

                                    pj   gr
The handle towards my hand ?—Come, let me clutch thee :—
R4   L2   r R2

    h q s   St
I have thee not;—and yet I see thee still !
R1
Dp   o pj
Art thou not, fatal vision, sensible
R2

                              ix
To feeling as to sight ?—or art thou but
                          R1

                          rb
A dagger of the mind ?—a false creation

          F
Proceeding from the heat-oppressed brain ?⌒

    e q
I see thee yet;—in form as palpable
R2
      Im
As this which now I draw.

—h c.......to.......q sl   —ix
Thou marshal'st me the way that I was going;
L3

—pp   —e q
And⌒such an instrument I was to use.
R1
  Sh²h con   ²pj⌒d
Mine eyes are made the fools o' the other senses,
  L1   L2
qk cl   e q   qk – h q ix
Or else worth all the rest :—I see thee still !
L1   R2   L3
—v as   —h q con   —pj h q   —c
And⌒on thy blade and dudgeon, gouts of blood . . .
                                          L5
—w
Which was not so before !—
  R2
                          Ar h q v   Sh
                                 There's no such thing :—
                                 L1
Kn   ch Bbr   —c q
It is the bloody business, which informs
                                    L2
—r l   N
Thus to mine eyes.   Now o'er the one-half world
                        R1

Nature seems dead, and wicked dreams abuse

The curtained sleep.   Now witchcraft celebrates
                        R2

Pale Hecate's offering, and withered murder

Alarumed by his sentinel the wolf
R1

Whose howl's his watch, thus, with his stealthy pace,
                        R2

With Tarquin's ravishing strides, toward his design
                                    l
                             ²d q
Moves like a ghost.   Thou sure and firm-set earth
ad   l   R2
  r:—l   shr ch
Hear not my steps which way they walk—for fear

          2 dx
The very stones prate of my whereabout !

      2 pj v   e f v
And take the present horror from the time
                      R1
     cl
Which now suits with It.

13

w   —h q p
I go, and it is done :⌒the bell invites me.⌒
R₂   —ad
Fr
Hear it not, Duncan, for it is a knell

          —z ix   —rv: d b
That summons thee . . . to heaven or to hell.

MARCO BOZZARIS.—*F. G. Halleck.*

d q ix
At midnight, in his guarded tent,
  L₁
          rb
  The Turk was dreaming . . . of the hour

          s   pp   d q ch sh
When Greece, her knee in suppliance bent,

          con   pj
  Should tremble at his power;

h q ix   c   to f   to   q⌒to   x s
In dreams, through camp and court he bore
          L₂   L₁
      rv   ev
  The trophies of a conqueror;
                  L₃
      ix   Sm
In dreams, his song of triumph heard—
  L₂
R   h q o
Then, wore that monarch's signet-ring—

      pp   ,d str   ²h ⌒ ‿eq
Then, press'd that monarch's throne—a king l—
                              r R₂
N
As wild his thoughts, and gay of wing,

      Sh
  As Eden's garden bird !⌒
      R₁

  —h q ix
At midnight, in the forest shades,
      R₂
—r p   —l p
Bozzaris ranged his Suliote band,

—s   nt
True as the steel of their tried blades,

  —rb   ch as   h q str
  Heroes in heart and hand.
      L₂ up   R₁

  —hq ix
There had the Persians' thousands stood,
   L1
 pp as   —d q ix str
There had the glad earth drunk their blood

   —ch rb
  On old Platæa's day;
    L2 up
qk—h q s: h f s pp   2e q o
And now these breathed that haunted air—
  L1
       rb
The sons of sires who conquered there—

   ch con str: —ch Br:
With arm to strike, and soul to dare,
   L2   L1
      2c⌢x
  As quick, as far as they !⌒
   2̱d L2

N   h q ix
An hour passed on :—the Turk awoke ;—
L1
 v as
  That bright dream⌒was his last ;—
        dn
 As   —w
He woke—to hear his sentries shriek—
re L3
  R e q v   —ix   x q
" To arms !—they come !—the Greek !—the Greek !"

   N   c   x
He woke—to die,⌒midst flame, and ⌒smoke,
   R1 dn   R2
—c ⌒x:
And shout, and groan, and sabre stroke,
   R2
2h con
And death-shots falling thick and fast,
  R 1

Like forest-pines before the blast,

  pj⌣z
Or lightnings from the mountain-cloud ; . . .
  R2
  cl L
And heard—with voice as trumpet loud,—
  . re L3
 —h q:
  Bozzaris cheer his band :—

  c⌒h⌣e q ch str
" Strike !—till the last armed foe expires—
(L4) L3
c⌣e q   tr
Strike—for your altars and your fires—
 stp

—d h‿z   tr
Strike!—for the green graves of your sires—

    ²z U   ²exp ou
God,—and your native land!"⌢

 ²h fs   p   x
They fought, like brave men, long and well,
        L4
      ²‿f s as
They piled that ground with Moslem slain,—

      e cl   con
They conquered! . . . but Bozzaris fell,
                L3
    Sh
Bleeding at every vein.

  ² h q
His few surviving comrades saw

    Sm —d f: wv
His smile, when rang their proud hurrah,
                                L4

    And the red field was won;

pp   h cr
Then saw in death his eyelids close,
                L1

Calmly as to a night's repose,

    N
Like flowers at set of sun.

D—w: f e
Bozzaris! She who gave thee birth
        R1

Will, by the pilgrim-circled hearth

                        rj ou
    Talk of thy doom without a sigh;
            R2
          ²d q exp   2 e q
For thou art Freedom's now, and Fame's;

        rb   z f
One of the few, the immortal names,
            R1
          —h to —d q
    That were not born to die!
                L2 (bw)

PRINCIPLES OF ELOCUTION.

PART SIXTH.

THE LANGUAGE OF PASSION.

1. A special search for illustrations of the Language of Passion resulted in the discovery that poets, and even dramatists—with the exception of Shakespeare—while they constantly speak *about* Passion, comparatively seldom give it direct utterance. The passages herein gathered from the wide fields of Shakespearean and general literature are embodiments of passionate *expression*, in all moods, "from grave to gay, from lively to severe." As such, they furnish the very best kind of material for elocutionary exercise.

2. The shades of sentiment in each passage—as apprehended by the student—should be noted in the margin, and the passages then delivered so as to express the sentiments indicated. This exercise will be found not only improving to style, but valuable for the development of critical acumen, and the formation of a habit of close attentiveness in general reading.

3. The emphatic words are denoted by *italics*. No attempt is made to show the relative force of the emphases. Something must be left for the reader's own discrimination. The most important distinction among the italicised words would be manifested by the reader's *underlining* such words as he conceives to be suggestive of more than they literally express.

4. In addition to the ordinary marks of punctuation, the *Clause* (⌈ ⌊ |), the *Break* (...), and the *Expressive Pause* (⌒), are occasionally introduced.

EMPHASIZED EXERCISES

IN THE

LANGUAGE OF PASSION.

ABSORBING LOVE.—*P. J. Bailey.*

The only music | he
Or learn'd or listened to, was from the lips
Of her he *loved ;*—and *that* he learnt by *heart.*
Albeit she would *try* to teach him tunes,
And put his *fingers* on the keys; but he
Could only *see* . . . *her* eyes, and hear . . . her *voice,*
And *feel* . . . her *touch.*

ADMIRATION.—*Shakespeare.*

What *you* do
Still *betters* what is done.   When you *speak,* sweet,
I'd have you do it *ever :* when you *sing,*
I'd have you buy and *sell* so; so give *alms ;*
Pray so; and, for the ordering your *affairs,*
To sing *them* too.⌒ When you do *dance,* I wish you
A wave of the *sea* . . . that you might ever do
Nothing *but* that: move still, still so,
And *own* no other function.   *Each* your doing—
So singular in each particular—
Crowns what you are doing, in the *present* deeds,
That *all* your acts are queens.

ADMONITION TO CONSISTENCY.—*Shakespeare.*

Remember *March,* the *Ides* of March remember !
Did not great *Julius* | bleed for *justice'* sake ?
What villain touch'd his body, that did stab,
And *not* for justice ?   What ! shall one of us,
That struck the foremost man of all this *world,*
But for *supporting* robbers—shall we now
Contaminate *our* fingers with base bribes,
And sell the mighty space of our large honours . . .
For so much . . . *trash* as may be grasped thus ?—
I had rather be a *dog,* and bay the moon,
Than . . . *such* a Roman.

A DREAM.—*Republic of Letters.*

Thus spoke I to a vision of the night ;—
" O, joy ! A *dream? Thank* heaven that it is fled !
For know you not, I dreamt that you were *dead :*—
And with the dream my soul was *sickened* quite.

But since you're *here*, and since my heart is light,
Come, as of old, and let us wandering seek
Yon high and lovely hill, upon whose height,
Which looks on all we value, we may speak
As we were *wont*, amid its bracing air,
And pluck the while its crowned jewels there :
For—|how I know not | but 'tis *long* ago
Since last we met . . *Ha !* *Wherefore* look you so?
And why this. . . *dimness?* ” ⌒—Horror! 'twas the *Ghost*
Alone I saw | of him I loved and lost!

ADVICE.—*Shakespeare.*

Give thy thoughts no *tongue,*
Nor any *unproportion'd* thought his *act.*
Be thou familiar, but by no means *vulgar.*
The *friends* thou hast, and their adoption *tried,*
Grapple them to thy soul with hooks of steel :
But do not dull thy palm with entertainment
Of each *new*-hatch'd and unfledg'd comrade. Beware
Of *entrance* to a *quarrel ;* but *being* in,
Bear it, that the *opposer* | may beware of *thee*
Give every man thine *ear,* but *few* thy *voice.*
Take each man's censure, but reserve *thy* judgement :
This above *all,* to thine own *self* be true,
And it must follow, as the night the day,
Thou *canst* not then | be false to *any* one.

AFFECTION.—*J. S. Knowles.*

Men go *mad*
To lose their hoards of *pelf,* when hoards as rich
With industry may come in time *again !*
Yet they go mad. . it happens every day.
Have not some *slain* themselves ? Yet, if a *maid,*—
Who finds that she has . . . *nothing* | garner'd up,
Where she believed she had a *heart* in store
For one she gave away—is desperate,
You *marvel* at her! *Marvel!*—when the *mines*—
Of all the earth—are poor as *beggary*
To make *her* rich again ! Am I *ashamed*
To tell thee this? No !—Save the love we pay
To *Heaven, none* purer, holier, than that
A virtuous woman feels for him she'd cleave
Through *life* to.   *Sisters* part from sisters—brothers
From *brothers*—children from their *parents*—but
Such woman from the *husband* of her choice . . .
Never.

AFFECTIONATE REMEMBRANCE. —*Wordsworth.*

She dwelt among the *untrodden* ways beside the springs of Dove—
A maid whom there were none to *praise,* and *very* few to *love :*—

A *violet*, by a mossy stone half *hidden* from the eye —
Fair as a *star*, when only *one* is shining in the sky.
She lived *unknown*, and few could know when Lucy *ceased* to be,
But . . . she is in her grave—and, oh, the *difference* to *me!*

AMBITION.—*Byron.*

Ay—father! I have *had* those earthly visions
And noble aspirations, in my youth,
To make my own the mind of *other* men,
The *enlightener* of nations; and to *rise* . . .
I knew not *whither*—it *might* be | to *fall;*
But fall, even as the mountain *cataract,*
Which, having leapt from its more dazzling height,
Even in the foaming strength of its abyss,
Lies low, but *mighty* still. ⌢ But . . . this is *past;*
My thoughts *mistook* themselves.

ANGER.—*Shakespeare.*

                    Not *speak* of Mortimer!
Zounds, I *will* speak of him; and let my soul
Want mercy, if I do not *join* with him.—
Yea, on his part, I'll empty all these veins,
And shed my dear blood, drop by *drop,* i' the dust,
But I will *lift* the down-trod Mortimer
As high i' the air as this unthankful *king;*
As this ingrate and *canker'd* Bolingbroke.
Those prisoners I shall *keep*—I *will;* that's flat.⌢
He said he would not *ransom* Mortimer;
Forbad my tongue to *speak* of Mortimer;
But I will find him when he lies *asleep,*
And in his ear I'll *holla*—Mortimer!
Nay,
I'll have a *starling* shall be taught to speak
Nothing *but*—Mortimer . . . and *give* it him,
To keep his anger *still* in motion.

ANGRY SURPRISE.—*Shakespeare.*

Gone. . . to be *married!*—gone to swear a *peace!*
False blood to false blood joined! Gone.   . to be *friends!*—
Shall *Lewis* have Blanch? and Blanch those *provinces?*
It *is* not so:—thou hast *mis*-spoke,—mis-*heard!* ⌢
Be well advised, tell o'er thy tale again . . .
It *cannot* be:—thou dost but *say* 'tis so,⌢
What dost thou mean by shaking of thy head?
Why dost thou look so sadly on my *son?*
What means that hand upon that breast of thine?
Why holds thine eye that lamentable rheum,—

Like a proud river peering o'er his bounds?
Be these sad signs *confirmers* of thy words?
Then speak again;... not *all* thy former tale,
But this *one* word,—whether thy tale be *true* ?

APPARITION.—*Shakespeare.*

How *ill* this taper burns!... *Ha!* who comes here? ⌒
I think | it is the weakness of mine eyes
That shapes this ... *monstrous* apparition—
It *comes* upon me: ⌒ *art* thou ... *any* thing?
Art thou some god, some angel, or some *devil*,
That mak'st my blood cold, and my *hair* to stare? ⌒
Speak to me ... *what* thou art.

APPREHENSION.—*Lee.*

When the sun *sets*, *shadows* that showed at noon
But small, appear most long and *terrible* :
So, when we think *fate* hovers o'er our heads,
Our *apprehensions* shoot beyond all bounds ;
 Owls, *ravens*, *crickets*, seem the watch of *death* ;—
Nature's worst *vermin* scare her godlike sons.
Echoes, [the very leaving of a voice. |
Grow babbling *ghosts*, and call us to our *graves*.
Each *mole*-hill thought swells to a huge *Olympus* ;
While we, fantastic dreamers, *heave* and puff,
And sweat... with an *imagination's* weight.

ASSUMED BLUNTNESS.—*Shakespeare.*

                    This is some fellow
Who, having been *praised* for bluntness, doth *affect*
A *saucy* roughness ; and constrains the garb,
Quite from his *nature*.—He *cannot flatter* ... he !
An *honest* mind and plain,—he *must* speak truth : ⌒
An' they will take it... so ; —if *not* ... he's plain. ⌒
These kind of knaves I *know*, which in this ... *plainness*
Harbour more *craft*, and more corrupter ends
Than *twenty* silly, ducking observants,
That stretch their duties nicely.
Fetch forth the *stocks*, ho ! ⌒
You *stubborn* ancient knave, you reverend *braggart*.
We'll *teach* you... *Fetch* forth the stocks :...
As I've life and honour, there shall he sit till *noon*.

AUTHORITY.—*Shakespeare.*

O, it is excellent
To have a giant's *strength* ; but it is tyrannous
To *use* it like a giant.
Could great men | *thunder*
As Jove himself does, Jove would ne'er be *quiet*:...

For *every* pelting petty officer,
Would use his heaven for thunder ; *nothing* ... but ... thunder.
Merciful *Heaven !*
Thou, rather, with thy sharp and sulphurous bolt,
Split'st the unwedgeable and gnarled *oak*,
Than the soft myrtle.—O, but *man*, proud man !
Drest in a little brief authority,
Most *ignorant* of what he's most *assured*—
His glassy essence,—like an angry *ape*,
Plays such fantastic tricks, before high Heaven,
As make the angels ... *weep*.

AVARICIOUS AGE.—*Young*.

Oh, my coevals ! *remnants* of yourselves !
Poor human *ruins*, tott'ring o'er the grave !
Shall we, shall aged men, like aged trees,
Strike *deeper* their vile root, and *closer* cling,
Still more enamour'd of this wretched soil ?
Shall our pale, wither'd hands, be still stretched out,
Trembling, at once with *eagerness* and age ?
With avarice and *convulsions* grasping hard ?
Grasping ... at *air !* for *what* has earth beside ?
Man *wants* but little ; nor that little *long :*
How *soon* must he resign his very *dust !*

BEAUTY.—*Blair*.

Beauty ! thou pretty *play*-thing ! dear *deceit !*
That steals so *softly* o'er the stripling's heart,
And gives it a new *pulse*, unknown before,—
The *grave* ... *discredits* thee.   Thy charms *expung'd*,
Thy roses faded, and thy lilies soiled.—
What had'st thou *more* to boast of ? Will thy lovers
Fiock round thee *now*, to gaze and do thee homage ?
Methinks I *see* thee, with thy head laid low ;
Whilst, surfeited upon thy damask cheek,
The high-fed *worm* in lazy volumes roll'd,
Riots unscar'd.   For *this* was all thy caution ?
For this, thy painful labours at the *glass*,
To improve those charms, and keep them in repair,
For which the spoiler *thanks* thee not ? Foul feeder !
Coarse fare and *carrion* please thee full as well,
And leave as keen a relish on the sense.

BEREAVEMENT.—*Alex. Bell*.

Each has his woe, and *I*, alas, have mine.
All *common* sorrows are in common *shared ;*
But there's a *climax* of calamity
Which settles in some *solitary* breast.

The angry winds and flooding rains oft spread
A *general* wreck; while the electric fire
A *single* victim strikes.—O, I *have* been
A *husband* and a *father!* ⌢ *Now*, alas!
I'm *childless, widowed, hopeless, aimless!*

BOASTFUL CHALLENGE.—*Shakespeare.*

     Show me what thou'lt do;
Woul't *weep?* woul't *fight?* woul't *fast?* woul't *tear* thyself?
Woul't drink up Esil? eat a crocodile?
I'll do't.—Dost thou come here to *whine*,
To *outface* me with leaping in her grave?
Be buried . . . quick . . . with her . . . . and so will *I:*
And if thou prate of *mountains*, let them throw
Millions of acres on us; till our ground,
Singeing its pate against the burning zone,
Make *Ossa* like a *wart!* Nay! ⌢ an' thou'lt *mouth,*
I'll rant as well as thou.

CHARITY.—*Crabbe.*

 An *ardent* spirit dwells with Christian love,—
The *eagle's* vigour in the pitying *dove:*
'Tis not enough that we with sorrow *sigh*,
That we the wants of *pleading* man supply,
That we in *sympathy* with sufferers feel,
Nor hear a grief without a *wish* to heal:
Not these suffice:—to sickness, pain, and woe,
The Christian spirit loves with aid to *go;* ⌢
Will not be *sought, waits* not for Want to plead,
But *seeks* the duty—nay, *prevents* the need;—
Her utmost aid to *every* ill applies,
And plans relief for *coming* miseries.

CHEERFULNESS.—*Shakespeare.*

 Now, my co-mates and brothers in exile,
Hath not old custom made this life *more* sweet
Than that of painted *pomp?* Are not these woods
More free from *peril* than the envious *court?*
Here feel we but the penalty of *Adam,*
The *season's* difference;—as the icy fang
And churlish chiding of the winter's *wind*,—
Which . . . when it bites and blows upon my body,
Ev'n till I *shrink* with cold, I *smile,* ⌢ and say,
This | is no *flattery;* these are counsellors
That feelingly persuade me . . . *what* . . . I *am.*
Sweet are the uses of Adversity;
Which, like the toad, ugly and venomous,
Wears yet a precious *jewel* in its head;
And this our life, ⌊exempt from public haunts, |

Finds *tongues* in *trees*, *books* in the running *brooks*,
Sermons in *stones*, and good in *every* thing.

CLOSE OF A GUILTY CAREER.—*Shakespeare.*

I have liv'd long enough : my *May* of life
Is fall'n into the *sear*, the yellow leaf;
And that which *should* accompany old age,—-
[As honour, love, obedience, troops of *friends*, |
I must not look to have; but, in their stead,
Curses... not loud, but *deep*,—*mouth*-honour,—*breath*, ⌢
Which the poor heart would *fain* deny, but dare not.

CONFIDENCE.—*Byron.*

That's *false* ! a *truer*, *nobler*, *trustier* heart,
More loving, or more loyal, *never* beat
Within a human breast.   I would not *change*
My exil'd, persecuted, mangled husband—
Oppress'd, but *not* disgraced, crushed, overwhelm'd—
Alive or *dead*, for Prince or Paladin,
In story or in fable—with a *world*
To back his suit ⌢ *Dishonour'd—He* dishonour'd !
I tell thee, Doge, tis *Venice* is dishonour'd.

CONFLICTING PASSIONS.—*Shakespeare.*

Thou think'st 'tis much that this contentious *storm*
Invades us to the skin :—so 'tis to *thee ;*
But | where the *greater* malady is fixed,
The lesser is scarce *felt.*   Thou'dst shun a *bear ;* ...
But if thy flight lay toward the raging *sea*,
Thou'dst *meet* the bear i' the mouth.   When the *mind s* free,
The body's *delicate :* the *tempest* ... in my mind
Doth from my senses take *all* feeling else
Save ... what . . beats there. ⌢ *Filial* ingratitude! ...
Is it not as this mouth should tear this *hand*
For lifting food to't?—But I will *punish* home! ⌢
No, I will *weep* no more. ⌢ In *such* a night
To shut *me* out!... Pour *on ;* I will endure : ⌢
In such a night as *this !* O Regan—Goneril!—
Your old kind *father*, whose frank heart gave *all*, . . .
O, that way *madness* lies : ⌢ let me *shun* that.
No more of that.—Prythee go in; seek thine own ease;
This tempest will not give me leave | to *ponder*
On things would hurt me *more.*—But I'll go in!—
In, boy; go first. ⌢ I'll *pray*, and then I'll sleep. ⌢
Poor *naked* wretches, wheresoe'er you are,
That bide the pelting of this pitiless storm.
How shall your houseless heads, and unfed sides,
Your loop'd and window'd raggedness, *defend* you
From seasons such as these? . . . O, I have ta'en

Too little *care* of this! ⌒ Take *physic*. pomp;—
Expose *thyself* to feel what wretches feel, . . .
That thou may'st shake the superflux to them,
And show the *heavens* more just.

CONTEMPTUOUS REPROACH.—*Shakespeare*.

Thou *slave*, thou wretch, thou *coward*,
Thou little valiant, *great* in villany!
Thou ever strong upon the *stronger* side!
Thou *Fortune's* champion, thou dost never fight
But when her humorous ladyship is *by*
To teach thee safety! ⌒ thou art *perjur'd* too,
And sooth'st up greatness.   What a *fool* art thou,
A ramping fool; to brag, and stamp, and *swear*
Upon my party! Thou cold-blooded slave,
Hast thou not spoke like thunder, *on* my side . . .
Been *sworn* my soldier? bidding me *depend*
Upon thy stars, thy fortune, and thy strength? . . .
And dost thou now | fall over to my *foes?* ⌒
Thou wear a *lion's* hide! *doff* it for shame,
And hang a *calf's* skin on those recreant limbs.

CONSTANCY.—*Milton*.

Certain, my resolution is—to *die*.
How can I live without *thee!* how forego
Thy converse sweet, and love so dearly join'd,
To live again in these wild woods . . . *forlorn!*
Should God create *another* Eve, and I
Another rib afford, yet loss of thee
Would *never* from my heart! no, no; I feel
The link of *nature* draw me; flesh of *my* flesh,
Bone of my bone thou art, and from thy state
Mine *never* shall be parted, . . . bliss or *woe*.

CONTRADICTION.—*Lloyd*.

" Here, Cicely. take away my *gun:*
How shall we have these starlings *done?* "
" —Done! what, my love? your wits are *wild!*
Starlings, my dear! they're *thrushes*, child. "
" Nay, now, but look, consider, wife,
They're *starlings*."—"No, upon my life!
Sure I can judge as well as *you* . . .
I *know* a thrush, and starling too."—
" —Who was it *shot* them, you or I?
They're *starlings!*"—" *Thrushes!*"—" Wife . . . you *lie*." —
" —Pray, Sir, take *back* your dirty word,
I *scorn* your language . . . as your *bird;*
It ought to make a husband *blush*,
To treat a wife so . . . 'bout a . . . *thrush*. "

"— *Thrush*, Cicely ? "—" *Yes*."—" A *starling !* "—" No."—
The lie *again*, and then . . . the *blow*.

CRAFTY ADVICE.—*Rowe*.

Learn to *dissemble* . . . *wrongs*, to *smile* at injuries,
And suffer . . . crimes thou want'st the power to *punish :*—
Be *easy*, affable, familiar, *friendly :*—
Search, and know all mankind's mysterious ways ;
But . . . trust the secret of *thy* soul | to *none !*
This is the way,
This *only*, to be *safe* in such a world as this is.

CRAFTY MALIGNITY.—*Milton*.

Let me not *forget* what I have gained
From their own mouths : *All* is not theirs, it seems ;
One fatal *tree* there stands,—of *knowledge* called,—
Forbidden them to taste. Knowledge forbidden ?
⌢ Suspicious . . . *reasonless !*   *Why* should their Lord
Envy them that ? Can it be *sin* to know ?
Can it be *death ?*   And do they only stand
By *ignorance ?*   Is *that* their happy state—
The proof of their obedience and their faith ?
O, fair foundation laid | whereon to build
Their *ruin !* Hence I will excite their minds
With more *desire* to know ; and to *reject*
Envious command, invented with design
To *keep* them low, whom knowledge might exalt
Equal with *gods :* ⌢ Aspiring to *be* such . . .
They taste and *die !*

DEATH.— *Young*.

Will *toys* amuse, when med'cines cannot cure ?
When *spirits* ebb, when life's enchanting scenes
Their lustre lose, and *lessen* in our sight ;
| As lands, and cities, with their glittering spires,
To the poor shatter'd *bark*, by sudden storms
Thrown off to sea, and soon to perish there ? |
Will toys amuse ? *No : thrones* will then be toys,
And earth and *skies* seem . . . *dust* upon the scale.

DESIRE AND DREAD OF DEATH.—*Byron*.

We are *fools*—of time and terror : days
Steal on us, and steal from us ; yet we live,
Loathing our life, and *dreading* still to die. ⌢
In all the days of this detested yoke—
This vital *weight* upon the struggling heart,
| Which sinks with sorrow, or beats quick with **pain**,
Or joy that *ends* in agony or faintness— |

In *all* the days—of past and future,—for
In life there is *no* present,—we can number
How *few*, how *less* than few—wherein the soul
Forbears to *pant* for death; and yet ... draws *back*
As from a stream in winter, though the chill
Be but a *moment's*.

DESPAIR.—*Byron*.

　　　　　　　To be thus—
Grey-hair'd with *anguish*, like the blasted pines,
Wrecks of a *single* winter, barkless, branchless;
A blighted trunk upon a *cursed* root,
Which but supplies a *feeling* to decay;—
And to be thus *eternally*; *but* thus,
Having been otherwise! Now furrow'd o'er
With wrinkles, plough'd by *moments*, not by years;
And hours ... all tortured into *ages*—hours
Which I *outlive! ⌒* Ye toppling crags of *ice*—
Ye *avalanches*,—whom a breath draws down
In mountainous o'erwhelming—*come* and crush me!
I *hear* you—momently, above, beneath,—
Crash with a frequent conflict; but ... ye *pass*,
And *only* fall | on things that still *would* live.

DISAPPOINTED ENVY.—*Shakespeare*.

Three great ones of the city,
In personal suit to make *me* his lieutenant,
**Off* capp'd to him;—and by the faith of man,
I know my *price*—I am worth no *worse* a place. ⌒
But he, as loving his own pride and purposes,
Evades them—with a bombast circumstance,
Horribly stuffed with epithets of war;
And, in conclusion, *nonsuits*
My mediators; for, certes, says he,
I have *already* | chose my officer.
And *what* was he?—
Forsooth, a great ... *arithmetician*,
One Michael Cassio, a Florentine ... a fellow
That never set a *squadron* in the field,
Nor the division of a battle | knows
More than a *spinster*—unless the bookish *theorick*,
Wherein the toged *consuls* can propose
As masterly as he:—mere *prattle*, without practice,
Is all his soldiership. But *he*, sir, had the election, ⌒
And *I*,—of whom his eyes had seen the *proof*,
At Rhodes—at Cyprus—and on other grounds,
Christian and heathen,—must be be-lee'd and calm'd

---

* Saluted him,—took off their caps.

By . . . debitor and creditor, this *counter*-caster ⌒
He, in good time, must his Lieutenant be,
And *I*, (O, bless the mark!) his Moorship's. . *Ancient*
But there s no remedy—'tis the *curse* of service ⌒
Preferment goes by letter and *affection ;*
Not by the *old* gradation, where each Second
Stood *heir* to the First.

DISDAINFUL SCORN.—*Byron.*

I could not *tame* my nature down : for he
Must *serve* who fain would sway,—and *soothe*—and *sue*—
And *watch* all time, and pry into all place,—
And be ⌒ a living *lie*,—who would become
A mighty thing amongst the mean ;—and such
The mass *are* —I *disdained* to mingle with
A herd, *though* to be leader,—and of *wolves*,
The *lion* | is *alone*, and so am *I.*

DISGUST.—*Shakespeare.*

There may be in the cup a *spider* steeped,
And one may drink, depart, and take no venom
For his *knowledge* is not infected ;—but
If one present the abhorred ingredient
To his *eye*—make known *how* he hath drunk,
He . . . cracks his gorge—his sides, with violent hefts ⌒
I . . . have drunk, and *seen* the spider !

DISINTERESTED LOVE —*J. Sheridan Knowles.*

Rank that *excels* its wearer, doth *degrade ;*
Riches *impoverish* that divide respect:
O, to be cherished for *one's self* alone !
To owe the love that cleaves to us, to naught
Which *fortune's* summer—*winter*,—gives or takes ;
To know that, while we wear the heart and mind,
Feature and form, high heaven endowed us with,—
Let the storm pelt us, or *fair* weather warm
We *shall* be loved ! *Kings.* from their thrones cast down,
Have *blessed* their fate, that they were valued for
Themselves, and not their stations, when some knee
That *hardly* bowed to them in plenitude
Has kissed the *dust* before them, *stripped* of all !

DISSEMBLED LOVE.—*Shakespeare.*

Think not I *love* him, though I ask for him ;
'Tis but a peevish *boy ;*—yet he talks *well :*—
But what care I for *words ?* yet words do well . . .
When he that speaks them *pleases* those that hear.
It is a pretty youth . . . not *very* pretty :—

But sure, he's *proud* . . . and yet his pride *becomes* him . . .
He'll make a *proper* man. ⌢ The best thing in him
Is his *complexion* : and faster than his tongue
Did make offence, his *eye* | did *heal* it up.
There was a pretty redness in his lip ; . . .
A little riper and more lusty red
Than that mix'd in his cheek : 'twas just the difference
Betwixt the *constant* red and mingled *damask*. ⌢
There be *some* women, Silvius, had they mark'd him
In parcels as I did, would have gone *near*
To fall in love with him ; ⌢ but, for my part,
I . . . love him *not*, ⌢ nor *hate* him not ;—and yet
I have more *cause* to hate him than to love him ;
For what had he to do to *chide* at me?
He said, mine eyes were *black*, and my *hair* black ;
And,—now I am remember'd,—*scorn'd* at me : . . .
I marvel why I *answer'd* not again ;—
But that's all one ; omittance is no *quittance*.

DISTRUST.—Shakespeare.

Glamis thou art, and *Cawdor ;*—and *shalt* be . . .
What thou art *promis'd :*—Yet do I fear thy nature ;
It is too full o' the milk of human *kindness*,
To catch the *nearest* way. ⌢ Thou *wouldst* be great ;—
Art not without ambition ; but without
The *illness* should attend it. What thou wouldst highly,
That wouldst thou *holily ;* wouldst not *play* false,
And yet wouldst wrongly *win* : thou'dst have, great Glamis,
That which cries,—*Thus* thou must do, if thou have it :
And that which rather thou dost *fear* to do,
Than wishest should be *un*done. ⌢ Hie thee *hither,*—
That I may pour *my* spirits in thine ear ;
And chastise with the valour of my tongue
All that impedes thee | from the golden round
Which fate and metaphysical aid doth seem
To *have* | thee crown'd withal.

EMULATION IN " GENTILITY."—Household Words.

Here's the . . . plumber-painter-and-glazier . . . come to take
the funeral *order*—which he is going to give to the *sexton*—who
is going to give it to the *clerk*—who is going to give it to the
carpenter—who is going to give it to the furnishing *undertaker*
—[who is going to *divide* it with the Black *Jobmaster.*
" Hearse and *four*, Sir?"—says he.—"No ; a *pair* will be
sufficient."—" I beg your pardon, Sir, but when we buried Mr.
Grundy, at number twenty, there were *four*. Sir . . . I think it
right to *mention* it."—" Well, perhaps there had *better* be four."
—" Thank you, Sir." ⌢
" Two *coaches* and four, Sir, shall we say ? "—" No, coaches

14

and *pair*." "You'll excuse my mentioning it, Sir, but pairs to the coaches, and four to the hearse. would have a *singular* appearance to the *neighbours*. When we put four to *anything*, we always carry four right *through*."—" Well! *say* four!"—" Thank you, Sir." ⌒

"*Feathers*, of course ?"—" No :—*No* feathers. They're *absurd*."—" Very good, Sir; *No* feathers!"—" No."—" *Very* good, Sir.—We *can* do fours without feathers, Sir - - - but it's what we never *do*.* When we buried Mr. *Grundy*, we had feathers - - - and—I only throw it out, Sir—*Mrs*. Grundy might think it strange."—" Very well! Feathers!"—" Thank you, Sir."

And so on through the whole . . . black job of jobs because of . . . Mrs. Grundy and . . . "*gentility!*"

ENCOURAGEMENT.—*Shakespeare.*

Great Lord, wise men ne'er sit and *wail* their loss,
But cheerly seek law to *redress* their harms.
What though the mast be now thrown overboard,
The *cable* broke, the holding *anchor* lost,
And half our *sailors* swallowed in the flood?
Yet lives our *pilot* still. Is't meet that he
Should *leave* the helm, and, like a fearful lad,
With tearful eye *add* water to the sea,
And give more strength to that which hath too much;
While, in his moan, the ship *split* on a rock,
Which industry and courage might have *saved ?*
Ah! what a *shame!* Ah, *what* a fault were this!

ENVIOUS CONTEMPT.—*Shakespeare.*

I was born free as *Cæsar ;* so were *you.* ⌒
We both have *fed* as well; and we can both
Endure the winter's *cold* . . . as well as he!
For once, upon a raw and gusty day,
The troubled Tiber chafing with her shores,
Cæsar said to me,—*Dar'st* thou, Cassius, now
Leap in with *me* into this angry flood,
And swim to *yonder* point? Upon the *word*,
Accoutred as I was—I plunged in,
And bade him *follow :* ⌒ so, indeed, he did.
The torrent roar'd; and we did buffet it
With *lusty* sinews; throwing it aside
And stemming it with *hearts* of controversy; . . .
But ere we could *arrive* the point proposed,
Cæsar cried, *Help* me, Cassius, or I sink.
I—as Æneas, our great ancestor,
Did, from the flames of Troy, upon his shoulder

---

* This emphasis on a word already used in the sentence may seem a violation of the Principle of Emphasis, but it is not so; " do " is here equivalent to " *do* do " as opposed to " *can* do."

The old Anchises bear—*so*, from the waves of Tiber
Did I . . the *tired* Cæsar! ⌒ And this man
Is now become a *God!* and *Cassius* is . . .
A *wretched* creature—and must bend his body
If Cæsar carelessly but *nod* on him. ⌒
He had a *fever* when he was in Spain,
And, when the fit was on him, I did mark
How he did *shake*. . . . 'Tis true,—this *god* did shake.
His coward lips did from their *colour* fly;
And that same *eye*, whose bend doth awe the world,
Did lose its lustre: ⌒ I did hear him *groan* :
Ay, and that tongue of his,—that bade the Romans
Mark him, and write his speeches in their books,—
Alas, (it cried,) Give me some *drink*, Titinius . . .
As a sick *girl*. ⌒ Ye gods! it doth *amaze* me,
A man of such a *feeble* temper should
So get the start of the majestic world,
And bear the palm alone.

EXALTED MISERY.—*Dowe.*

O royalty! *what* joys hast thou to boast,
To recompense thy *cares?* Ambition *seems*
The passion of a *God.* Yet from my throne
Have I, with *envy*, seen the naked *slave*
Rejoicing in the music of his chains,
And singing toil away; and then at eve
Returning peaceful to his couch of *rest* :—
Whilst *I* | sat anxious and *perplexed* with cares :
Projecting, plotting, *fearful* of event;
Or, like a wounded snake, lay down to writhe
The *sleepless* night, upon a bed of state.

EXCULPATION.—*Shakespeare.*

Friends, Romans, *Countrymen!* lend *me* your ears;
I come to *bury* Cæsar, not to *praise* him.
The *evil* that men do lives after them;
The *good* | is *oft* interred with their bones. ⌒
So *let* it be with Cæsar! ⌒ The noble *Brutus*
Hath told you, Cæsar was *ambitious*—
If it were so, it was a *grievous* fault;
And grievously hath Cæsar *answered* it ⌒
Here—under *leave* of Brutus . . . and the rest—
For Brutus is an *honourable* man . . .
So are they *all!* all . . . honourable men—
Come *I* to speak in Cæsar's funeral.
 He was my *friend*—faithful and *just* to me—
But Brutus says, he was *ambitious* . . .
And Brutus is an honourable man! ⌒
He hath brought many *captives* home to Rome . . .
Whose ransoms did the *general* coffers fill :

Did *this* in Cæsar *seem* ambitious? ⌢
When that the *poor* have cried, Cæsar hath *wept;*—
Ambition should be made of *sterner* stuff! . . .
Yet Brutus *says* he was ambitious;
And Brutus is an honourable man ! ⌢
You *all* did see, that, on the Lupercal,
I, thrice, presented him a kingly *crown,*
Which he did thrice *refuse*: was *this* ambition?
Yet Brutus says he *was* ambitious . . .
And *sure* he *is* . . . an *honourable* man ! ⌢
I speak not to *disprove* what Brutus spoke;
But here I am to speak what I do *know.*
You *all* did love him once—not without *cause !*
What cause withholds you, then, to *mourn* for him?
O *Judgement !* thou art fled to brutish *beasts,*
And men have *lost* their reason ! ⌢ *Bear* with me :
My heart is in the *coffin* there . . . with Cæsar . .
And I must pause ⌢ till it come *back* to me !

EXHORTATION AGAINST AMBITION. —*Shakespeare.*

Cromwell, ⌢ I did not think to shed a *tear*
In all my miseries, . . . but thou hast *forced* me—
Out of thy honest *truth,* to play the woman. ⌢
Let's *dry* our eyes : and thus far hear me, Cromwell ;
And,—when I am *forgotten ;* . . . as I *shall* be,
And sleep in dull cold marble, where no *mention*
Of me more must be heard of,—say I *taught* thee,
Say,—Wolsey,—that once trod the ways of *glory,*
And sounded *all* the depths . . . and *shoals* of honour,—
Found *thee* a way, out of his wreck, to *rise* in ;
A safe and *sure* one. *though* thy master miss'd it.
Mark but my fall, and *that* that ruin'd me. ⌢
Cromwell. I charge thee. fling away *ambition ;*
By that sin fell the *Angels :* how can man then—
The image of his Maker.— *hope* to win by't ?
Love thyself *last ; cherish* those that *hate* thee :—
Corruption wins not more than *honesty.*
Still in thy right hand carry gentle *peace.*
To silence envious tongues.   Be *just,* and *fear* not :
Let *all* the ends thou aim'st at—be thy *country's,*
Thy *God's,* and truth's. ⌢ *then,* if thou fall'st, O Cromwell,
Thou fall'st a *blessed* martyr !   Serve . . . the *king ;*
And, . . . ⌢ prythee, lead me in. ⌢
There take an *inventory* of all I have, . . .
To the last *penny,* 'tis the *king's ;* my *robe,*
And my *integrity* to Heaven. is *all*
I dare—now—call mine *own.* O Cromwell. Cromwell,
Had I but served my *God* with *half* the zeal
I served my King. . . . *He* would not, in mine age
Have *left* me—naked—to mine *enemies.*

EXHORTATION TO COURAGE.—*Shakespeare.*

But wherefore do you *droop ?* Why look you sad ?
Be great in *act.* as you have been in thought;
Let not the world see fear and sad distrust
Govern the motion of a *kingly* eye :
Threaten the threatener, and *outface* the brow
Of bragging horror; so shall inferior eyes,
⌊That borrow their behaviours from the great, ⌋
Grow great by your *example ;* ⌒ and put on
The dauntless spirit of *resolution ;*
Show boldness and aspiring *confidence.*
What, shall they seek the lion in his *den,*
And *fright* him . . . there ;—and make him tremble *there?*—
Oh *let* it not be said ! ⌒ Forage and run. . . .
To meet displeasure *farther* from the doors,
And grapple with him *ere* he come so nigh.

FAREWELL TO GREATNESS.—*Shakespeare.*

Farewell, a *long* farewell, to all my greatness !
⌒ This is the state of man :—to-day he puts forth
The tender leaves of *hope,* to-morrow *blossoms,*
And bears his blushing honours *thick* upon him :
The third day comes a *frost.* a killing frost;
And,—when he thinks, ⌊good easy man, ⌋ full *surely*
His greatness is a-*ripening,*—nips his *root,*
And then . . . he *falls . . . as—I* do. ⌒ I have ventured—
Like little wanton boys that swim on bladders,—
These many summers in a sea of glory . . .
But *far* beyond my depth. ⌒ My high-blown pride
At length *broke* under me . . . and now has left me,
Weary, and old with service, to the mercy
Of a rude stream, that must for *ever* hide me. ⌒
Vain pomp and glory of this world, I *hate* ye !
I feel my heart *new* open'd. ⌒ O, how wretched
Is that poor man that hangs on *princes'* favours !
There is, betwixt that smile he would aspire to—
That sweet aspect of princes. and his *ruin,*
More pangs and fears than wars or *women* have ⌒
And—*when* he falls, he falls like *Lucifer* . . .
Never to *hope* again.

FEAR OF DEATH. — *Young.*

Why *start* at death? Where *is* he? Death arrived
Is *past ; not* come. or *gone*—he's never *here.*
Ere hope. *sensation* fails : black-boding man
Receives—not suffers—death's tremendous blow.
The knell, the shroud, the mattock. and the grave,
The deep damp vault. the darkness. and the worm,—
These are the *bugbears* of a winter's eve,
The terrors of the *living,* not the dead.

Imagination's fool, and *error's* wretch,
Man *makes* a death which Nature *never* made;
Then on the point of his own fancy falls;
And feels a *thousand* deaths in fearing one.

GRATITUDE:—*Shakespeare.*

         I have five hundred crowns,—
The thrifty hire I saved under your father,
Which I did store to be my *foster*-nurse,
When service should in my *old* limbs lie lame,
And unregarded age in *corners* thrown;—
Take that: and . . . He that doth the *ravens* feed,
Yea, providently caters for the *sparrow,*
Be comfort to my age! Here is the gold;
All this I *give* you. ⌢ Let me be your *servant ;—*
Though I look old, yet I am *strong* and lusty:
For in my youth I never did apply
Hot and rebellious *liquors* to my blood;
Nor did not, with unbashful forehead woo
The *means* of weakness and debility:
Therefore my age is as a *lusty* winter,
Frosty but *kindly :* ⌢ let me go with you . . .
I'll do the service of a *younger* man
In all your business and necessities.

GRIEF.—*Byron.*

He asked *no* question—*all* were answered now,
By the first glance on that *still* marble brow.
It was enough—she *died*—what recked it *how?*
The love of youth, the hope of *better* years,
The *only* living thing he could not hate,
Was reft at once :- and he *deserved* his fate . . .
But did not *feel* it less.—The *good* | explore
In peace—those realms where guilt can *never* soar:
The *proud*—the wayward—who have fixed *below*
Their joy—and find this earth *enough* for woe,
Lose *in* that one . . . their *all*—perchance a mite—
But who in patience parts with all delight?
Full many a stoic eye and aspect stern
Mask . . . hearts where *grief* hath little left to learn;
And many a *withering* thought lies *hid,* not lost,
In *smiles* . . . that *least* befit who wear them *most.*

GUILTY CONSCIENCE.—*Byron.*

    The mind that broods o'er *guilty* woes,
      Is . . . like the scorpion girt by *fire :*
    In circle *narrowing* as it glows.
    The flames around their captive close;

Till, inly searched by thousand throes
　　And *maddening* in her ire,
One, and a *sole* relief she knows :
The *sting* . . . she nourished for her foes,
⌊Whose venom never yet was vain,
Gives but one pang. and cures *all* pain, ⌋
She darts into her desperate *brain.* ⌒
So do the dark in soul expire,
　　Or *live* . . . like scorpion girt by fire ;
So writhes the mind *remorse* hath riven—
Unfit for earth, undoomed for *heaven* ;
Darkness above, *despair* beneath,
Around it *flame,* within it . . . *death !*

HATRED.

Why, get thee *gone,* . . . *horror* and night go with thee !⌒
Sisters of *Acheron,* go hand in hand,
Go dance about the bower, and close them in ;
And tell them that *I* sent you to salute them.
Profane the ground, and—for the ambrosial rose
And breath of jessamin,—let *hemlock* blacken
And deadly *night-shade* poison all the air :
For the sweet nightingale may *ravens* croak,
Toads pant, and *adders* rustle through the leaves :
May *serpents*, winding up the trees, let fall
Their hissing necks upon them from above,
And mingle *kisses* . . . such as *I* would give them.

HONESTY TRUE NOBILITY.—*Alex. Bell.*

I shall not grieve your lordship by a claim
Of *kindred* blood, which often brings *disgrace.*
I prize *gradations* in the social scale :
They mainly tend to harmony and *peace ;*
But there exists a rank which far *transcends*
The stars and coronets that shine in courts :
It takes no sounding *name* to make men stare ;
No blazoning *heraldry* proclaims its pomp ;
Its modest title is—plain *honesty.*
Though homely be its garb, though coarse its fare,
And though it live *unnoticed* by the crowd ;
Still, *spite* of fashion's fools, the honest man
Is yet the *highest* noble of the land !
Yes, honesty's the poor man's *best* estate,
And *still* is his when other gifts take *wing.*
'Tis regal breath makes *lords,*—but honest men
Receive *their* honour from the *King* of kings !

HONOUR.—*Shakespeare.*

Well, 'tis no matter ;—*honour* pricks me on. Yea, but how if
honour prick me *off* when I come on ? How *then ?* Can honour

set-to a *leg?* No. Or an *arm?* No. Or take away the *grief* of a wound? No. Honour hath *no* skill in surgery then? No. ⌢ What *is* honour? A word. What is *in* that word? *Honour!* What *is* that honour? *Air.* ⌢ A trim reckoning! ⌢ Who *hath* it? He that *died* o' Wednesday.—Doth he *feel* it? No.—Doth he *hear* it? No.—Is it *in*sensible, then? Yea, to the *dead.* But will it not live with the *living?* No. Why? *Detraction* will not suffer it:—therefore I'll *none* of it.—Honour is a mere *'scutcheon* . . . and so ends my catechism.

IGNORANT CRITICISM.—*Sterne.*

"And how did Garrick speak the *soliloquy* last night?"—"Oh, against all *rule*, my Lord; most *ungrammatically!* Betwixt the substantive and the *adjective*, which should agree together in number, case, and gender, he made a *breach* thus—⌢—stopping as if the point wanted *settling;* and after the *nominative* case, which ⌊your Lordship knows⌋ should govern the verb, he suspended his voice in the *epilogue*, a *dozen* times,—*three* seconds and three-*fifths*, by a stop-*watch*, my Lord, each time."—"Admirable *grammarian!* "

" But ⌋ in suspending his voice was the *sense* suspended likewise? Did no expression of *attitude* or *countenance* fill up the chasm? Was the *eye* silent? Did you *narrowly* look?"—" I . . . looked only at the stop-*watch*, my Lord."—"*Excellent* observer!"

O, of all the *cants* which are canted in this canting world,— though the cant of *hypocrisy* may be the *worst*,—the cant of *criticism* is the most *tormenting!*—I would go fifty *miles* . . . on *foot* . . . to *kiss* the hand of that man whose generous heart will give up the reins of his imagination into his *author's* hands, be pleased he knows not *why*, and *cares* not wherefore.

INCREDULOUS HORROR.—*Mrs. Norton.*

Thou dost but *jest*—thou couldst not tell it me
So *calmly*, were it true; thy lip would *quiver*,
Thine eye would shrink, thy hand would tremble,
Thy voice would *falter* forth the horrid words—
Even as a tale of blood is *ever* told;
Thy brow . . . but ah! that grave and gloomy *smile*
Sends a *chill* poison creeping through my veins! ⌢
And yet it *is* not true! ⌢ *He* . . . dead! Oh no!
Young, proud, brave, beautiful; but yesternoon
The chief of thousands, who would all have given
Their life's-blood, drop by *drop*, for love of him.—
He *could* not die!—⌢ Who *told* me he was dead? ⌢
Oh! horrible *dreams* are maddening my poor brain . . .
Hark! there are voices ringing through the air.—
They call thee . . . *murderer!* ⌢ Thou answerest not!
'Tis true!—And now that rivulet of blood
Which flows between us, parts our souls for *ever!*

INDIFFERENCE.—*Literary Treasury.*

There was in our town a certain Tom Ne'er-do-well—an honest fellow, who was brought to ruin by . . . too readily crediting that *care* will kill a *cat*. Poor fellow! he never considered that he was *not* a cat;—and, accordingly, he made it a point not to care for *anything*. He did not care for his father's *displeasure*—and he was *disinherited*. He did not care for *money*—and he was *always* distressed. He did not care for other people's *feelings*—and he was severely winged in a *duel*. He did not care for a notice to *trespassers*—and he walked into a *man-trap*. He did not care for his *wife*—and she ran *away* from him. He did not care for his *health*—and he became *bedridden*. He didn't care . . . for *any body*—and every body left him to his sorrows. ⌒ And lastly, he didn't care . . . for *himself*—and he died in a *workhouse*.

INDIGNANT CONTRAST.—*Burns.*

See yonder poor *o'erlaboured* wight,
So *abject*, mean, and vile,
Who *begs* a brother of the earth
To give him *leave* to toil;
And see his lordly fellow-worm
The poor petition *spurn*—
Unmindful though a weeping *wife*
And helpless *offspring* mourn.

If I'm *designed* yon lordling's slave—
By Nature's law designed—
Why was an independent *wish*
E'er planted in my mind?
If not, why am I *subject* | to
His cruelty, or scorn?
Or why has man the will, and *power*,
To *make* his fellow mourn?

INDIGNATION.—*Moore.*

To think that *man*, thou just and gentle God!
Should stand before Thee, with a *tyrant's* rod,
O'er creatures like himself, with souls from Thee,
Yet dare to boast of perfect *liberty!*
Away, away! ⌒ I'd rather hold my neck
By doubtful tenure from a *Sultan's* beck,
In climes where liberty has scarce been *named*,
Nor *any* right but that of ruling claimed,
Than *thus* to live, where *bastard* freedom | waves
Her fustian flag | in *mockery* . . . over *slaves!*

JEALOUSY.—*Shakespeare.*

Think'st thou, I'd make a *life* of jealousy,
To follow still the changes of the moon

With *fresh* suspicions? No: to be *once* in doubt,
Is   . once to be *resolv'd.* ⌢ Exchange me for a *goat*
When I shall turn the business of my soul
To such exsufflicate and blown surmises,
Matching *thy* inference. 'Tis not to make me jealous,
To say . . my wife is *fair—feeds* well—loves *company—*
Is *free* of speech—sings—plays—and *dances* well.
Where virtue is, these are *more* virtuous!—-
Nor, from mine *own* weak merits, will I draw
The *smallest* fear, or doubt of her revolt—
For, she had eyes and *chose* me. ⌢ *No,* Iago;—
I'll *see,* before I doubt; *when* I doubt . . . *prove :*
And, on the proof, there is no more but this,—
Away at once with *love,* or . . . *jealousy.*

JOY.—*Shakespeare.*

               O! my soul's *joy!*
If after *every* tempest come such calms,
May the winds blow . . . till they have wakened *death !*
And let the labouring bark climb hills of seas
Olympus high, and duck again as low
As *hell's* from heaven! ⌢ If it were now to *die,*
'Twere now to be *most* happy; for I fear
My soul hath her content so *absolute,*
That not another comfort *like* to this
Succeeds in unknown fate.

JUSTIFICATION.—*Shakespeare.*

Romans, *Countrymen,* and Lovers!— Hear me for my *cause;*
and be *silent* that you may hear. *Believe* me, for mine honour:
and have *respect* to mine honour, that you may believe. Censure
me in your *wisdom;* and awake your senses, that you may the
better judge. ⌢ If there be any in this assembly, any dear *friend*
of Cæsar's, to him I say, that *Brutus'* love to Cæsar was no *less*
than his. If, then, that friend demand, why Brutus rose *against*
Cæsar, *this* is my answer;—*not* that I loved Cæsar less, but that
I loved *Rome* more. Had you rather Cæsar were living, and die
all *slaves,* than that Cæsar were dead, to live all *freemen ?*—As
Cæsar loved me, I *weep* for him; as he was fortunate, I *rejoice* at
it; as he was valiant, I *honour* him; but . . . as he was *ambitious,*
I slew him! There are ⌢ tears for his love, joy for his fortune,
honour for his valour, and *death* for his ambition!—Who's here
so base, that would be a *bondman ?* if any, speak! for him have
I *offended.* Who's here so rude, that would not be a *Roman? if*
any, speak! for *him* have I offended. Who's here so vile, that
will not *love* his country? if any, speak! for him *have* I offended.
—I pause for reply. ⌢ None? then *none* have I offended!

LAUGHTER.—*Shakespeare.*

A *fool !* ⌢ a fool!—I met a fool i' th' forest . . .
A *motley* fool;—a miserable varlet!—

As I do live by food, I met a fool ↷
Who laid him down, and bask'd him in the sun,
And rail'd on Lady Fortune in *good* terms . . .
In good *set* terms,—and yet a motley fool;
" Good *morrow*, fool," quoth I ; " No, sir," quoth he ;
" Call me not fool, till heav'n hath sent me *fortune !* " ↷
And then he drew a *dial* from his poke,
And—looking on it with lack-lustre eye—
Says very wisely . . . " It is . . . *ten* o'clock ! "—
" Thus may we *see*," quoth he, " how the world wags ;
'Tis but an hour ago since it was *nine*,
And after one hour more 'twill be *eleven !*—
And so from hour to hour we *ripe* and ripe,
And then ↷ from hour to hour we *rot* and rot . . .
And . . .↷ thereby hangs a tale." When I did hear
The motley fool thus *moral* on the time,
My lungs began to crow like *chanticleer*,
That fools should be so *deep* contemplative :—
And I did laugh, sans intermission,
An *hour* . . . by his dial. O *noble* fool !
A worthy fool ! ↷ Motley's the *only* wear.

LISTENING.—*Wordsworth.*

I have seen
A curious child who dwelt upon a tract
Of *inland* ground, applying to his ear
The convolutions of a smooth-lipped *shell ;*
To which ↷ in silence hushed ↷ his very *soul*
Listened intently ; and his countenance soon
Brightened with joy ; for *murmurings* from within
Were heard—sonorous cadences ! whereby,
To his belief, the monitor expressed
Mysterious *union* with its native sea. ↷
—Even *such* a shell the *universe* itself
Is to the ear of *Faith.*

LISTENING TO DISTANT MUSIC.—*Republic of Letters.*

What strain is this ↷ that comes upon the sky
Of moonlight, as if yonder gleaming *cloud*
Which seems to wander to the melody,
Were *seraph*-freighted !—Now ↷ it *dies* away
In a most far-off tremble ↷ and is *still ;*
Leaving a charmèd silence on each hill
Flower-covered, and the grove's minutest spray.
Hark ! ↷ one *more* dip of fingers in the wires !
One scarce-heard *murmur* . . . struggling into sound,
And fading—like a sunbeam from the ground,
Or gilded\vanes of dimly visioned spires !
But it hath tuned my *spirit*, which will *recall*
Its magic tones, in memory treasured *all.*

LOWLINESS OF MIND.—*H. K. White.*

O! I would walk
A weary journey, to the farthest verge
Of the big *world*, to *kiss* that good man's hand,
Who, in the blaze of wisdom and ot art,
Preserves a *lowly* mind; and to his God,—
Feeling the sense of his own littleness,—
Is as a *child* in meek simplicity! ⌐
What is the pomp of *learning ?* the parade
Of letters and of tongues? ⌐ Even as the *mists*
Of the grey morn before the rising sun,
That pass away and perish.—Earthly things
Are but the transient pageants of an *hour ;*
And earthly *pride* is like the passing *flower,*
That springs . . . to *fall,* and blossoms *but* to die.

MALICIOUS REVENGE.—*Shakespeare.*

There I have *another* bad match : a *bankrupt,* a prodigal, who dare scarce show his head on the Rialto;— a *beggar,* that used to come so *smug* upon the mart;—let him look to his *bond !* he was wont to call me . . . *usurer ;—let* him look to his bond ! he was wont to lend money for a . . . Christian *courtesy ;*—let him *look* to his bond ! ⌐ He hath *disgrac'd* me, and hinder'd me of half a *million ;* laugh'd at my losses.—mock'd at my *gains,*— scorn'd my *nation,*—thwarted my bargains,—*cool'd* my friends, —heated mine *enemies ;* ⌐ And what's his *reason ?* I . . . am . . . a *Jew :* Hath not a Jew *eyes ?* hath not a Jew hands? organs, dimensions, senses, affections, *passions ?—fed* with the same food, *hurt* with the same weapons, subject to the same *diseases, heal'd* by the same means, warm'd and cool'd by the same winter and summer as a . . . *Christian* is? If you *prick* us, do we not *bleed ?* if you *tickle* us, do we not *laugh ?* if you *poison* us, do we not *die ?* and if you *wrong* us, shall we not *revenge? ⌐* If we are like you in the rest, we will resemble you in *that.* ⌐ If a Jew wrong a Christian, what is his . . . *humility ?—Revenge.* If . . . a Christian . . . wrong . . . a *Jew,* what should his . . . *sufferance* be, by . . . Christian *example ?— Why, revenge.* The villainy you teach me, I will *execute :* and it shall go hard, but I will *better* the instruction.

MATERNAL LOVE.—*A. Bethune.*

Unlike all *other* earthly things,—
Which ever shift and ever change,—
The love which a fond *Mother* brings,
Nought earthly can estrange.
All that by mortal *may* be done
A mother ventures for her son.
If marked by worth and *merit* high,
Her bosom beats with *ecstacy ;*
And though he own *nor* worth nor charm,
To him *her* faithful heart is warm :

Though wayward *passions* round him close,
And fame and *fortune* prove his foes;
Through *every* change of good and ill
*Un*changed, . . . a mother loves him *still*.
And when those kindred cords are *broken*
  Which twine around the heart;—
When friends their *farewell* word have spoken,
  And to the grave depart :—
When parents, brothers, husband, die, . . .
  And *desolation* only
At every step meets her dim eye,
  Inspiring visions lonely :—
Love's last and *longest* root below,
Which widowed mothers *only* know,
Watered by each successive grief,
Puts forth a fresher, *greener* leaf.
Divided streams unite in one,
And *deepen* round her only son;
And when her *early* friends are gone,
She lives and breathes in him *alone*.

MELANCHOLY REFLECTIONS.—*Shakespeare.*

                         Poor lord! is't *I*
That chase thee from thy country, and expose
Those tender limbs of thine to the event
Of the none-sparing *war ?* and is it I
That drive thee from the sportive court, where thou
Wast shot at with fair *eyes*, to be the mark
Of smoky *muskets ?* O you leaden messengers,
That ride upon the violent speed of fire,
Fly with *false* aim; move the still-piercing air,
That *sings* with piercing . . . *Do* not touch my *lord !*⌢
Whoever shoots at him, *I* set him there :
Whoever charges on his forward breast,
I am the caitiff that do *hold* him to it;
And, though I kill him not, I *am* the cause
His death was so effected.⌢ Better 'twere
I met the raven *lion*—when he roar'd
With sharp constraint of hunger; better 'twere
That *all* the miseries which nature owes,
Were mine at once . . . I will be *gone*,
My *being* here it is that holds him hence ;
Shall I stay here to do't? *No*, no, although
The air of *paradise* did fan the house,
And *angels* officed all ! ⌢ I will be gone.

MERCY.—*Shakespeare.*

The quality of *mercy* is not *strain'd ;*
It droppeth, as the gentle *rain* [from heaven
Upon the place beneath : | It is *twice* bless'd;—

It blesseth him that *gives, and* him that takes :
'Tis *mightiest* in the mightiest; it becomes
The thronèd monarch *better* than his crown :
His sceptre shows the force of *temporal* power,—
The attribute to awe and majesty,
Wherein doth sit the dread and *fear* of kings ;—
But mercy is *above* this scepter'd sway;
It is enthronèd in the *hearts* of kings ;
It is an attribute of *God* himself:
And earthly power doth then show *likest* God's,
When mercy *seasons justice.*

MISERY IN ROYALTY.—*Shakespeare.*

Of *comfort . . . no* man speak :
Let's talk of *graves,* of worms, and epitaphs ;
Make dust our paper, and with rainy eyes
Write *Sorrow* on the bosom of the earth.
Let's choose executors, and talk of *wills* . . .
And yet not so,—for what can we bequeath,
Save our deposèd *bodies* to the ground?
Our lands, our *lives,* and all . . . are *Bolingbroke's ;*
And nothing can we call our own . . . but *death,*
And that small model of the barren earth
Which serves as paste and *cover* to our bones.
For heaven's sake, let us sit upon the ground,
And tell sad stories of the *death* of kings :—
How some have been *deposed,*—some slain in *war ;*—
Some haunted by the *ghosts* they have deposed ;—
Some poison'd by their *wives,*—some *sleeping* kill'd ;—
All murder'd ; for within the hollow crown
That rounds the mortal temples of a king
Keeps Death his *court :* and there the antic sits,
Scoffing his state, and grinning at his pomp;
Allowing him a *breath,* a little scene
To monarchize, be fear'd, and kill with looks;
Infusing him with self and vain *conceit,*—
As *if* . . . this flesh, which walls about our life,
Were brass *impregnable ;* and humour'd thus,
Comes at the last, and with a little pin
Bores *through his* castle wall, and . . . *farewell* king !
Cover your heads, and mock not flesh and blood
With solemn reverence; throw *away* . . . respect,
Tradition, form, and ceremonious duty,—
For you have but *mistook* me all this while.
I live with *bread* like you, feel *want,* taste *grief,*
Need *friends :*— *subjected* thus,
How can you say to me I am a *king ?*

MUSIC.—*Shakespeare.*

Note but a wild and wanton *herd,*
Or race of youthful and unhandled colts,

Fetching mad bounds, bellowing, and neighing loud,
⌊Which is the hot condition of their blood; ⌒
If they perchance but hear a *trumpet* sound,
Or *any* air of music touch their ears,
You shall perceive them ⌒ make a mutual stand,⌒
Their savage eyes turn'd to a *modest* gaze,
By the sweet power of music.—Therefore, the poet
Did feign, that Orpheus drew *trees, stones,* and *floods ;*—
Since *naught* so stockish, hard, and full of rage,
But music, for the time, doth *change* his nature.
The *man* that hath *no* music in himself,
Nor is not *mov'd* with concord of sweet sounds,
Is fit for *treasons,* stratagems, and spoils ;—
The motions of his spirit are dull as *night,*
And his affections dark as *Erebus :*
Let *no* such man be *trusted.*

MUTABILITY OF LOVE.—*Moore.*

Alas ! how *light* a cause may move
Dissension between hearts that love !—
Hearts that the world in *vain* had tried,
And *sorrow* but more closely tied !
That stood the *storm*—when waves were rough—
Yet, in a *sunny* hour fall off ;—
Like ships that have gone down at sea,
When heaven was all *tranquillity !* ⌒
A something, light as *air*—a *look,*
A *word* . . . unkind, or wrongly taken—
Oh ! Love, that tempests *never* shook,
A breath, a touch like this, *hath* shaken.
And ruder words will soon rush in,
To *spread* the breach that words begin ;—
And eyes forget the gentle ray
They wore in *courtship's* smiling day ;—
And *voices* lose the tone that shed
A tenderness round all they said . . .
Till,—fast declining—one by one
The sweetnesses of Love are *gone :*—
And hearts, so lately mingled, seem
Like broken *clouds,*—or like the *stream*
That smiling left the mountain's brow,
As though its waters *ne'er* could sever,
Yet—ere it reach the plains below—
Breaks . . . into floods that part for *ever.*

NATURAL FREEDOM.—*Cowper.*

But *slavery !* virtue dreads it as her *grave,*
Patience itself is *meanness* in a slave :
Or,—if the will and sovereignty of God
Bid suffer it *awhile,* and kiss the rod,—

Wait for the dawning of a brighter day,
And snap the chain the *moment* that you may.
Nature imprints upon whate'er we see
That has a heart and *life* in it—be *free* !

PERVERSITY.—COURTING A SHREW.—*Shakespeare.*

                              I will attend her here,—
And woo her with some *spirit* when she comes.
Say, that she *rail* . . . why, then, I'll tell her plain,
She sings as sweetly as a *nightingale.* ⌒
Say, that she *frown* . . . I'll say she looks as clear
As morning *roses* newly wash'd with dew. ⌒
Say, she be *mute*, and will not speak a word, . . .
Then I'll commend her *volubility,*—
And say—she uttereth piercing *eloquence.*
If she do bid me *pack* . . . I'll give her thanks,—
As though she bid me stay by her a *week* :⌒
If she *deny* to wed, . . . I'll crave the *day*
When I shall ask the bans, and when be married.

PITY.—*Crabbe.*

What *cutting* blast! and he can scarcely crawl:
He *freezes* as he moves,—he *dies* if he should fall!
With cruel fierceness drives this icy sleet . . .
And must a Christian perish . . . in the street,
In *sight* of Christians? ⌒ There! at *last*, he lies,—
Nor, unsupported, can he *ever* rise.—
He cannot live.—In pity *do* behold
The man affrightened, weeping, trembling, cold:
Oh! how those flakes of snow their entrance win
Through the poor rags, and *keep* the frost within!
His very *heart* seems frozen, as he goes
Leading that starved companion of his woes.
He tried to *pray*—his lips, I saw them move,
And he so turned his piteous eyes above;
But the fierce wind the willing heart opposed,
And, ere he spoke, the lips in misery *closed.*
Poor suffering object! yes, for *ease* you prayed,
And *God* will hear,—He *only*, I'm afraid. ⌒
When reached his home, to what a cheerless fire
And *chilling* bed will those cold limbs retire!
Yet ragged, wretched as it is, that bed
Takes *half* the space of his contracted shed.
I saw the *thorns* beside the narrow grate,
With *straw*, collected in a putrid state:
There will he, kneeling, *strive* the fire to raise,
And *that* will warm him, rather than the blaze;
The sullen, smoky blaze, that cannot last
One *moment* after his attempt is past: ⌒
And *I*, so warmly and so purely laid,
To sink to *rest!* . . . indeed, I am *afraid!*

POVERTY.—*Hartley Coleridge.*

'Tis sweet to see
The *day*-dawn creeping gradual through the sky :
The silent sun at *noon* is bright and fair,
And the calm *eve* is lovely; but 'tis sad
To sink at eve on the dark dewy turf,
And feel . . . that *none* in all that countless host
Of glimmering stars, beholds one little spot,
One humble *home* of thine.   The vast void sky,
In all its trackless leagues of azure light,
Has not one *breath* of comfort for the wretch
Whom houseless *penury* enfranchises ;
A brother freeman of the midnight *owl*,
A sworn acquaintance of the howling *winds*,
And flaggy pinion'd *rain*.

PRAYER.—*Tennyson.*

More things are wrought by *prayer*
Than this world dreams of.   Wherefore let thy voice
Rise like a *fountain* for me night and day.
For what are men better than sheep or *goats*,
That nourish a *blind* life within the brain,
If, knowing God, they lift *not* hands of prayer,
Both for themselves and those who call them friend?
For so, the *whole* round earth is every way
Bound by gold chains about the feet of *God*.

PROUD INDEPENDENCE.—*Shakespeare.*

Your grace shall pardon me,—I *will* not back;
I am too high born to be *propertied ;*
To be a *secondary*—at control,
Or useful serving-man and instrument
To *any* sovereign state throughout the world.
Your breath first *kindled* the dead coal of wars
Between this chastised kingdom and myself,
And brought in matter that should *feed* this fire :—
And now 'tis far too huge to be blown *out*
With that same weak wind that enkindled it.
You taught me how to know the face of right,
Acquainted me with interest to this land :
Yea. *thrust* this enterprise into my heart;
And come ye now to tell me John hath made
His *peace* with Rome?   What is that peace to *me ?*
I, by the honour of my *marriage*-bed,
After young Arthur, claim this land for *mine ;*
And, now it is half *conquered*, must I back, . . .
Because that " John hath made his peace with Rome?"
Am *I* Rome's slave?   What *penny* hath Rome borne,—
15

What men provided,—what munition sent,
To under-*prop* this action? Is't not *I*
That undergo this charge? Who else *but* I,—
And such as to my claim are liable,
Sweat in this business, and maintain this war?
Have I not here the best *cards* for the game,
To *win* this easy match played for a crown?
And shall I now give *o'er* the yielded set?—
No, on my soul; it *never* shall be said.

RAVING.—*Dickens.*

" Nobody shall go *near* her," said the man, starting fiercely up, as the undertaker approached the recess. " Keep *back!* keep back! if you've a *life* to lose."

" *Nonsense*, my good man." said the undertaker. who was pretty well used to misery in *all* its shapes—" nonsense! "

" I *tell* you," said the man—clenching his hands, and stamping furiously on the floor.—" I tell you I *won't* have her put into the ground! She couldn t *rest* there. The worms would *worry* —not eat her,—she is so *worn* away."

The undertaker offered no *reply* to this raving; but producing a tape from his pocket, knelt down for a moment by the side of the body.

" Ah! " said the man,—bursting into tears, and sinking on *his* knees at the feet of the dead woman;—'*kneel* down, kneel down; kneel round her, *every* one of you, and mark my words. I say, she *starved* to death. I never *knew* how bad she was, till the *fever* came upon her. and then ⌒ her bones were starting through the *skin*. There was neither fire nor *candle ;* she died in the *dark*—in the dark! She couldn't even see her *children's* faces, though we heard her gasping out their *names.*⌒ I *begged* for her in the streets,⌒ and . . . they sent me to *prison !* When I came back, she was dying; and all the blood in my heart is *dried* up, for they starved her to *death !* I *swear* it before Heaven that saw it,—they *starved* her! " He twined his hands in his hair, and, with a loud scream, *rolled* grovelling upon the floor; his eyes fixed, and the *foam* gushing from his lips.

REBELLION.—*Moore.*

Rebellion! foul *dishonouring* word.
  Whose wrongful blight so oft has stained
The *holiest* cause that tongue or sword
  Of mortal *ever* lost or gained.
How many a spirit, born to bless,
  Hath *sunk* beneath that withering name,—
Whom but a day's, an hour's *success*,
  Had wafted to eternal *fame !*
As *exhalations*. when they burst
From the warm earth, if *chilled* at first,

If checked in soaring from the plain,
Darken to fogs, and *sink* again; —
But.—if they once triumphant spread
Their wings above the mountain-head—
Become *enthroned* in upper air,
And turn to sun-bright *glories* there!

REGRETFUL PITY.—*Shakespeare.*

Alas! poor Yorick! I knew him, Horatio: a fellow of infinite
jest, of most *excellent* fancy; he hath borne me on his *back* a
thousand times; and now... how *abhorred* in my imagination it
is; ⌒ my *gorge* rises at it. Here hung those lips that I have
kissed I know not how oft. Where be your gibes *now?* Your
gambols? Your songs? Your flashes of merriment that were
wont to set the table on a *roar?* Not *one* now . . . to mock your
own grinning? *Quite* chop-fallen? ⌒ Now get you to my *lady's*
chamber, and tell her, let her paint an *inch* thick, to this favour
she . . . must come; make her *laugh* . . . at that.

REJECTING COUNSEL.—*Shakespeare.*

I pray thee; *cease* thy counsel,—
Which falls into mine ears as profitless
As water in a *sieve;* give not *me* counsel;
Nor let no *comforter* delight mine ear . . .
But . . . such a one whose *wrongs* do suit with mine.
Bring me a father that *so* loved his child,
Whose joy of her is *overwhelmed* like mine,
And bid *him* speak of patience. ⌒
Measure his woe the length and breadth of mine,
And let it answer every strain for strain;
As thus for thus, and such a grief for such.
In every lineament, branch, shape, and form . . .
If such a one will smile, and stroke his beard;
Cry—Sorrow, wag! and hem when he should groan;
Patch grief with proverbs; . . . *bring* him yet to me,
And I of him *will* gather patience.
But there is *no* such man; ⌒ for men
Can counsel, and *speak* comfort to that grief
Which they *themselves* not feel; but, tasting it,
Their counsel turns to *passion*—which before
Would give preceptial *medicine* to rage—
Fetter strong madness in a *silken* thread—
Charm ache with *air*—and agony with words . . .
No, no; 'tis all men's office to *speak* patience
To those that wring under the load of sorrow:
But no man's virtue, nor sufficiency,
To *be* so moral, when he shall endure
The like himself: therefore give me *no* counsel: ⌒
My griefs cry *louder* than advertisement.

REMEMBERED LOVE —*Hon. Mrs. Norton.*

Oh, while the heart, where *her* head hath lain
In its hours of joy, in its sighs of pain;
While the *hand,* which so oft hath been clasped in hers,
In the twilight hour, when nothing stirs,—
Beat with the deep full pulse of *life;*
Can he *forget* his departed wife?
Many may love him, and *he,* in truth,
May love, but not with the love of his *youth;*
Ever, around his joy, will come
A stealing sigh for *that* long-loved home;
And *her* step and her voice will go glidingly by,
In the desolate halls of his *memory!*

REMONSTRANCE—WITH INDIGNATION.—*Mrs. Hemans.*

What! let the foe *engird* us—that our bands
May *rest? Forget* that last disastrous day!
Forget it! Rest! *Bethink* you, noble knights,
Whence we must now draw strength! send down your thoughts
Into the very depths of grief and *shame,*
And bring back courage *thence!* To *talk* of rest! ⌒
How do *they* rest, unburied on their field,
Our *brethren,* slain by Gaza? Had we time
To give them *funeral* rites? and ask we now
Time to *forget* their fall? My *father* died. . . .
I cannot speak of him! . . . What! and forget
The infidel's fierce *trampling* o'er our dead ?
Forget his scornful *shout?* ⌒ give battle *now,*
While the thought lives, as *fire* lives! *There* lies strength!
Hold the dark memory *fast!* Now, now—this *hour;*
Gather your forces to the western gate!
Let *none* forget that day! Our field was lost—
Our city's strength laid low,—*one* mighty heart,—
Your Chief's . . . my father's—*broken!* Oh! let none
Forget it! *Arm!* Way for *remorse!* Arm! arm!
Free way for *vengeance!*

REMORSE—FOR COMMITTING MURDER.—*Shakespeare.*

O, my offence is *rank* . . . it smells to heaven;—
It hath the primal *eldest* curse upon't,—
A *brother's* murder; ⌒ *Pray* can I not.
Though inclination be as sharp as 'twill
My stronger guilt *defeats* my strong intent;
And—like a man to double business bound,—
I stand in pause where I shall *first* begin . . .
And *both* neglect. ⌒ What if this cursèd hand
Were thicker than *itself* with brother's blood?
Is there not rain enough in the sweet heavens
To wash it white as *snow?* Whereto *serves* mercy,
But to confront the visage of offence ?

And what's in *prayer*, but this two-fold force,—
To be forestalled ere we *come* to fall,
Or pardon'd, *being* down? Then I'll look up,
My fault is past.   But, O, what *form* of prayer
Can serve my turn?... *Forgive* me... my foul *murder ?* ...
That *cannot* be, since I am still possess'd
Of those *effects* for which I did the murder—
My crown, mine own ambition, and my queen.
May one be pardon'd, and *retain* the offence? ⌢
In the corrupted currents of *this* world,
Offence's gilded hand *may* shove by justice ;—
And oft 'tis seen, the wicked prize itself
Buys out the *law*.   But 'tis not so *above*—
There is no shuffling—there the action lies
In his *true* nature; and we ourselves compell'd,
Even to the teeth and forehead of our faults,
To give in *evidence*.   What then? what rests? ⌢
Try what *repentance* can : ... what can it *not ?*
Yet what *can* it, when one can *not* repent?
O wretched state? O bosom, black as death!
O *limèd* soul, that, struggling to be free,
Art *more* engaged!   *Help*, angels ! ⌢ Make *essay !* ...
Bow, stubborn knees ! and heart, with strings of steel,
Be soft as sinews of the new born *babe.* ⌢
All *may* be well!

REMORSE—FOR DRUNKENNESS.—*Shakespeare.*

I remember. ... a mass of things ... but nothing *distinctly :* a
quarrel ... nothing *wherefore.* O that men should put an enemy
in their mouths to steal *away* their brains! that we should ...
with joy, pleasure, revel, and applause, transform ourselves into
beasts ! I will ask him for my place again ... he shall tell me I
am ... a *drunkard.* ⌢ Had I as many months as *Hydra*, such an
answer would stop them all. ⌢ To be now a sensible man, by and
bye a *fool*, and presently ... a *beast !* ⌢ O strange ! *every* inor-
dinate cup is unblessed—and the ingredient ... is a *devil !*

REMORSELESS HORROR.—*Baillie.*

Alone ... with thee! but thou art *nothing* now.
'Tis *done*,—'tis numbered with the things o'erpast;
Would—*would* it were to come !—
What fated end, what darkly gathering cloud,
Will *close* on all this horror?
O, that dire *madness* would unloose my thoughts,
And fill my mind with wildest fantasies,
Dark, restless, *terrible ! Aught*, aught ... but this ! ⌢
How with convulsive life he *heaved* beneath me,
E'en with the death's wound gored ! O *horrid*, horrid !
Methinks I feel him *still.* ⌢ What sound is that?

I heard a smothered *groan*. ⌢ It is impossible ! . . .
It *moves !* It moves ! the cloth doth heave and swell.
It moves again ! I *cannot* suffer this,—
Whate'er it be, I will *un*cover it. ⌢
All *still* beneath.
Nought is there here but fixed and grisly *death*.
How sternly fixed ! Oh ! those glazed eyes !
They *look* upon me still.
Come, madness ! come unto me, senseless *death !*
I *cannot* suffer this !

REPROACH WITH WANT OF FRIENDSHIP.—*Shakespeare.*

You *have* done . . . that, you *should* be sorry for.
There is no terror, Cassius, in your *threats ;*
For I am arm'd so strong in *honesty,*
That they pass by me as the idle *wind,*
Which I respect not.   I did send to you
For certain sums of gold, which *you* . . . *denied* me ;
For *I* can raise no money by vile means ;
No, Cassius, I had rather coin my *heart,*
And drop my blood for drachmas, than to wring
From the hard hands of peasants their vile trash
By *any* indirection.   I did send
To you for gold . . . to pay my *legions,*
Which you . . . *denied* me. ⌢ Was that done *like* Cassius ?
Should *I* have answer'd Caius Cassius so ?
When Marcus Brutus grows so covetous,
To lock such rascal-counters from his friends,
Be ready, *gods*, with all your thunderbolts,
Dash him to pieces !

REPROACH, WITH WANT OF MANLINESS.—*Shakespeare.*

O proper *stuff !*
This is the very painting of your *fears ;*
This is the . . . *air*-drawn dagger, which you said
Led you to Duncan.   O, these flaws and starts
(*Impostors* to true fear) would well become
A *woman's* story, at a winter's fire,
Authoriz'd by . . . her *grandam*. ⌢ *Shame* itself !
Why do you make such faces ?   When all's done,
You look but on a *stool.*

REPROACH WITH STUPIDITY AND INCONSTANCY.

That Cæsar comes in *triumph !*
Wherefore *rejoice ?*—What *conquest* brings he home ?
What *tributaries* follow him to Rome,
To grace in captive bonds his chariot wheels ?
You *blocks*, you stones, you *worse* than senseless things ! ⌢

O, you hard hearts, you *cruel* men of Rome.—
Knew ye not *Pompey ?* Many a time and oft
Have you climbed up to walls and battlements,
To towers and windows, yea, to *chimney tops,*—
Your *infants* in your arms,—and there have sat
The live-long day, with patient expectation,
To *see* great Pompey pass the streets of Rome :
And when you saw his *chariot* but appear,
Have you not made a universal *shout,*
That *Tiber* trembled underneath her banks,
To hear the replication of your sounds,
Made in her concave shores ? . . .
And do you *now* put on your best attire?
And do you now cull out a *holiday ?*
And do you now strew *flowers* in *his* way
That comes in triumph over Pompey's *blood*
Be *gone !* ⌒
Run to your houses ; fall upon your *knees ;*
Pray to the gods to *intermit* the plague,
That *needs* must light on this ingratitude.

REPROOF OF SERVILITY.—*Byron.*

Approach, thou craven crouching *slave,*
  Say, is not this *Thermopylæ ?*
These *waters* blue that round you lave—
  O servile offspring of the *free*—
Pronounce what sea, what shore is this : ⌒
The gulf, the rock of *Salamis !* ⌒
These scenes, their story not unknown,
Arise, and make again your *own :*
Snatch from the ashes of your sires
The embers of *their* former fires :
And he who in the strife *expires*
Will add to theirs a name of fear
That Tyranny shall *quake* to hear :
And leave his sons a *hope,* a fame,
They too will rather *die* than shame!
For Freedom's battle once begun,
Bequeathed by bleeding sire to son,
Though baffled oft, is *ever* | *won.*

SAD FOREBODING.—*Shakespeare.*

This man's brow, like to a *title*-leaf,
Foretells the nature of a *tragic* volume
To *fright* our party.—How does my *son,* and *brother ?*
Thou *tremblest,* and the whiteness of thy cheek
Is apter than thy *tongue* to tell thy errand. ⌒
Even such a man,—so faint, so spiritless,
So dull, so dead in look, so woe-begone,—

Drew *Priam's* curtain in the dead of night,
And would have told him, half his *Troy* was burn'd . . .
But Priam *found* the fire, ere he his tongue;—
And I . . . my Percy's *death*, ere thou report'st it.
This thou would'st say. Your son did thus, and thus;
Your brother, thus: so—fought the noble Douglas ;
Stopping my greedy ear with their bold deeds . . .
But in the end,—to stop mine ear *indeed*,—
Thou hast a sigh to blow *away* this praise,
Ending with—brother, son, and *all* . . . are *dead*.

SARCASTIC EXPOSTULATION.—*Shakespeare*.

Signior Antonio, *many* a time—and oft
On the *Rialto*—you have rated me
About my *moneys*, and my *usances:* ⌒
Still have I *borne* it with a patient shrug;
For sufferance is the badge of *all* our tribe.
You call me—*misbeliever, cut-throat—dog*,
And *spit* upon my Jewish gaberdine . . .
And all for use of that which is mine *own*.
Well, then, it now appears you *need* my help:
Go to, then; you come to me, and you say,
Shylock, we would have *moneys:* . . . *You* say so;
You, . . . that did void your rheum upon my beard,
And foot me, as you spurn a stranger *cur*
Over your threshold; Moneys is your *suit !* ⌒
What *should* I say to you? Should I not say
Hath a *dog* money? is it *possible*
A cur can lend three thousand ducats? *or*, . . .
Shall I bend low, and in a *bondsman's* key,
[With bated breath, and whispering humbleness, |
Say *this*,—
Fair sir, you . . . *spit* on me on Wednesday last;
You *spurn'd* me . . . such a day; another time
You called me . . . *dog ;* and for these . . . *courtesies*
I'll . . . *lend* you thus much moneys.

SCORN.—*Byron*.

Pardon is for *men*,
And not for *reptiles*,—we have none for *Steno*,
And no *resentment ; things* like him *must* sting,
And higher beings suffer,—'tis the charter
Of life. The man who dies by an *adder's* fang
May have the crawler crush'd. but feels no *anger ;*
'Twas the worm's *nature :* and some *men* are worms
In *soul* . . . *more* than the living things of tombs.

SELFISH HATRED.—*Shakespeare*.

How like a fawning *publican* he looks !
I *hate* him ⌒ for he is a . . . *Christian ;*

But *more*, for that, in low simplicity,
He lends out money *gratis*,—and brings down
The rate of usance here with *us*, in Venice.
If I can catch him once upon the hip,
I will feed *fat* the ancient grudge I bear him.
He hates our sacred *nation*, and he *rails*,—
Even there where merchants most do congregate.—
On *me*, my bargains, and my well won *thrift*,
Which he calls ... *interest :* ⌒ Cursèd be my *tribe*,
If I *forgive* him!

SHUFFLING REFUSAL.—*Shakespeare.*

They answer in a joint and corporate voice,
That now *they* are at fall,—want treasure,—*cannot*
Do what they *would* ... are *sorry:* ... you are *honourable* ...
But yet ... they could have *wish'd* ... they know not ...
Something hath been amiss ... a noble nature
May catch a wrench ... *would* all were well ... 'tis *pity.* ⌒
And so, intending *other* serious matters,
After distasteful looks, and these hard fractions,
With certain *half*-caps, and cold moving *nods*,
They *froze* me into silence.

SICKNESS.—*Shakespeare.*

And wherefore should this good news make me *sick ?*
I should *rejoice* now at this happy news,
And now my sight fails, and my brain is giddy, ...
O me! ... come *near* me, ... now I am *much* ill. ⌒
I pray you take me up, and bear me hence
Into some other chamber. ⌒ *Softly*, pray—
Let there be no *noise* made, my gentle friends,—
Unless some dull and favourable hand
Will whisper *music* to my weary spirit.

SORROW CAUSING FORGETFULNESS.—*Shakespeare.*

Yet one word more :—grief *boundeth* where it falls, ...
Not with an *empty* hollowness, but *weight ;*
I take my leave before I have *begun*,
For sorrow ends not when it *seemeth* done ;—
Commend me to my *brother*, Edmund York—
Lo, this is *all :* ... nay, yet depart not so;
Though this be all ... do not so *quickly* go. ⌒
I shall *remember* more. Bid him ... Oh, *what ?* ⌒
With all good speed at *Plashy* visit me. ⌒
Alack, and what shall good old York there see,
But *empty* lodgings, and unfurnish'd walls,
Unpeopled offices, *untrodden* stones?
And what *hear* there for welcome but my *groans ?*

Therefore commend me . . . let him *not* come there—
To seek out sorrow that dwells *every* where;
Desolate, desolate! I will hence. and *die :*⌢
The *last* leave of thee takes my weeping eye.

STERN REPROACH.—*Shakespeare.*

Enforced thee! art thou king, and *wilt* be forced?
I *shame* to hear thee speak. Ah, *timorous* wretch!
Thou hast *undone* . . . thyself, thy son, and me;
And given unto the house of *York* such head
As thou shalt reign but by *their* sufferance.
To entail *him* and his heirs unto the crown,
What is it but to make thy *sepulchre*,
And creep into it far before thy time?
Warwick is chancellor, and the lord of Calais;
Stern *Faulconbridge* commands the narrow seas;
The *Duke* is made protector ot the realm,
And yet shalt thou be *safe ?* Such safety finds
The trembling *lamb* environèd with wolves.
Had *I* been there, which am a silly woman,
The soldiers should have tossed me on their *pikes*
Before I would have granted to that act.
But *thou* preferr'st thy life *before* thine honour.
And, seeing thou dost, I here *divorce* myself—
Both from thy table, Henry, and thy bed,—
Until that act of parliament be *repealed*
Whereby my *son* is disinherited.
The *northern* lords, that have forsworn thy colours,
Will follow *mine*, if once they see them spread:
And spread they *shall* be; to thy foul disgrace,
And utter *ruin* of the house of York. ⌢
Thus do I *leave* thee. Come, son, let's away.

SULLENNESS.—*Byron.*

I have not *loved* the world, nor the world *me ;*
I have not *flattered* its rank breath, nor bowed
To its idolatries a *patient* knee,—
Nor coin'd my cheeks to *smiles.*—nor cried aloud
In worship of an *echo ;* in the crowd
They could not deem *me* one of such; I stood
Among them, but not *of* them; in a shroud
Of thoughts which were not *their* thoughts ;—and *still* could,
Had I not *filed* my mind, which thus *itself* subdued.

I have not loved the world, *nor* the world me.—
But let us part *fair* foes. I do believe—
Though I have *found* them not—that there *may* be
Words which *are* things—hopes which will *not* deceive,

And virtues which are merciful, nor weave
Snares for the failing : I would also deem,
O'er others' griefs, that *some* sincerely grieve ;
That two, or *one*, are *almost* what they seem,—
That *goodness* is no *name*, and *happiness* no *dream*.

SUSPICION.—*Shakespeare.*

Let me have men about me that are *fat ;*
Sleek-headed men, and such as *sleep* o'nights :
Yond' *Cassius* has a lean and *hungry* look ;
He *thinks* too much :—such men are *dangerous*.
'Would he were fatter ! . . . But I *fear* him not :
Yet if my name were *liable* to fear,
I do not know the man I *should* avoid
So soon as that spare Cassius. ⌒ He *reads* much ;
He is a great *observer*, and he looks
Quite *through* the deeds of men : he loves no *plays*,
As thou dost, Antony ; he hears no *music :*
Seldom he *smiles ;* and smiles in such a sort,
As if he *mock'd* himself,—and scorn'd his spirit
That could be mov'd to smile at *any* thing. ⌒
Such men as he | be never at heart's ease
While they behold a *greater* than themselves ;
And therefore are they *very* dangerous. ⌒
I rather tell thee what *is* to be fear'd,
Than what *I* fear . . . for *always* I am . . . Cæsar. ⌒
Come on my *right* hand.—for this ear is deaf,—
And tell me truly what *thou* think'st of him.

SYMPATHY, WITH ADMIRATION.—*Baillie.*

O ! I have seen a sight, a *glorious* sight !
Thou would'st have *smiled* to see it —
Yes, smil'd ! although mine eyes are wet with *tears*.
Faith, so they are ; well, well, but *I* smiled too.
O, *had* you seen it !
Drawn out in goodly ranks—*there* stood our *troops ;*
Here, in the graceful state of manly youth,
His dark face brightened with a generous smile,—
Which to his eyes such *flashing* lustre gave,
As though his soul, like an unsheathèd *sword*,
Had through them gleamed—our noble *General* stood ;
And to his soldiers, with *heart*-moving words
The veteran showing. his brave deeds rehearsed ;
Who, by his side stood like a *storm*-scathed oak
Beneath the shelter of some noble tree,
In the *green* honours of its youthful prime.
I cannot tell thee how the veteran *looked !*
At first he bore it up with *cheerful* looks,
As one who *fain* would wear his honours bravely,
And greet the soldiers with a comrade's face :

But when Count Basil, in such *moving* speech,
Told o'er his actions past, and bade his troops
Great deeds to *emulate*, his countenance *chang'd* ;
High heav'd his manly breast, as it had been
By inward strong emotion half-*convuls'd* ;
Trembled his nether lip; he shed some *tears*,
The General *paus'd*—the soldiers *shouted* loud ;
Then hastily he brushed the drops *away*,
And wav'd his hand. and clear'd his tear-chok'd voice,
As though he would some grateful *answer* make ;
When *back* with double force the whelming tide
Of passion came; high o'er his hoary head
His arm he toss'd, and. heedless of respect,
In Basil's *bosom* hid his agèd face,
Sobbing aloud. ⌒ From the admiring ranks
A cry arose; still *louder* shouts resound ; ⌒
I felt . . . a sudden *tightness* grasp my throat
As it would *strangle* me; such as I felt,—
I knew it well,—some twenty years ago,
When my good *father* shed his blessing on me.
I hate to *weep*, and so I came *away*.

TERROR.—*Moliere.*

Ah ! *mercy* on my soul ! What is that?—My old friend's . . .
ghost ? They say none but *wicked* folks *w-a-lk* . . . I wish I
were at the bottom of a *coal-pit.* ⌒ La ! how pale and *long* his
face is grown since his death : he *never* was handsome : and
death has improved him very much the *wrong* way ⌒ Pray . . .
do not come *near* me !—I wished you very well when you were
alive ;—but I could never abide a *dead* man cheek-by-jowl with
me . . . *Ah !*—Ah—mercy on us ! . . . *No* nearer, pray !⌒ If it be
only to take *leave* of me that you are come back, I could have *ex-
cused* you the ceremony with all my heart.—Or if you . . . mercy
on us !—no nearer—*pray*—or if you have *wronged* anybody. as
you always loved money . . . a *little,*—I give you the word of a
frighted Christian, I will pray as long as you *please* for the de-
liverance or repose of your departed soul. My good—worthy—
noble friend, do pray—*dis*appear . . . as ever you would wish
your old friend to come to his *senses* again.

TERRORS OF DEATH.—*Shakespeare.*

To *die*, and go . . . we know not *where* :—
To lie in cold obstruction. and to *rot:*—
This sensible—warm—motion, to become
A kneaded *clod ;* and the delightful spirit
To bathe in *fiery* floods, or to reside
In thrilling regions of thick-ribbed *ice ;*—
To be imprison'd in the viewless winds,
And *blown* ⌒ with restless violence about

The pendent world; *or* . . . to be . . . worse than worst
Of those, that lawless and uncertain thoughts
Imagine *howling !* ⌒ O .'tis *too* horrible !
The weariest and most *loathèd* worldly life—
That *age, ache, penury,* and *imprisonment*
Can lay on nature. . . is a *Paradise*
To what we *fear* of Death.

THREATENED REVENGE.—*Shakespeare.*

If they speak but *truth* of her . . .
These hands shall *tear* her; if they *wrong* her honour,
The *proudest* of them shall well hear of it.
Time hath not yet so *dried* this blood of mine,
Nor age so ate up my *invention.*
Nor fortune made such havoc of my *means,*
Nor my bad life 'reft me so much of *friends,*
But they shall *find* awak'd in such a kind,
Both strength of limb, and policy of mind,
Ability in means, and choice of friends—
To *quit* me of them *thoroughly.*

TIES OF LOVE.—*P. J. Bailey.*

I loved her, for that she was *beautiful ;*
And that she seemed to be . . . all *Nature,*
And all *varieties* of things in one :
Would *set* at night in clouds of *tears,* and rise
All light and *laughter* in the morning : fear
No petty customs or *appearances,*
But think what others only *dreamed* about,
And *say* what others did but think, and *do*
What others would but say, and *glory* in
What others *dared* but do.   So *pure* withal
In soul ; in heart and act such conscious, yet
Such careless *innocence,* she made round her
A halo of *delight !*—'twas *these* which won me ;
And that she never schooled *within* her breast
One thought, or feeling, but gave *holiday*
To all ; and she made all even *mine*
In the communion of love ; and we
Grew *like* each other.

UNTOLD LOVE.—*J. A. Hillhouse.*

The soul, my lord, is fashioned like the lyre ;
Strike *one* chord suddenly, and *others* vibrate.
Your *name* abruptly mentioned, casual words
Of *comment* on your deeds, *praise* from your uncle,
News from the armies, talk of your *return,* . . .
A word let fall touching your youthful passion,
Suffused her cheek, called to her drooping eye

A momentary *lustre ;* made her pulse
Leap headlong, and her bosom *palpitate.*
I could not long be *blind ;* for love *defies*
Concealment, making every glance and *motion*
Speech—and *silence* a tell-tale.
  These things, though trivial in themselves, begat
Suspicion. But long *months* elapsed
Ere I knew all. She had, you know, a *fever.* ⌒
One night, when all were weary and at rest,
I. sitting by her couch, tired and o'erwatched,
Thinking she slept, suffered *my* lids to close. ⌒
Waked by a voice, I found her . . . Never, signor,
While life endures, will that scene *fade* from me !—
A dying lamp winked on the hearth, that cast
And snatched the shadows. — *Something* stood before me !
In *white.* My flesh began to *creep.* I thought
I saw a *spirit.* It was my *lady* risen
And standing with clasped hands like one in prayer.
Her pallid face, in the dim light, displayed
Something, methought. *surpassing* mortal beauty.
She presently turned round, and fixed her large wild eyes
Brimming with *tears* upon me ; fetched a sigh
As from a *riven* heart, and cried, ''He's *dead !*
But, hush !—*weep* not :—I've bargained for his *soul ;*
That's safe in bliss !" ⌒ Demanding *who* was dead,—
Scarce yet *aware* she raved,—she answered quick,
Her *Cosmo,* her beloved ! for that his *ghost,*
All pale and gory, thrice had passed her bed.
With that, her passion breaking *loose,* my lord,
She poured her lamentation forth in strains
Pathetical beyond the reach of *reason.*
'' *Gone,* gone, gone to the grave, and never *knew*
I loved him !" ⌒ I'd no power to speak or *move.*—
I sat *stone-*still.—A horror fell upon me.
At last, her little strength ebbed out : she sank ;
And lay, as in *death's* arms, till morning.

UPBRAIDING—WITH WANT OF DUTY.—*Shakespeare.*

Fie, fie ! *un*knit that threatening, un*kind* brow ;
And dart not *scornful* glances from those eyes,—
To wound thy *lord* . . . thy *king* . . . thy Governor. ⌒
It *blots* thy beauty, as *frosts* bite the meads ;
Confounds thy fame, as *whirlwinds* shake fair buds ;
And in *no* sense is meet, or amiable.
A woman moved is like a *fountain* troubled,
Muddy, ill seeming, thick, bereft of beauty :
And, while it is so, *none* so dry or thirsty
Will deign to sip, or touch one *drop* of it.
Thy husband is thy lord, thy *life,* thy keeper,
Thy head, thy sovereign ; one that *cares* for thee,

And for thy maintenance : commits his body
To painful *labour*, both by sea and land ;
To watch the night in storms, the day in cold,
While thou liest warm at *home*, secure and safe ;
And craves no *other* tribute at thy hands,
But love, fair looks, and true *obedience* ;—
Too *little* payment for so great a debt.
Such duty as the subject owes the *prince*,
Even such—a woman oweth to her *husband ;*
And when she's *froward*, peevish, sullen, sour,
And *not* obedient to his honest will,
What is she but a foul contending rebel,
And graceless *traitor* to her loving Lord ?—
I am *ashamed* that women are so simple
To offer *war* where they should kneel for peace ;
Or seek for *rule*, supremacy, and sway,
When they are *bound* to serve, love, and *obey*.

VALOUR.—*Moore.*

He *read* their thoughts . . . they were his *own.*⌒
    What ! while our arms can wield these blades,
Shall we die *tamely ?* die *alone ?* . . .
    Without one *victim* to our shades—
One *Moslem* heart, where, buried *deep*,
The sabre from its toil may sleep ?
No ! . . . God of Iran's burning skies !
Thou *scorn'st* the inglorious sacrifice. ⌒
No ! . . . though of all earth's *hope* bereft,
Life, swords. and *vengeance*, still are left !
We'll make yon valley s reeking caves
    Live in the awe-struck minds of men,
Till tyrants *shudder*, when their slaves
    Tell of the Ghebers' bloody glen.—
Follow, brave hearts ! ⌒ this *pile* remains
Our refuge still . . . from *life* and chains ;
But his the best, the *holiest* bed,
Who sinks entombed in *Moslem* dead !

VENGEANCE.—*Dugald Moore.*

There is an order in the race of men,
Who, being smit by fortune's shafts, sit down,
And—like a *statue* on a pedestal—
Seem chill'd to *marble !* or, they *whine* away
Their manhood—like sick maidens. ⌒ *I* . . . was not
Made of such *moping* matter ! I was not
Fashion'd to walk the earth, and bear about
A *rainy* eyeball and a *nerveless* heart !
The wild materials that are gathered *here*
Could only yet be quench'd in showers of *blood*, . . .
Not smothered in salt rheum !—I have been *wrong'd*,

Ay, *trampled* on!—but they who smote me, yet
May feel—when least expected—the keen tooth—
The *adder's* fang,—sharp, cutting, edg'd with death,
In what they deem'd a *worm*.

VIRTUE.—*Rowe.*

Yes! to be *good* is to be *happy :—angels*
Are happier than mankind, *because* they're better.
Guilt is the source of *sorrow :* 'tis the fiend,
The *avenging* fiend, that follows us behind
With whips and stings.   The *blest* know *none* of this;
But rest in everlasting *peace* of mind,
And find the height of all their *heaven* is goodness.

WARNING.—*Cotton.*

To-morrow, didst thou say?
Methought I heard Horatio say, To-morrow.
Go to—I will not *hear* of it. ⌢ *To-morrow !*
'Tis a *sharper*,—who stakes his *penury*
Against thy plenty; who takes thy ready cash,
And pays thee *nought*, . . . but wishes, hopes and *promises,*
The currency of *idiots :* injurious *bankrupt,*
That gulls the easy creditor!—*To-morrow !*
It is a period *no-where* to be found
In all the hoary registers of Time,—
Unless, perchance, in the *fool's* calendar !
Wisdom disclaims the word, nor holds *society*
With those who own it.   No, my Horatio,
'Tis Fancy's child, and *Folly* is its father;
Wrought of such stuff as *dreams* are, and *baseless*
As the fantastic visions of the evening.
But, soft, my friend; ⌢ arrest the *present* moments;
For, be assured, they all are arrant *tell-tales :*
And—though their flight be silent, and their path
Trackless as the wingèd couriers of the air—
They post to heaven, and there *record* thy folly.
Because, though stationed on the important watch,
Thou, like a sleeping, faithless sentinel,
Didst let them pass, *un*noticed, unim*proved.*
And know, for that thou slumberedst on the guard,
Thou shalt be made to *answer* at the bar
For every fugitive; and ⌢ when thou thus
Shalt stand impleaded at the high tribunal
Of hood-winked Justice, who shall *tell* thy audit !
Then, stay the *present* instant, . . . dear Horatio !
Imp it the marks of *wisdom* on its wings;
'Ti more worth than *kingdoms ! far* more precious
Th   all the crimson treasures of *life's* fountain !—
     t it not *elude* thy grasp; but—like
     good old *patriarch* upon record,—
   ld the fleet angel *fast*, until he *bless* thee !

THE END.

PROF A. MELVILLE BELL'S WORKS.

ELOCUTION.

ELOCUTIONARY MANUAL—PRINCIPLES OF ELOCUTION. *Sixth Edition. Price $1.50.*
ESSAYS AND POSTSCRIPTS ON ELOCUTION. *Price $1.25.*
EMPHASIZED LITURGY. *Price $1.00.*
SERMON READING AND MEMORITER DELIVERY. *Pamphlet. Price 15 cents.*

DEFECTS OF SPEECH.

PRINCIPLES OF SPEECH, DICTIONARY OF SOUNDS, AND CURE OF STAMMERING. *Price $1.50.*
THE FAULTS OF SPEECH. *Price 60 cents.*

PHONETICS.

UNIVERSITY LECTURES ON PHONETICS. *Price 60 cents.*
ENGLISH LINE-WRITING. *Price 60 cents.*
UNIVERSAL STENO-PHONOGRAPHY. *Price 75 cents.*
SPEECH READING AND ARTICULATION TEACHING. *Price 25 cents.*
WORLD-ENGLISH—THE UNIVERSAL LANGUAGE. *Price 25 cents.*
HANDBOOK OF WORLD-ENGLISH. *Price 25 cents.*

VISIBLE SPEECH (Inaugural Edition).

VISIBLE SPEECH—UNIVERSAL ALPHABETICS. *Price $4.00.*
CLASS PRIMER OF ENGLISH VISIBLE SPEECH. *Price 20 cents.*
EXPLANATORY LECTURE ON VISIBLE SPEECH. *Pamphlet. Price 15 cents.*

VISIBLE SPEECH (Revised Edition).

SOUNDS AND THEIR RELATIONS. *Price $2.00.*
POPULAR MANUAL OF VISIBLE SPEECH AND VOCAL PHYSIOLOGY. *Price 50 cents.*
VISIBLE SPEECH READER. *Price 40 cents.*
ENGLISH VISIBLE SPEECH IN TWELVE LESSONS. *Price 50 cents.*

The above Works may be obtained, by order, through any bookseller, or—post free on receipt of price,—from

N. D. C. HODGES, 874 Broadway, New York.
EDGAR S. WERNER, 28 West Twenty-third Street, New York.

See special notice to booksellers, p. vi.

*** On parcels ordered directly from the Author, teachers receive wholesale discount. Address 1525 Thirty-fifth Street, Washington, D. C.